Meetings That Get Results

Meetings That Get Results

A FACILITATOR'S GUIDE TO BUILDING BETTER MEETINGS

Terrence Metz

BERRETT-KOEHLER PUBLISHERS, INC

Berrett-Koehler Publishers, Inc.
1333 Broadway, Suite 1000
Oakland, CA 94612-1921
Tel: (510) 817-2277
Fax: (510) 817-2278
www.bkconnection.com

ORDERING INFORMATION
Quantity sales. Special discounts are available on quantity purchases by corporations, associations, and others. For details, contact the "Special Sales Department" at the Berrett-Koehler address above.

Individual sales. Berrett-Koehler publications are available through most bookstores. They can also be ordered directly from Berrett-Koehler: Tel: (800) 929-2929; Fax: (802) 864-7626; www.bkconnection.com.

Orders for college textbook / course adoption use. Please contact Berrett-Koehler: Tel: (800) 929-2929; Fax: (802) 864-7626.

Distributed to the U.S. trade and internationally by Penguin Random House Publisher Services.

Berrett-Koehler and the BK logo are registered trademarks of Berrett-Koehler Publishers, Inc.

Printed in the United States of America

Berrett-Koehler books are printed on long-lasting acid-free paper. When it is available, we choose paper that has been manufactured by environmentally responsible processes. These may include using trees grown in sustainable forests, incorporating recycled paper, minimizing chlorine in bleaching, or recycling the energy produced at the paper mill.

CIP data for this book is available at the Library of Congress.
ISBN 978-1-5230-9315-1

First Edition

27 26 25 24 23 22 21   10 9 8 7 6 5 4 3 2 1

Book producer: Westchester Publishing Services
Cover designer: Howie Severson

This book is dedicated to several important family members:

To my best friend, partner, and wife, LoriJo, whose expertise remains hidden on every page. She is all about doing the next right thing. LoriJo walks her talk, spending most of her time serving others and not herself. She is clear thinking, exceptionally bright, highly practical, and a truly spiritual humanitarian—on top of being beautiful, inside and out. It takes a special kind of person, someone who loves life, to look forward to Monday mornings.

To my daughter, the classy professional Georgia Jean, for her edits, keen observations, constant encouragement, and unconditional love.

To my sedulous son, Joshua Cincinnati, for expanding our loving family with the addition of our vivacious daughter-in-law, Katie; and to both of them for bringing Michael Thomas, our resolute grandchild, into this existence.

Finally, to Henry, our 16-year-old cockapoo, for his reminders, as regular as clockwork, that it is time to eat.

Contents 🚀

Foreword 🚀

In the course of our lives, we should deeply reflect on the sheer amount of time we spend in meetings. A majority of meetings in business are a critical mechanism for generative conversations to clarify the why, what, who, how, and when around producing a coherent shared understanding of the work at hand that needs to be executed. However, meetings are also a gateway to building trusted relationships and the magical world of tapping greater insights and knowledge than we could access by ourselves.

In the world we see now emerging in 2020 and beyond, meetings will become ever more frequent, virtual, and critical as the rate of change continues to accelerate and we have shorter prediction windows with more volatility and unexpected outcomes. In short, we are now witnessing an existential shift in the process of planning and problem solving that will require many more working professionals to master meeting management skills, both virtually and face-to-face, to be far more effective.

In this book, Terrence Metz lays out an integrated practicum that is both useful and intentional, to build better meeting outcomes and establish viable skills for every leader of groups, large or small. He does so by elevating the key competencies of facilitation as the lever for experiencing meetings as a value-creating human experience that also leaves the participants confident in their contributions as well as the outcome of their conversations.

Fifteen years ago, I introduced Terrence's set of facilitation practices to a group of highly experienced project managers who were also instructors in the Stanford University Advanced Project Management Program. The conversion time for upgrading their meeting skills was very short, but having access to a set of easy-to-use meeting tools to plan and facilitate workshops built a cohort of very confident trainers and facilitators who were called upon consistently for facilitating very complex and strategic program planning meetings.

Based on many of the skills and tools now available to you in this book, my own practice of meeting facilitation was forever changed, because my own confidence and effectiveness became very evident. And, even today, when I reflect on ways I could do better and make more impact, I am always curious about how I could have made my meetings and client workshops more powerful. I am very appreciative that Terrence has taken the time to get this knowledge codified to share with the whole world at a time of major transformation. As many have said, every leader is only as good as the toolbox they know how to use, so this book is a timely must-have.

Enjoy the read and the reflections!

William Malek
Senior Director
Southeast Asia Innovation Management Research Center

Introduction

Launching

LET'S GET STARTED

There's nothing more frustrating than an unproductive meeting—except one that leads to another unproductive meeting. This book is dedicated to the millions of people right now who are leading meetings without any training in facilitation or meeting design. Within the book's pages are solutions to ensure that your meetings produce clear and actionable results. I show you how to run meetings that are profitable and productive—and that ultimately lead to fewer meetings.

In addition to basic information-exchange meetings (such as staff meetings and board meetings), I focus on three important forms of frequently challenging meetings:

- **Decision-making**—focusing on prioritization and ranking

- **Planning**—that is, consensual agreement and shared ownership (*who* does *what* by *when*?)

- **Problem solving**—for example, focusing on innovative solutions *during* the meeting

It's All about You

I understand that in a world of back-to-back meetings, you barely have time to find the right resources and training to become a better leader. Yet, while you would not attempt to build a boat without the proper training, equipment, and support, every day millions of people are conducting meetings without critical understanding of or formal training on how to be an effective meeting leader in person or online. Meetings whose deliverables affect tens, hundreds, or even thousands of jobs, or determine the success or failure of a department or company, regularly cost organizations more money than all the boats, ships, and skyscrapers being built today. This book gives you a significant edge:

- The book empowers you to help your groups create, innovate, and break through the barriers of miscommunication, politics, and intolerance.

- The book makes it easier for you to help others reach consensus and shared understanding, while never yielding to the easy answer.

- The book provides you with specific *Agenda Steps* and *Tools* to avoid the worst possible result of any meeting: another meeting.

MAKING IT EASY

Facil in Latin means "easily accomplished." The word *facilitaera* evolved from the Latin verb *facilius reddo*, meaning "easily accomplished or attained." When a group of subject matter experts manages to stay focused, miracles can happen. Therefore, I define business facilitation as a method that removes all distractions, *making it easy or attainable* for a group of experts to gain traction by focusing on the same question at the same time, led by a meeting facilitator who knows how to sequence questions, ask questions with precision, and guide consensual understanding and agreement around optimal solutions for that specific group of experts.

THE TOUGH PART

Rarely do events, meetings, or workshops proceed in a linear fashion. They don't just "start here" and then "end there." Rather, they continually loop and twirl—for reasons such as these:

- Someone joins the meeting late, online or in person.

- A subject matter expert gets called away unexpectedly and upon return discovers that some critical information was not included.

- You are asked to go back and add something.

- Someone changes her mind because her introspection has found a connection between a few things previously not considered.

- Someone comes back from break with added information obtained from a subject matter expert who is not in attendance (or from the internet).

- You are asked to substitute or combine something.

- Someone wakes up and cannot understand something decided earlier.

- Two people start arguing because they refuse to agree with each other based on "principle."

- You need to fully define something.

- You do a poor job handling participants' electronic leashes (cell phones, laptops, etc.) and when everyone wakes up, they quickly unravel what has already been accomplished.

Sound familiar? If so, the remedies in this book are meant for you. I cannot promise you a method to *resolve* everything you encounter in meetings. But I do promise to give you a method and additional confidence to *manage* anything that develops or erupts during your meetings.

When you see the term "meetings" you might substitute the generic term "sessions." Meeting leadership skills allow you to pivot among ceremonies, conferences, events, meetings, and workshops—wherever groups assemble in session to decide, plan, prioritize, and solve problems. I want to make it easier for you to be a credible meeting leader and meeting facilitator[1] when leading diverse types of meeting sessions, for all types of groups, organizations, teams, and tribes.[2]

RELAX

The style of this book supports quick reading and cross-referencing. Conventions include the following:

- Lists of items (such as bullet points) are typically alphabetically ordered. If not, lists are sorted by chronology, dependency, frequency, or importance (impact).

- *Meeting Approaches*, *Agenda Steps*, and *Tools* appear in *italics*, with cross-references to the chapters or sections where they appear.

LEGACY

Like you, I know how it feels to sit in a meeting and think, "this is a waste of the organization's time and money." To solve this problem, I've spent years improving a structured method to design and lead better meetings. Once you have read this book, you will have the knowledge I wish I had earlier in my career. The book is the result of more than 15,000 hours invested in training thousands of people on four different continents. These people now plan and run better meetings using disciplined, holistic meeting design, based on proven techniques such as structured conversations, with an ever-vigilant eye toward decision quality and collaborative ownership.

How to Navigate This Meeting Design Guide

- **Read the first four chapters** to understand and reinforce meeting leadership; the core skills and discipline of effective facilitation; and how to manage group collaboration, meeting conflict, and personality dysfunction. When you need a refresher, refer to the table of contents

---

[1] Meeting facilitator is one of four roles performed by the meeting leader; the other three roles commonly performed by the meeting leader include meeting coordinator, meeting documenter, and meeting designer.

[2] Teams reassemble every season with new players. Tribes stay together through thick and thin, over the long haul.

to isolate the topic you need to reinforce, such as "How to Manage Arguments."

- For your meetings and events, **use the Quick Reference sections and *Tool* selection guide** at the end of the book to remind you about suitable activities for structuring your agenda and meeting design. The Quick Reference sections prompt you with detailed instructions to use when building your *Launch*, *Agenda Steps*, and *Wrap* (fully detailed and scripted in chapter 5).

- **For specific agendas, tools, and procedures** that you can use repeatedly when conducting meeting sessions, **turn to these chapters** (also see table I.1):
  - Planning sessions—chapter 6
  - Decision-making and prioritization sessions—chapter 7
  - Problem-solving and innovation sessions—chapter 8
  - Online sessions and differences—chapter 9
  - Staff meetings and other information-exchange sessions—chapter 9
  - Board meetings and "Robert's Rules" situations—chapter 9

- After identifying your situation and locating the appropriate *Agenda Steps*, **adapt the prescribed procedures** to your personal taste and environmental constraints by considering the following factors:
  - Duration or amount of available time
  - Monetary impact of your meeting deliverable on organizational objectives
  - Number of participants, expected and optimal
  - Physical space or online ease of using breakout rooms
  - Your ability to adapt the tools to both in-person and online settings
  - Your experience and confidence with the recommended tools

- **Script your *Annotated Agenda*** (chapter 5) **from start to finish.** For best results, follow the seven activities of a professional introduction (*Launch*) using the prescribed sequence. Script them and follow your script. According to *New York Times* best-selling author Daniel Pink,[3] the four activities of a professional conclusion (*Wrap*) are even more important than a smooth *Launch*. So thoroughly prepare for your four

---

[3] Daniel Pink, *When: The Scientific Secrets of Perfect Timing* (2018).

Table I.1. Meeting Design That Supports Servant Leadership

Chapter	Topic
1	**Serving:** Resistance to change, importance of knowledge transfer, and the immense value of meetings based on clear thinking, servant leadership skills, and structured meeting design
2	**Leading:** Critical disciplines including line of site, consciousness about different meeting roles, the nature of organizational alignment, and foundation of structure
3	**Facilitating:** The indispensable servant skills that make it easier for meetings to get *DONE* faster through active listening, precise questioning, and timely challenging
4	**Collaborating:** How to transform conflict into consensus leveraging the objectives of the product, project, department, business unit, and organization
5	**Structuring:** Using a masterful *Launch* and *Wrap* for all sessions, modifying pre-built agendas and creating your own, and building fully scripted *Annotated Agendas* through structured conversations and vigorous preparation
6	**Planning:** A fully integrated session that builds consensual plans about *who* does *what* by *when* to meet or exceed goals, key results, and other objectives
7	**Deciding:** Proven *Tools* for galvanizing decisions and consensual agreement around purpose, criteria, options, and priorities throughout simple, complicated, and complex situations
8	**Solving:** Field-tested *Meeting Approaches* and *Tools* using numerous creative activities for securing consensual agreement around innovative actions and solutions to embrace
9	**Controlling:** Live and real-time sessions, hybrid in-person and online sessions, remote sessions, and virtual sessions and their differences. Support from "hip-pocket" *Intervention Tools* for special and unplanned meeting challenges
Appendix	**Supporting:** Substantial and vital supplements such as the golden rule and the "silver rule," *Quick References*, and a list of *Tools* and where to find them, followed by a glossary and bibliography

concluding *Review and Wrap* activities, which ensure clear and actionable results.

- **Prepare your participants**. For major initiatives or workshops, send out a *Participants' Package* (chapter 5). For 50-minute meetings, prepare a one-page description of the meeting purpose, meeting scope, meeting objectives, and basic agenda.

- Once your *Annotated Agenda* (chapter 5) is complete, and even while you are working on it, **prepare supplementary material** and **visual support** such as a glossary, slides, legends, posters, and screens (illustrated throughout this book) to help you explain the tools and procedures you will use to build deliverables and get DONE.

1

Serving

DISCIPLINE OF SERVANT LEADERSHIP

If the thought of change instills in you the "FUD" factor—fear, uncertainty, and doubt—you're not alone. Fear of change keeps people in relationships they've outgrown, jobs they don't like, and even hairstyles that no longer suit them.

FEAR: F#©% Everything and Run

Likewise, even when organizations understand that change is necessary if they are to add value and remain competitive, they also suffer from FUD. They fear that they may fail; face uncertainty about how to change or, rather, what actions will lead to successful change; and, finally, doubt whether all the time, money, and effort it takes to implement change will be worth it.

That's where you come in. The truth is, people don't change their minds; they make new decisions—sometimes frequently—based on new or added information. This new and added information accelerates change by influencing decision-making in both individuals and groups.[1]

With that truth in mind, it becomes clear that "servant leaders" (like you) are not engaged to change peoples' minds, but rather to make it easier for people to choose appropriate change supported with more informed decisions. By speaking *with*

> —**Charles Darwin**
> *It is* not *the strongest of the species that survives, nor the most intelligent, but the one most responsive to change.*

---

[1] For the past 30 years, most changes have been both digital and dynamic, constantly shifting—based on things that are "in-formation." As much of life is "in-formation," change is both inherent and inevitable—only growth is optional.

Table 1.1. Knowledge Transfer Molds the Optimal Leadership Technique

Information Storage	Knowledge Transfer	Leadership Technique
Bard	Oral	Steward
Book	Print	Manager
Documentary	Broadcast	Executive
Cloud	Digital	**Facilitator**

people rather than *at* them, servant leaders create environments that foster breakthrough solutions.

In most organizations, this change begins during meetings. The problem is that meetings often fail for one of three reasons:

1. The wrong people are attending (rare).

2. The right people attend but are apathetic and don't care (rarest).

3. The right people care but they don't know how to conduct an effective meeting (bazinga!).

We know that groups can make higher-quality decisions than the smartest person in the group alone, so why don't we invest in learning how to run better meetings? Part of the problem can be found in our muscle memory. When part of a group or team, we are more attuned to taking orders than creating collaborative solutions.

> *You can complete a project without facilitation, but you could also cut your own hair.*

Historically, leadership techniques have evolved based on where information was stored and how knowledge was shared—from rural stewards who knew about crops and animal behavior to complex urban environments layered with infrastructure and technology.

In recent centuries we relied on executives and managers for their experience and machine knowledge. As leaders, they told us what to do. Today's complex knowledge base and knowledge transfer technique, however, requires a new breed of servant leaders. Most of them are trained to avoid problems attributable to weak meeting leadership, poor facilitation, and lack of meeting design. This new breed is not a person, but a role—the role of the meeting facilitator (see table 1.1).

From this point on, I use the following terms and understanding:

- **All servant leaders are leaders, but not all leaders are servant leaders.**

  - Servant leaders accept the likelihood of more than one right answer and serve others to help them find the best answer for their own situation.

- Early on I frequently use the term "servant leader," because much of the material in the first four chapters applies to both servant leaders and meeting facilitators.

- **All skilled meeting facilitators are servant leaders, but not all servant leaders facilitate meetings.**

  – Servant leaders may also be found as advisers, arbitrators, coaches, consultants, and ombudspersons and in other roles in which they share primary skills with meeting facilitators, such as active listening, maintaining content neutrality, observing, questioning, and seeking to understand.

- Beginning in chapter 5, I refer more frequently to the meeting designer—a title that frequently also designates the meeting leader, distinguished from the "meeting facilitator."

- **To be precise, being a meeting leader requires managing three additional roles—meeting coordinator, meeting documenter, and meeting designer—that are quite independent of the role of meeting facilitator.**

  – In a practical sense, however, people often act as meeting leaders because they usually perform all four roles, although not all the time—especially in more complicated meetings, frequently called "workshops."

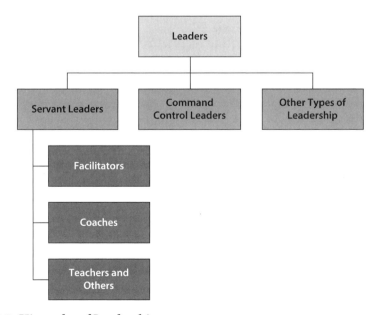

Figure 1.1. Hierarchy of Leadership

The Servant Leader Solution

As the workplace transforms, leadership techniques change. Today, instead of dealing mostly with individuals (one-on-one conversations), servant leaders work frequently with people in groups (ceremonies, events, meetings, and workshops). Instead of supervising hours of workload, servant leaders help their teams become self-managing (see figure 1.1). Instead of directing tasks, servant leaders motivate people to achieve results.

Facing consecutive days of back-to-back meetings, meeting participants value well-run meetings that focus on aligning team activities with organizational goals. Professionally trained facilitators solve communication problems in meetings or workshops by ensuring the group stays focused on the meeting objectives while applying meeting designs that lead to more informed decisions.

—Robert Moran,
Futurist **(2013)**
With technology empowering the individual, the battle for the twenty-first century could be the battle of the self-organizing swarm against the command and control pyramid.

Compared to traditional or historic leaders, modern leaders exhibit many of these positive traits. A further shift is required, however, for many of these leaders to become truly facilitative, so that teams and groups realize the full potential of their commitment, consensus, and ownership.

Have you ever led a meeting? I'll assume that you have. Ask yourself, **What changed from the moment your participants walked into the meeting until the meeting ended?**

As a servant leader and meeting facilitator, you become the change agent, someone who takes meeting participants from where they are at the beginning of the meeting to where they need to be at the conclusion. All leaders must know where they are going. They must know what the group is intending to build, decide, or leave with when the meeting is done. Effective servant leaders also start with the end in mind.

The servant leader does not have answers but rather takes command of the questions (see table 1.2). Optimal questions are scripted and properly sequenced. If you were designing a new home, for example, you would consider the foundation and structure long before you decide on the color of the grout. By responding to appropriate questions, meeting participants focus and generate their collective preferences and requirements.

A neutral meeting leader values rigorous preparation, anticipates group dynamics, and designs the meeting accordingly. The meeting leader becomes responsible for managing the entire approach—the agenda, the ground rules, the flow of conversations, and so on—but not the content developed during the

Table 1.2. Characteristics of the Facilitative Leadership Difference

Modern Leaders	Servant Leaders
Are content experts, based on position and power	Are context experts, based on credibility, genuineness, and inspiration
Are involved in directing tasks	Facilitate plans and agreements based on group input
Communicate and receive feedback	Structure activities so that stakeholders and team members evaluate them, their leaders, and one another
Have some meeting management skills	Are skilled in using groups to build complex outputs by structuring conversations based on a collaborative tone
Remain accountable for results	Transfer ownership so that members are highly skilled and accountable for outcomes
Value teamwork and collaboration	Focus on removing impediments while providing procedures that fortify self-organizing teams

meeting. Effective meetings result from building a safe and trustworthy environment, one that provides "permission to speak freely" without fear of reprisal or economic loss.

Ironically, the more structured the meeting, the more flexible you (the meeting facilitator) can be. For without structure, a meeting design, or a road map, you can never tell exactly where you are or, more important, how much remains undone. With structure, you can take the scenic route, because you have a plan that references your original design—whereas groups without structure who take the scenic route get lost or, worse, cannot agree on where to go next.

With that said, I will not waste your time by covering the background and history of facilitation, giving you an overview of facilitation, or mentioning any other material not directly applicable to helping you become a better servant leader (or meeting facilitator). I'll focus on critical thinking and how a structured method of facilitation generates the highest level of flexibility. As I noted earlier, structure does not hamper or restrict flexibility; structure makes it easier for you, as the servant leader, to be flexible and practical.

In addition, I will not spend much time on activities designed to improve teamwork, increase trust, and so on—in other words, what most other resources publish about "facilitation." Rather, this book focuses on meeting objectives and outputs of business meetings, frequently referred to as "deliverables."

Benefits of Embracing a Facilitative Leadership Technique

When organizations support skilled and facilitative leadership for product development, project management, process improvement, and so on, they are allocating human capital to ensure the success of their single most expensive investment: meetings. Organizations do so in these ways when:

- context is carefully managed, teams are free to focus on greater quality and value—quality being defined as satisfying customer expectations and value being defined as exceeding customer expectations.

- staff are treated like partners and collaborators, commitment and motivation increase.

- stakeholders' ideas are sought, meetings become collaborative, innovative, and vibrant.

The value of embracing the servant leader–facilitative leadership technique extends beyond meetings to benefit a widening circle of people:

- *You benefit by*

  - earning respect and recognition for leading better meetings

  - increasing your leadership consciousness, facilitation competence, and meeting design confidence

  - learning how to modify and adapt proven agendas, procedures, and tools for information gathering, analyzing, and decision-making

- *Your organization benefits by*

  - expediting the output of highly sought deliverables

  - improving the culture and team spirit while enabling outstanding individual performances

  - reducing the cost of omissions and issues subject to normal oversight

  - reducing the cost of wasted meetings and wasted time in meetings

- *Your community benefits by*

  - encouraging shared planning efforts to improve the distribution of resources

  - improving volunteerism

  - increasing decision transparency

  - solidifying shared ownership

- *All society benefits by*
  - increasing eco-effectiveness through reducing wasted time and resources
  - improving the likelihood of win-win scenarios
  - motivating hitherto unused or underused intellectual capacity

Throughout this book, I aim to shift your thinking from "facilitation" (a noun, representing a static way of *being*) to "facilitating" (a verb, representing a dynamic way of *doing*)—that is, truly making it easier for your meeting participants to make more informed decisions. Leading is about stimulating and inspiring people, and facilitating skills are part of the DNA of servant leaders.

Facilitation Liberates Leaders

In the past, leaders needed to be experts on content. Today, organizations already employ and engage a wealth of subject matter experts. What organizations need are leaders who know how to be facilitative while managing context. In the past, leadership was about giving answers. **Today, leadership is about asking precise and properly sequenced questions while always providing a safe environment for everyone's response.**

Imagine the following scenario: Your team is tasked with developing a plan to solve the problem of employee burnout in the cybersecurity department. To assess the value of proposed solutions, the team needs to know the purpose of the cybersecurity department—why it exists.

WHICH OF THE FOLLOWING MAKES BETTER SENSE?

A **"presenter"** might access the cybersecurity department charter from Human Resources. In most organizations, this task would take from 15 minutes to five hours or longer. Then the presenter might spend another 15 minutes putting together PowerPoint slides and then take five minutes to present the slides and another 10 to 20 minutes to manage questions and answers about content on the slides. Call it one hour total, minimum. At the conclusion, the presenter owns the content on the slides.

Alternatively, you, as the meeting leader, can use a procedure, such as my *Purpose Tool* (chapter 7).[2] The *Purpose Tool* distills a consensual expression about the purpose of the cybersecurity department directly from the subject matter experts who understand both the purpose and the problems in the department today. In 15 minutes or less, you can lead the team to build an expression of shared purpose using the *Purpose Tool*. Most important, at the end of the 15 minutes, the meeting participants, not you, own the results.

---

[2] One of dozens of facilitation tools supplied in this book, the *Purpose Tool* captures a consensual understanding of *why* something is being done before stepping into further analysis or design about *what* to do and *how* to do it.

A structured technique bestows ownership on your participants right from the beginning. But the real joy is that once you understand how to use a particular tool (for example, how to manage the context), you can use it repeatedly. Moreover, you don't need to have detailed expertise on specific content. You need to have only a conversational understanding about the terms being used.

RAISE YOUR CONSCIOUSNESS ABOUT MEETING ROLES

From this point on, I'll raise your consciousness around the roles of meeting designer, meeting facilitator, and meeting leader by helping you understand these concepts:

- As meeting leader, how to think separately about facilitation and meeting design

- How critical it is for facilitators to remain content-neutral—passionate about results, yet unbiased about path

- How to apply facilitator skills, such as precise questioning, keen observing, and active listening, to improve meetings

- The fact that the meeting coordinator, meeting documenter, meeting facilitator, and meeting designer are not persons but rather roles that are frequently performed by one person

2

Leading

BE A SERVANT, NOT A SENATOR

Clear leadership consciousness integrates the *why*, *what*, and *how*. Exceptional meeting leadership also requires keen awareness and the ability to describe to participants . . .

- *Where* they are going (so they know what "done" looks like)

- *Why* the meeting is important (if it is not, it should not take place)

- *What* questions they need to answer and in what sequence

- Meeting roles and rules, leading to *who* does what

- Planned activities and procedures, leading to *how* participants will get done

Meeting Leadership: Where *Comes before* Why

Technically, leaders do *not* have to know why they are going somewhere to be successful at arriving. They must, however, be clear about where they are going. All leaders—command control leaders, meeting leaders, and servant leaders— must have line of site, or a straight line leading to the target: the "deliverable" (or output) from the meeting, or what DONE looks like.

After you can describe where you are leading your group, first seek agreement about why the deliverable is important. If your participants cannot agree on why the object of their endeavors is important, it is unlikely that they will arrive at consensus during subsequent analysis or design activities.[1]

Let me be clear, you are not seeking to have everyone playing the same note on the same instrument. That would be quite boring and uneventful. Rather,

---

[1] I define the term "consensus" as "a result you can live with." It may not be anyone's favorite result. But reaching consensus does mean that everyone agrees to support the result professionally and that no one will personally lose any sleep over it.

you are seeking the harmony of different notes being played on different instruments—something akin to music, whether a symphony or hip-hop.

Your role, as the meeting facilitator, is to dictate tempo, volume, and who plays when. Do not, however, pick up an instrument and start playing on behalf of your meeting participants. It is their responsibility to provide music from their instruments; they are the experts. They do not have to play the same note, but you must keep them harmonious.

The balance of this chapter on meeting leadership explains how mastering three concepts will enable you to lead any group in any type of situation. The three concepts seem complicated yet are vital to collaborative meetings around complex topics. You may not completely understand them immediately, but they will crystallize by the end of the book after you use these three concepts over and over:

1. The **holarchy** or graphical view (discussed in the next section) operating throughout an organization[2]

2. The **trichotomy** or first-cut analytical method for applying structure that immediately divides complex issues into three manageable portions (discussed later in the chapter)

3. The **meeting roles** that must be respected because you want subject matter experts to strive for objectivity and, therefore, leave their egos and titles in the hallway

NOTE: Jan Smuts (prime minister of the Union of South Africa) coined the term "holism" in 1926. In his book *Holism and Evolution*, Smuts defined holism as "the tendency in nature to form wholes that are greater than the sum of the parts through creative evolution."[3]

Holarchy: It Begins with DONE

Unclear speaking and writing indicate unclear thinking. If you are acutely aware of where you are leading your group, then express this objective in a written statement, for your benefit and theirs. If you are unable to articulate your meeting objective in writing, you need more time or understanding.

Meetings need to be documented. If they are not documented, nothing happened. Therefore, an effective leader begins by documenting the meeting objectives, frequently called deliverables. To understand the value of a deliver-

---

[2] Arthur Koestler, in his book *The Ghost in the Machine* (1967), defines a holarchy as a hierarchy of self-regulating holons that function first as autonomous wholes in relation to their parts, second as dependent parts in relation to controls from higher levels, and third in coordination with other holons.

[3] Howard Esbin, "Holism: A Brief History," https://www.linkedin.com/pulse/holism-brief-history-howard-b-esbin-phd/.

able, it should be viewed with respect to its impact on all other objectives of an organization, as part of the *organizational holarchy* shown in figure 2.1.

The organizational holarchy represents the web of interdependent connections throughout an organization. The root "arch" in the terms "holarchy" and "hierarchy" means "governance or rule"; "hier" means "sacred or holy," while "holos" means "whole." Thus, in a holarchy, each cell is both a whole and a part; systems are nested within one another. One well-known phrase calls the holarchy of humankind the "butterfly effect." Einstein labeled his mathematical holarchy "relativity."

An organization may be called a corporation, a government body, or something else. An organization may represent a collection of business units. Not all organizations are large enough to be separated into discrete business units. And in some organizations, the departments are so large, they would be called business units in other organizations. Please be flexible when drawing lines about the terms being used.

In both commercial and governmental organizations, business units control departments or programs that are ongoing. Each ongoing department or program commands a collection of products or projects that come and go, with discrete starting and stopping points. Thus, the organization frequently executes its strategy through investments it makes toward new or renewed products and projects, some lasting longer than others.[4]

The holarchy represents the unity of all the objectives, from business units to answers developed in meetings. The purpose of any meeting ought to support the organization's purpose, scope, and objectives. If not, the meeting should be canceled. To know which products or projects are most important, leaders use their awareness of what else is going on in and around the organization to ascertain the extent to which a particular initiative supports the purpose, scope, and objectives of everything else going on in the organization.

1. Harmonious **purpose** means everything being done should support the purpose of the organization—or else should not be done. The purpose of any question asked in a meeting should support the purpose of the *Agenda Step*. The *Agenda Steps* should support the purpose of the meeting, which supports the product, the project, and so on. Each of these in turn should also support the programs, departments, and business units dependent on them.

2. **Scope** represents boundaries and is usually framed by the organization. For example, a manufacturer of regenerative electric engines will avoid setting up a chain of ice cream parlors (although I'm sure

---

[4] A wise man once said, "I don't care what you claim your strategy is, follow the money. Where are you making investments? What projects and products are being approved? There's your strategy."

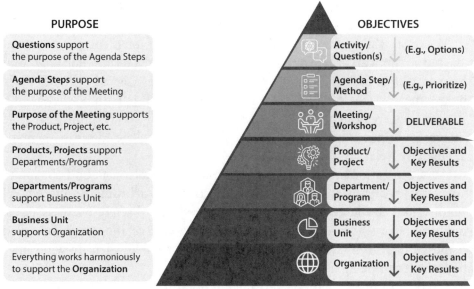

SCOPE increases until it reaches the level of the entire organization.

Figure 2.1. Organizational Holarchy of Alignment

more unusual things have happened). Regardless, it's unlikely that a project team for some engine manufacturer will venture into ice cream parlors without clear and explicit approval from its program office, business unit, and organization.

3. **Objectives** provide measurements of progress and success. They influence the priorities for approving labor and material resources. Although given various names, the family of objectives represents the aims for each operation (that is, each row in figure 2.1).[5]

NOTE: What is the difference between purpose and objectives since the purpose is to reach or exceed the objectives? Objectives or objects are nouns—that is, things. Purpose gives reason and rationale for the value of something. Purpose provides context for the value of the objects.

A change in any one of the cells of the holarchy causes a ripple throughout an organization, whether subtle or profound. The success or failure of new products affect the development of subsequent new products (or projects). Likewise, a project's success or failure affects the sponsoring department or program, and those ripples are felt by its business unit and organization.

---

[5] In the English language alone, we have the terms "criteria," "CTQ" (critical to quality), "goals," "key results," "KPI" (key performance indicators), "milestones," "objectives," "targets," and so on. They all represent measurements of how well an operation is performing, from the entire organization down to specific products and projects.

Understanding the organizational holarchy requires one to "begin with the end in mind," as Steven Covey put it.[6] If actions taken or decisions made within an organization do not harmonize with the organization's purpose, stay within the organization's scope, and support the organization's objectives, the actions or decisions are unwarranted.

The equivalent idea among practitioners who call themselves Agilists states that before we begin our meeting, we need to know what DONE looks like.[7] In other words, where are we going? The combined objectives of projects, products, programs, departments, and business units represent an aggregate of the organizational objectives. The collection might also be referred to as the organizational strategy, because it provides leadership with line of site about the relationship of these objectives and reflects the ability to make investment and operational decisions.

> NOTE: David Spangler writes, "Thus in a hierarchy, participants can be compared and evaluated based on position, rank, relative power, seniority and the like. But in a holarchy each person's value comes from his or her individuality and uniqueness and the capacity to engage and interact with others to make the fruits of that uniqueness available to the entire organization."[8]

As the meeting leader and meeting facilitator, you must also possess line of site. You need to know where you are going. Are we building a narrative list, a paragraph, or pages of documentation? Are we building a chart of roles and responsibilities or a process flow diagram, or both? In other words, do you know where you are leading this group and what they need to build during this meeting to get DONE? Can you estimate the value and impact your deliverable has on the entire organization?

> NOTE: If a meeting fails, it puts the product or project it supports at risk. Consequently, a failed meeting has immediate impact on departments and business units reaching their objectives. In turn, if reaching their objectives has been jeopardized, the organization is also put at risk. Wall Street frowns, and the stock price drops—all because of lousy meetings.

Connections between all the parts of the holarchy are vitalized through communications and the exchange of information, which dramatically affect

---

[6] The second habit Stephen Covey covers in *The 7 Habits of Highly Effective People* is "Begin With the End in Mind."

[7] Agilists are practitioners who promote an Agile mindset, which commonly relies on project management frameworks such as Scrum, Lean, Kanban, and so on. The Agile mindset is highly attentive toward the definition of "DONE."

[8] David Spangler, "A Vision of Holarchy," *Seven Pillars: House of Wisdom*, https://web.archive.org/web/20120218163022/http://www.sevenpillarshouse.org/index.php/article/a_vision_of_holarchy1.

decision-making. The decisions involved may include decisions to buy or sell; whom to hire; how to define "pay," including the full package of benefits; and so on.

> NOTE: For each operation in the holarchy, information requirements are distinct, yet communicated objectively through common objectives such as currency, duration, frequency, precision, and so on.

From the boardroom to the boiler room, decisions should harmonize with the purpose of the organization and support reaching (or exceeding) organizational objectives. Thus, making decisions represents the most important action taken every day by employees, executives, and others. Those decisions optimally favor the purpose, scope, and objectives of the entire organization.

The most crucial decisions, involving copious amounts of funding or affecting quality of life for a lot of stakeholders, need to appeal to specific organizational objectives. In other words, in most organizations, to promote appropriate and consistent decision-making, appropriate stakeholders should be able to access the purpose, scope, and objectives of the organization—in writing.

Many would call that document the strategic plan. Likewise, most departments and program offices have their own purpose, scope, and objectives in writing as well. Again, these may frequently be called strategic or departmental plans. To gain investment and organizational support, projects and products also rely on written documents that stipulate their purpose, scope, and objectives; these documents are frequently called team or product charters.

Therefore, meeting leaders must understand and articulate the purpose, scope, and objectives for each meeting they lead, before the meeting begins. Meeting leaders must also understand and articulate the purpose, scope, and objectives for each *Agenda Step* and each question that needs to be answered during the meeting. Leaders first need line of site to explain how the output from each question and *Agenda Step* aligns and supports all objectives—from meeting objectives, through organizational objectives.

A meeting leader who is incapable of writing down the meeting purpose, scope, and objectives is not prepared to lead the meeting. Furthermore, the leader should understand the impact of the meeting. What is the meeting worth? How important is it? Prove it. If we fail, what have we lost or put at risk (typically dollars or personnel hours—for example FTPs[9])?

I will use the holarchy in chapter 4 to help you manage arguments and conflict. Again, in chapter 6, I will use the holarchy to show you how to facili-

---

[9] "FTP" stands for "full-time person"; some use "FTE" for "full-time employee" or "equivalent." Calculated as the value of one person for one year, the contribution of an FTP is approximately 2,000 hours of work. For example, a project might require four FTP, but using 16 people, it is completed within three months.

tate *Alignment*, analyzing to what extent meeting results support organizational objectives. In practice, the holarchy demands that we maintain vigilance around the terms people use. The terms that most often cause organizational confusion or disagreement, whether you have a clear organizational holarchy or not, include "purpose," "scope," and "objectives."

When a participant says, "But I thought the purpose was to _____?," you must first ask the participant, "the purpose of what?" Is the participant referring to the purpose of the organization, program, product, meeting, activity, or question? While these purposes should harmonize, they are discretely different from one another.

> NOTE: The following series of examples (business, product, meeting) illustrates the holarchy using the analogy of the fictitious THRIVE LLC[10] as it builds a new financial product designed to help people better manage their personal assets and liabilities.

HARMONIOUS PURPOSES

The purpose of something defines why it exists. The purpose is different for each department, project, and meeting, as can be seen in the following examples:

- *Product development department purpose:* The purpose of the THRIVE product development department is to research, develop, and commercialize products that appeal to households aspiring to make their lives easier.

- *Product purpose:* The purpose of the THRIVE financial product supports managing household finances by providing services that monitor, track, and automate the management of financial assets and liabilities and thoroughly improve the handling of household financial accounts.

- *Meeting purpose:* The purpose of the meeting is to define the activities that household personnel perform to support their own objectives and obligations with respect to assets and liabilities.

A NARROWING SCOPE

The scope defines what is included in or excluded from a department, project, or meeting. Scope describes boundaries: reach and breadth. Purpose and scope wording sometimes overlaps, because purposes focus on what is included within the scope.

---

[10] THRIVE LLC is a fictitious for-profit greenfield company that provides to residential households products and services intended to make life easier and more manageable.

- *Product development department scope:* The department scope includes products and services that appeal directly to households aspiring to make their personal lives and lifestyles easier and more rewarding.

- *Product scope:* The product scope includes managing financial assets and liabilities in households using account management, accounts payable, accounts receivable, budgeting, investments, and tax management.

- *Meeting scope:* The scope of this meeting includes only those activities that specifically support account management activities and requirements within the financial realm of people in North America, including Canada, Mexico, and the United States (but not Greenland and parts of Iceland), over the next five years.

SHARED OBJECTIVES

Objectives (goals) define what is to be accomplished. Enterprise-wide objectives are defined by the organization, are translated into operational plans by business units, and give rise to department and program objectives that drive discrete product, project, and personnel goals and objectives. Objectives furnish depth and detail about direction, as in these examples:

- *One of many product development department objectives:* Provide the sales and marketing department with shippable product and support collaterals for three new financial products to be launched by the end of fiscal year 20__.

- *One of many product goals:* Develop a solution that allows real-time access to account information and eliminates the need for monthly reconciliation across different financial accounts.

- *Meeting deliverable (for meetings, the objectives are called deliverables):* A SIPOC model of personal account management activities, inputs, and outputs that support financial account management requirements.[11]

Once each purpose and all objectives are clear, a group can make consistent decisions about alignment, priorities, and resource allocation. Tom Sommer accurately touches upon alignment when he claims that to measure alignment, "we should ask four questions: 1. What does success look like for you personally (in your role)? 2. What does success look like for the team? 3. What does success look like for the department? 4. What does success look like for the company?"[12]

---

[11] SIPOC (which stands for "source, input, process, output, client") represents a "use-case" model used to build process flow diagrams and support value-stream analysis, among other reasons.

[12] Tom Sommer, "Increasing Alignment: Ideas and Approaches to Increase Alignment across the Whole Organization," *Redbubble*, February 26, 2019, https://medium.com/redbubble/increasing-alignment-a33203fe8687.

His logic suggests we must appeal to the objectives of each of these stake-holders, minimizing the tension and maximizing the results. Indeed, if someone in a meeting suggests something that does not harmonize with our shared organizational purpose, we should not do it (unless we are participating in a *Visioning* session). If two people argue over which method to follow, we can appeal to the Objectives column of the holarchy to best determine which argument should win, based on the level of support it provides in reaching objectives from the product throughout the entire organization (more on this in chapters 4 and 6).

STILL WITH ME?

You were just exposed to the most difficult concept in the entire book. The holarchy may not resonate fully until you see how the holarchy is applied to help manage arguments, conduct alignment, and so on. Please be patient; the idea is worth taking the time to understand. Powerful concepts like the holarchy cannot be explained simply.

Trichotomy: Foundation of Structure

In ancient Greece, Plato's "trivium" served as the necessary foundation entitling citizens to vote. The three tests of the "trivium" were logic, rhetoric, and grammar—spanning the transformation from the abstract to the concrete. Aristotle, Immanuel Kant, Søren Kierkegaard, Sigmund Freud, Sir Francis Bacon, and dozens of other famous minds have built systems of thought and critical thinking based on the concept of the trichotomy.

> **—Aristotle**
> *Express yourself like the common people but think like a wise person.*

Through critical thinking, the structure of trichotomy helps you break down complex issues into manageable pieces. To build traction, you can sharpen your questions to keep your meetings focused. Structure begins with the trichotomy as a function of will, wisdom, and activity. It conveys in a mathematical sense that $Y = (f) X + X + x + x$, with our meeting deliverable, Y, being a function of answers to the big X's (will, wisdom, and activity) that further deconstruct into answers about little x's. As you know, we must first agree on *why* something is important before agreeing on *what* to do about it and then arguing about *how* to do it.

After meetings conclude, the thoughts and words expressed become the impetus for shaping upcoming deeds and actions. If nothing changes, the meeting was a waste of time. Notice how over the course of meetings, the abstract (we begin with thoughts, or will) converts into words for sharing and arguing (wisdom), that eventually change our actions or behavior (activity). Will, wisdom, and activity equate to the *why*, the *what*, and the *how* that justify the time

Table 2.1. Trichotomy: Structuring Thoughts (Abstract) into Actions (Concrete)

Level of Structure / Topic	First	Second	Third
Trichotomy	Will	Wisdom	Activity
Apocryphal	Thoughts	Words	Deeds
Beliefs	Head	Heart	Hands
Governance	Policy	Rules	Procedures
Intelligence	Strategic	Tactical	Operational
Life cycle	Planning	Analysis	Design
Plato	Logic	Rhetoric	Grammar
Logic	Why	What	How
Use case	Input	Process	Output

and expense of meetings. Meetings are validated when thoughts are transformed into actions (table 2.1).

During meetings, participant thoughts are converted into words that are shared with other participants. The exchange of ideas catalyzes the stimulation and discovery of ideas that did not walk into the meeting but were created during the meeting.

The leader-posed questions in meetings direct and stimulate participant thinking. Notice that when a participant asks a question during a meeting, and we focus on the question, we are in danger of following that participant's agenda. Remember that scope creep begins in meetings—usually in meetings with weak or ignorant scope control.

Structure tells us not to ask for the deliverable Y, but rather to ask detailed questions that aggregate into a deliverable, the X's or the x's. As we aggregate the responses to the X's and the x's, we generate the deliverable, Y. Let's look at two examples.

EXAMPLE 1: MARKETING PLAN

If your deliverable is a marketing plan, you cannot simply ask "What is the marketing plan?" You must know in advance that the marketing plan (Y) is a function of segmentation, targeting, positioning, message, medium, and so on (some little x's). So you might start out by asking, "What are the three primary target customers for _____ product or service?" Since detailed questions stimulate participants and are easier to answer, we might even narrow our question to a specific geographical area or a stratified customer type.

EXAMPLE 2: GLOBAL HUNGER

If your deliverable is a solution for global hunger among children, you do not ask, "What should we do to fix global hunger among children?" That question is so broad that people could respond by bringing up anything from global warming to genetically modified plants. Structure tells us to sharpen our questions so that we might ask, "What could we do to improve food storage capacity in coastal Somalia?"—a question specific enough to generate helpful responses such as "repurpose low-yield mine shafts," "convert abandoned rail cars," and so on.

STRUCTURE GIVES RISE TO FLEXIBILITY

With structure, you can always take the scenic route. You can explore unplanned tangents with reckless abandon because you have a path to take when the detour ends or goes nowhere. With no structure, people are not flexible; they are simply untethered.

Structure provides a way to design meeting sessions so that issues are not forgotten or overlooked, and participants can measure how much work was accomplished and how much more effort might be required to get DONE. Structured and focused questions consistently enable faster and more flexible responses than unstructured discussions that go "around and around."

Most people would not try to multiply 4,693 times 2,349 in their heads; they would write the problem down or use a calculator. Yet groups and teams always tackle far more complicated business problems such as entering new markets or launching new products. Unstructured meetings proceed with unfacilitated discussions that conclude when the time runs out, not when actionable results are clear.

In summary and in sequence, the trichotomy of meeting discipline fundamentally looks like this:

- Will: Why is something important? (abstract thoughts)

- Wisdom: What are we going to do to support it? (transformation of the abstract into the concrete)

- Activity: How are we going to get it done? (clear and concrete actions and results)

Here is a straightforward example:

- The frayed collar on my shirt is uncomfortable and socially embarrassing. (abstract)

- I could replace the collar, change shirts, go shirtless, buy a new shirt, or take some other relevant action. (transformation)

- I am going to the Bricks & Clicks store to purchase a replacement shirt. (concrete)

Become a disciplined leader by applying structure *before* your meeting begins. Once you develop awareness about *where* and *why* you are leading a group, apply critical thinking and discipline to understand *what* is needed. Then you can determine *how* you are going to lead a group to build it consensually. Effective leaders cycle groups through the *why*, the *what*, and the *how*, leading groups from where they are today to where they want to be tomorrow. To ensure consensus and innovation, effective leaders rely on structured meetings.

Consciousness: Meeting Roles

We behave differently as a manager than we do as a spouse, parent, or child, even if we long to be 29 years old again. We constantly switch roles to accommodate needs and expectations, both from ourselves and others. For example, a barista has different expectations and behaviors when making coffee drinks for customers than when off work and purchasing coffee as a customer.

Roles do not even need to be performed by people, as "expert systems" may substitute for people. Note how, on the internet, the role of travel agent has been replaced by "expert systems" such as Orbitz. When we use the self-checkout lane in a grocery store, the role of cashier has been replaced by another type of expert system that integrates bar codes, radio frequency identification (RFID) tags, and so on.

Meeting leaders are required to understand distinct meeting roles and to be able to switch between them quickly. The following lists three traditional roles found among most participants; the next section discusses four discrete roles typical to most meeting leaders. Keep in mind that roles represent a set of expected attitudes and behavior and do not equate with a person. People perform most roles, and we all perform multiple roles.

EXECUTIVE SPONSOR OR PRODUCT OWNER

The executive sponsor (which may be a steering team) pays for the business initiative, project, or product. The executive sponsor may participate in planning workshops and in early analysis workshops defining the business scope and measurements.

OBSERVER(S)

Observers are people with a tangential interest (such as advisory councils, auditors, contractors, customers, suppliers, team members, and vendors). Observers are *not* meeting participants. Observers stay out of conversations and do not distract other participants:

- They always keep silent during meeting time.

- They ask questions during breaks, lunches, or other periods between meetings.

PARTICIPANTS (SUBJECT MATTER EXPERTS, OR SMES)

Your meeting participants are members from the business and technical communities who contribute their subject matter expertise, also known as content.

Participant responsibilities include the following:

- Communicating meeting results to others as appropriate

- Owning the results of meetings in which they participate

- Preparing and participating actively

- Representing their business needs and goals

POWER OF PLURALITY

Nobody is smarter than everybody, because groups of people can develop more ideas (options) than individuals on their own. Any person or group with more options at their disposal will statistically make higher-quality decisions. By leveraging one another's minds, we are capable of breakthrough and innovation not realized when working alone.

For optimal group decision-making, empirical evidence suggests a meeting of between five and nine participants.[13] Although meetings with fewer participants may be common, be aware that fewer participants put you at risk of failing to realize innovative breakthroughs. Any more than nine participants can generate a poor return on investment because highly paid professionals are passively sitting, not making frequent contributions. Have you ever sat in a full-day meeting and spoken only once or twice throughout the day?

Planning workshops tend to have more participants than design workshops. Practically speaking, limiting some meetings to only nine participants may be impossible. However, a meeting of five to nine participants remains optimal and provides a range for you to target.

Four Roles Fulfilled by Meeting Leaders

Effective meeting leaders frequently perform four roles. When all four roles are performed by one individual it makes that person much, much more than a facilitator; that person becomes the meeting leader. The four roles include these:

- Meeting coordinator

- Meeting documenter

---

[13] The Agile community calls this "seven: plus or minus two," mathematically equivalent to a range of five to nine.

- Meeting facilitator

- Meeting designer

MEETING COORDINATOR

This role is part-time and may be performed partly by administrative support. Responsibilities include reserving meeting rooms and arranging for coordination, refreshments, supplies, and travel. The meeting coordinator role is not formal, but the responsibilities must be performed by some individual or individuals.

Meeting coordinator responsibilities include these tasks:

- Arranging for equipment and supplies and ensuring operable, reliable technology

- Ordering (and receiving and setting up) refreshments

- Reserving the meeting room or setting up the online technology platform

- Supporting participant requests such as log-in credentials or travel coordination, or providing technology training tips and resources for online meetings

MEETING DOCUMENTER (SCRIBE)

Frequently the person who is the meeting facilitator also serves as the meeting documenter, but the role could be assigned to someone else who documents the meeting results. Meeting documenters do not edit, paraphrase, or change documentation on their own.

NOTE: Neutrality is important. The meeting documenter(s) must maintain an objective and neutral role throughout the meeting. Judgment or evaluation of the content may lead to a skewed deliverable. The goal is not recording verbatim meeting minutes but documenting the agreed-upon outputs with enough detail to ensure accurate reviews.

Meeting documenter responsibilities include these tasks:

- Documenting outputs and inflection points, not verbatim conversations

- Distributing the meeting notes

- Managing edits, document versioning, and archiving

MEETING FACILITATOR

To be effective, the meeting facilitator's role is frequently defined to include the traditional roles of both "meeting facilitator" and "meeting designer." These are discrete roles; you could provide me with the meeting design, while I could facilitate. However, very few people understand the difference. So let's begin with the meeting facilitator's role.

As meeting facilitator, you establish an atmosphere of freedom and trust to allow for the exchange and challenge of ideas. The meeting facilitator enables and supports the discovery and evolution of ideas.

Both discovery and evolution rely heavily on challenging underlying assumptions. The meeting facilitator leads a group to consensus by building understanding around the assumptions and objective evidence (*why*) that support individual and subjective perspectives (*what*). Meeting facilitators conduct meetings.

These are the guiding principles of the meeting facilitator role:

- Diplomatically channels a diverse set of ideas into meaningful action

- Directs the group toward shared purpose and objectives

- Galvanizes consensus about what is known, remaining resilient about managing uncertainty and other open issues

- Liberates the group to concentrate on the content (answers) rather than the context (questions), thus providing traction to get DONE

The most effective meeting facilitators will be the ones who develop traction by getting the entire group to focus on the same thing at the same time.

Meeting facilitator responsibilities include these tasks:

- Actively listening to the conversation and challenging assumptions

- Creating synergy by removing distractions

- Ensuring that participants have an equal opportunity to participate

- Explaining and enforcing the roles

- Keeping the content within scope

- Managing the documentation person or process

- Observing group interactions and adjusting

- Questioning to achieve clarity—aiding communication among participants

- Recognizing disruptive behavior and creating positive corrections

- Working to manage conflicts quickly

Being of Service

The meeting facilitator role creates an environment where every participant can collaborate, innovate, and excel. Effective facilitators listen to understand, rather than listen to respond.

Servant Skills

Keep in mind that "consensus" does not imply "casualness." As an effective servant, it is your job to be to be kind, rather than nice. The words "kind" and "kin" are related to the same root, meaning "family." Being kind means to treat like family—so it is not always necessary to be nice, although it is always necessary to be professional. All the core skills associated with being an effective meeting facilitator are also required of every servant leader.

MEETING DESIGNER

The meeting designer's role determines the *Meeting Approach*, stipulates the questions to use, and provides an optimal sequence for answering those questions. The meeting designer's role is functional and not necessarily to be performed by a single individual or even by a person. For example, the executive sponsor could be the meeting designer in planning. The meeting design for buying travel tickets could rely on a system such as Expedia, rather than a person. The meeting design could derive from an established life cycle framework such as Kanban, Lean, SAFe, Scrum, and so on.

The individual performing the role of meeting facilitator usually performs the role of meeting designer as well. The meeting designer is an expert for the deliverable, who clearly understands the product to build, the *Meeting Approach*, and specific questions that need to be answered to create the deliverable.

> NOTE: Notice how family reunions seldom change from year to year. Who is the designer? Typically, the family matriarch or patriarch. The risk in using the same person as designer is that you will get the same old answer. This year's family reunion looks like last year's. People don't know what they don't know.
>
> Notice how rarely teenagers look forward to family reunions. Why? Because we do not obtain their input on what they would like to have or do. We assume that since we have all been teenagers, we already know what they want. How's that working out for you, by the way?
>
> At work, people rely on their "matriarch" or "patriarch" for meeting design support. Using your supervisor, mentor, partner, or person across the hall offers both risk and reward.
>
> The reward, of course, is that such people (think of mentors) are inexpensive. They don't send you an invoice for their time. More important, they take little of your energy to contribute by providing instant airtime. If you simply need to get your work done and get on with it, use the matriarch. But if you are seeking innovation or breakthrough, use a fresh or unique source for your meeting design, because innovation begins with the questions being asked. So stir up your design.

The meeting designer provides the *Meeting Approach* for building the deliverable by structuring the meeting to produce output in the most effective and expeditious manner. To transfer ownership to meeting participants, the meeting design ensures meaningful participant involvement during the meeting preparation and design.

The meeting designer structures the *Meeting Approach* and ensures that the output produced meets organizational standards of quality and consistency, so that others, such as product or project development or Scrum development teams, can act on the deliverable effectively.

The meeting designer reaches this result by doing the following:

- Helping stakeholders codify the deliverable and draft appropriate agenda steps

- Developing succinct questions that need to be answered

- Structuring the sequence of the questions

- Specifying primary and backup *Tools* and procedures for converting answers into final form such as a decision, a plan, a recommended solution, and so on

Note that questions drive a group's attention and focus. So, when participants ask questions, they have shifted roles from subject matter expert to meeting designer. If we follow their line of thought during a meeting and answer their questions, we may be "going down their agenda."

It is best to know what questions participants would like to address before the meeting starts. However, addressing their questions is not necessarily good nor bad. Sometimes it is a wise course to pursue, and sometimes it's not. For you to decide, you must first be aware of the meeting dynamics and how someone in the role of subject matter expert has taken over the role of meeting designer by asking a question.

We have all heard some people described as "having their own agenda." This is how meetings get derailed: participants ask questions that shift the group's focus. Most facilitators are unaware of this reaction as it is occurring. If you are conscious of the roles and have the structure to get you back on track, you can enjoy an occasional detour if time permits.

Quick Summary on Leading

This book shows you how to facilitate consensual agreement in the best manner for supporting all stakeholders. This chapter stresses the importance of knowing *why* you are meeting (leadership). Even great facilitators fail if they don't know where they are going.

The holarchy reminds us that resources such as time and money are finite, so we prioritize everything from individual actions to group projects. To prioritize effectively, we establish line of site from the product or project objectives to the business department and business unit objectives. Ultimately, we appeal to shared and consensual understanding as to which decisions, positions, or solutions best support the organizational purpose, scope, and objectives.

The trichotomy provides structure that enables the transformation from critical thinking into concrete actions. For meetings, structure helps us develop the questions we need to answer. The structure of the holarchy illustrates the impact meeting deliverables have on quality of life for participants and the organization or organizations your meeting supports.

Most meeting leaders perform four discrete roles, and the toughest is meeting designer. While everyone performs multiple roles within an organization (such as peer, mentor, and subordinate), all employees have a duty (fiduciary responsibility) and should view all their actions and decisions as having positive impact, strategically, tactically, and operationally, every moment of every day.

3

Facilitating

MAKING IT EASIER WITH THREE CORE SKILLS

This chapter focuses on detailing three core skills for meeting leaders who value facilitation, servant leadership, and getting DONE faster (structure). As meeting facilitator, you need to command these core skills but, at the same time, remember to always reduce or eliminate distractions so that your group stays focused.

Three Core Skills of Meeting Leaders

The following are three core skills vital to effective meeting leadership:

1. **Speaking and Questioning Clearly**

   - Being parsimonious—expressing the most with the least

   - Clarifying the meaning of terms—timely expanding and focusing conversation

   - Commanding the language—properly applying the parts of speech

   - Discovering the objective evidence, examples, facts, and logic

   - Distilling content contributions accurately, if not verbatim

   - Seeking objective measurements behind subjective biases

2. **Actively Listening and Observing Constantly**

   - Contacting and absorbing—noticing participants' verbal, nonverbal, and paraverbal (such as tone) aspects

   - Confirming—ensuring accuracy

   - Monitoring time, pace, and other environmental "noise" that might get in the way

- Reflecting emotions, feelings, opinions, and other supporting rationale

- Scanning for acceptance, rejection, or uncertainty from any participant

3. **Remaining Neutral and Controlling Context without Fail**

- Applying ground rules to get more done faster

- Creating a climate of acceptance and trust

- Documenting options or action plans without bias

- Helping participants decide and prioritize without your judgment

- Instructing participants how to structure their doubts or fears

- Stimulating conversations about *an* answer, not *the* answer

ROSETTA STONE OF FACILITATION

Meetings reflect a complex blend of issues, personalities, and proposals. As the meeting facilitator, when these issues cause you to question what you should do, ask yourself this question: **"If _____ happens, is it a distraction or not?"**

Because this question provides a key or a way of shaping any question you have about what you should or should not do, I call this question the Rosetta stone of facilitation.[1] If the answer is yes—whatever issue you are wondering about is a distraction—then it is your responsibility to remove the cause of the distraction so that your group can remain sharp and focused. However, if the answer is no, it is not a distraction, then don't worry about it.

The most formidable challenge for you and most facilitators is to get an intelligent group of people to *focus on the same thing at the same time.* Telling participants to focus will not work. Rather, you must persist in removing distractions so that whatever remains becomes the focal point. **From start to finish, to create traction, removing distractions remains the essential discipline.**

The Core Skill of Speaking Clearly

Clarity represents the extent to which a speaker's intent secures the understanding they seek. Unfortunately, numerous filters and obstacles stand between a speaker's intent and a listener's understanding, such as these:

- Biases and prejudices

- Perceptual challenges

---

[1] The Rosetta stone is a large stone carved and discovered in Egypt that enabled the deciphering of Egyptian hieroglyphs. Facilitators use the imaginary Rosetta stone of "distractions" to arrive at an answer about behavior. If something is a distraction, it should not happen; if it's not a distraction, don't worry about it.

- Speaking mannerisms
- Technology hiccups
- Vague word choice (lack of rhetorical precision)

Power struggles between various departments or business units often result from language differences and word choice. Power struggles may not be intentional but may occur because of differing perspectives and definitions of terms and expressions.

In meetings, facilitators do not work with "words" so much as with the intent and meaning behind the words. Frequently, graphs, illustrations, and models are better universal sources of content than narrative descriptions.

—Hafez (also known as Hafiz)
If you think that the Truth can be known From words,
If you think that the Sun and the Ocean Can pass through that tiny opening called the mouth.
O' someone should start laughing!
Someone should start wildly laughing—Now!

FACILITATE MEANING, NOT WORDS

Meeting participants most frequently express and extract meaning from the world of words, which I refer to as "narrative." Five common techniques, including narrative, express intent and meaning:

1. Narrative
2. Nonverbal
3. Illustrative
4. Iconic (symbols)
5. Numeric

NARRATIVE

Oral and written (narrative) rhetoric relies on words, the primary means of communicating in meetings. However, nonnarrative methods may be equally effective and sometimes preferred, especially when explaining complex topics and issues.

NONVERBAL

Substantial information during meetings transfers through body signals, openness (or closeness), shifting eyebrows, frowns of disapproval and grins of approval, and the like. Hand gestures help explain the passion and intensity behind some meeting participants' claims, along with cadence, tone, and other paraverbal traits.

ILLUSTRATIVE

Drawings, illustrations, and pictures reflect intent and meaning and are particularly effective in explaining complex relationships. Pictures of birds provide much clearer understanding about birds than using words alone. Likewise, process flow and value stream diagrams may provide quick overviews more effectively and efficiently than verbal explanations.

ICONIC (OR SYMBOLIC)

Icons and symbols extend intent and meaning. Many icons are now universally acceptable and leapfrog the challenges associated with language challenges. Street signs, restroom symbols, and public transportation indicators do not leave much room for confusion or misunderstanding (take the stop sign, for example).

NUMERIC

Scorecards, spreadsheets, and other weighted ranking systems should be familiar. Additionally, I built my *Quantitative TO-WS Analysis* (chapter 6) to describe the *Current Situation* numerically, thus avoiding some of the emotion and passion that can bog people down in searching for the right words. By using numbers instead of words, participants strive to understand in addition to trying to be understood.

OTHER TECHNIQUES

Dance, movies, music, storytelling, and other formats also communicate intent and meaning. Most of us, however, rarely engage other formats for expressing our intent when we are working with business groups.

Rhetorical Precision: Why It Can Be Tricky

Languages are remarkably dynamic. The English language is particularly rich, with a heritage of diversity. Unlike French or Italian,

> *—Economist* **blog (2010)**
> *Enron's document-management policy simply meant shredding. France's proposed solidarity contribution on airline tickets is a tax. The IMF's relational capitalism is corruption. The British solicitor-general's evidentiary deficiency was no evidence, and George Bush's reputational problem just means he was mistrusted.*

Table 3.1. English: A Mash-Up of Words from Major Languages

National Origin	Term	Original Meaning
Arabic	**Sofa**	Seat
Cantonese	**Ketchup**	Tomato juice
Japanese	**Shogun**	General
Malaysian	**Amok**	Rushing in a frenzy
Mayan	**Hurricane**	Mayan god, Huracan
Persian	**Caravan**	Traveling company
Turkish	**Kiosk**	Pavilion

English is not a fixed or static language. The meanings of English words are "not established, approved, and firmly set by some official committee charged with preserving its dignity and integrity." Influenced heavily by other languages, the English language is renowned for its "capacity for foxy and relentlessly slippery flexibility."[2]

Between 1590 and 1610 alone, more than 100,000 new words were added to the English language. Over time, some words do not survive, and others mutate into existence (for example, "Google" used as a verb). Because society itself introduces added terms, English becomes a hodgepodge of diverse and multicultural languages (see table 3.1).

I often ask students—and you may do the same before proceeding—to write down a single English term that describes the opposite of "life." Most write down "death." I then ask them to write down the opposite of "birth" and see a lot of smiles. Most would argue that the term "death" best answers the second challenge, and a better answer to the first challenge might be "lifelessness."

Of the eight parts of speech in English grammar[3] (the number varies for other languages), four are particularly problematic for facilitators working in English: adjectives, adverbs, prepositions, and pronouns. Collectively we call these words "modifiers" (although prepositions may be better viewed as "containers").

For example, if Sally claims she added value at her place of employment last week, few will dispute her statement. But if Sally claims she added a *lot* of value

---

[2] Simon Winchester, *The Meaning of Everything: The Story of the Oxford English Dictionary* (2003), 29.
[3] Noun, pronoun, verb, adjective, adverb, preposition, conjunction, and interjection.

last week, guess which term we will talk about?

> NOTE: When facilitating, be particularly careful with dialogue that includes "nyms": anto*nyms,* contro*nyms,* hom-o*nyms,* or syno*nyms.* Challenge and precision are required to build solid consensus around synonyms, especially when they are used as modifiers such as adjectives and adverbs.[4] With homonyms, someone in the group is most assuredly hearing the "wrong" term.[5]

> **—Jodi Picoult,**
> ***Country Living***
> *Words are like nets—they'll cover what we mean, but we know they can't possibly hold that much joy, or grief, or wonder.*

Similar words may express substantive differences as well. Consensual understanding is challenged by the similarities and at the same time the differences in meaning among terms derived from Anglo-Saxon, French, and Latin or Greek origins, as shown in table 3.2.

Dictionary definitions are not enough. Dictionaries describe what something means but do not prescribe which meaning was intended. Grammar determines how words are converted to the intent or meaning behind them.

Grammar reflects part but not all the context required to determine meaning. The context surrounding words and intent has tremendous influence on our translation of words into meaning. For example, without context, I could use my dictionary's fourth definition of "had," third definition of "little," and first definition of "lamb" to interpret the sentence "Mary had a little lamb" to mean that Mary may have eaten lamb for dinner! (Or maybe she took a small bite of lamb and did not like it!)

Even with supporting context, individual terms challenge people and cost organizations. Supposedly, the word "occurrence" cost the insurance policy consortium for the World Trade Center Towers nearly US$5 billion of additional risk, because the entire property was insured per "occurrence."

> NOTE: Was the situation on 9/11 involving New York's World Trade Center destruction one "occurrence" or two "occurrences"? For a compelling discussion on this topic, see *The Stuff of Thought: Language as a Window into Human Nature,* by Steven Pinker.

Even a basic term like "country" becomes surprisingly difficult to define. At one time, US Homeland Security offered 251 choices for the "country where

---

[4] A synonym is a word or phrase that means nearly the same as another word or phrase in the same language, for example, "begin" can be a synonym of "start."

[5] A homonym is each of two or more words having the same spelling but different meanings—for example, "lie" (recline) or "lie" (untruth).

Table 3.2. Similar Yet Different

Anglo-Saxon	French	Latin / Greek
Ask	Question	Interrogate
Dead	Deceased	Defunct
End	Finish	Conclude
Fair	Beautiful	Attractive
Fast	Firm	Secure
Help	Aid	Assist
Meeting	Reunion	Convention

you live," each one with its own unique number and recognized as a valid country.

For example, combining multiple sources at the start of the new millennium, the Sovereign Military Order of Malta had only two buildings in Rome but had diplomatic relations with 100 countries. The Vatican is cloistered in four hectares in the middle of Italy's capital but remained only an observer in the United Nations. Israel joined the world body in 1949, but twenty to thirty of the 192 UN members did not accept the Jewish state's existence. One-half of UN members recognized Kosovo at a time when the UN itself did not recognize Kosovo. Your organization may have similar cultural challenges when defining even basic terms, such as "customer" or "goal."

Moreover, context alone does not ensure consensual understanding, because the English language even permits contronyms, or words that mean the opposite of themselves, in context. For example, "garnish" can mean to furnish, as with food preparation, or to take away, as with wages; "refrain" could be to repeat or to halt; "screen" can mean to show (a movie) or conceal.

Are you beginning to see the importance of rhetorical precision?

NOTE: As a contronym, the term "consult" is nebulous and vague. When you say "consult" does that mean you are giving me something or that I need to give you something? Your guess is as good as mine!

KEEP IT SIMPLE

Regarding vocabulary, less is more. I should know; I struggle with this issue every day. Just ask my significant other. One trick I use is to remind myself to speak so that my grandmother will understand me. In other words, use the term "bunch" instead of "plethora."

Much can be expressed using very few words. Or as my grandmother would have told you, "I've heard good sermons and I've heard long sermons, but I've never heard a good, long sermon."

EMPHASIS ON PRECISION

Strive for precision, especially with your questions. For example, it is better to ask open-ended versions of questions than the ones we convert (unconsciously) to close-ended versions.

> **—Albert Einstein**
> *If you can't explain it simply, you don't understand it well enough.*

- "Anything else?" This common and vague question opens the floor to a plethora—oops, sorry, Grandma!—I mean, a bunch of out-of-scope and often confusing replies. Rather, contrast vagueness with the ease of repeating an entire question, such as "What are other ways we can improve food storage capacity in coastal Somalia?"

- "Do we all agree?" and "Do we have consensus?" are both unanswerable unless you are clairvoyant. However, "Will you support _____?" is answerable, both in the singular and the plural. "If we do _____, will you lose any sleep over it?" is also answerable by all participants.

- "Under what circumstances . . . ?" is immediately more effective than "Are there any circumstances . . . ?"

- "Who would like to share their thoughts . . . ?" does not compel a detailed response as well as "What are the arguments supporting [or against] . . . ?" (the question is also irrelevant since we care about *what* participants think and not *who* is doing the thinking).

Substance over Style

When training facilitators, I always stress substance over style. That said, effective presentation skills stimulate unique ideas, impressions, and intuitions. Presenting comes alive with qualities you bring:

- Cadence and tempo

- Eye contact (looking at participants increases trust)

- Gestures (no pointing at or turning your back on participants, for example)

- Inflections (avoid sounding monotone)

- Passion, pitch, and tone

- Pauses (do not fill them with meaningless words)

- Posture and movement—presenting yourself in a way that evokes credibility and respect (do not slouch or stand in one place, and do not hide behind the tables, podium, or flip charts)

VERBAL BLUNDERS

Being natural is more important than being polished. In the natural course of speech, people slip, stumble, and make verbal blunders (disfluencies).[6] Strive to be conscious of disfluencies so that they do not become distractions. Repeated blunders, rather than one-time slips, should be particularly avoided and carefully monitored. But never fall short of being natural and trustworthy. A speaker whose style is too smooth comes across as fake and untrustworthy, because speaking in public scares most people.

In 2004, Robert Eklund estimated that about 6 percent of spoken words count as disfluent:

- Filled pauses (such as "uh," "um")—found in every language, even American Sign Language, and an important disfluency to monitor, if a distraction

- Mispronunciations—can be natural and solicit nonverbal response; don't be bashful about asking for correction

- Prolongations of individual sounds—typically natural

- Truncations—careful with slang and proper pronunciation

Researcher Sharon Oviatt counted between 1.7 and 8.8 disfluencies per 100 words spoken. She found that 60 to 70 percent of disfluencies could be eliminated if the speaker's questions and responses were simply shorter and more specific.

PUBLIC SPEAKING

Public speaking is the number one fear of Americans. Fear of dying rates number two. Comedian Jerry Seinfeld suggests that, statistically, more Americans attending a funeral would rather be in the casket than delivering the eulogy.

As the brain senses a threat in the environment, the amygdala (the gray matter inside each cerebral hemisphere, involved with the experiencing of emotions) responds by activating the "fight or flight" response. The response includes other biological changes like a faster heart rate and increased blood flow to the brain. When speaking in front of others, speakers with a fear of public speaking have more active amygdalae. For those who fear public speaking, additional scripting and practice help tremendously.

> NOTE: Regarding fear of public speaking—scientists at 23andMe identified 802 genetic markers that are associated with fear of public speaking. Genetics and other factors like age, sex, and ancestry also influence fears.

According to the National Speakers Association (2006), the principles and practice of facilitating, rather than preaching, provide the most effective means

---

[6] Michael Erard, *Um: Slips, Stumbles, and Verbal Blunders, and What They Mean* (2007).

to establish clear messaging. In other words, lead with questions rather than answers.

Toastmasters International helps speakers deliver clear messages using voice, vocabulary, and delivery that are fully under control and disciplined through rehearsal and practice. The organization's founder (in 1907), Ralph Smedley, called the style "amplified conversation": you do not speak *to* an audience but *with* an audience. According to Smedley, the two notable features are brevity and eye contact, combined with avoiding "um." I also suggest taking up refereeing or coaching as a method to improve your public speaking skills and confidence.

NONVERBAL MISUNDERSTANDINGS

Keep your elbows tucked in, your hands below your heart, and your hands open, facing up. Be cautious with anything else.

For example, extending the index and little fingers upward from the fist to form a *V* (with the middle and pointer fingers tucked down into the palm, along with the thumb) can signify victory or good luck in the Americas but is considered quite vulgar in Italy.

A single thumb up, commonly used to express "fine with me" in the United States, counts as the number one in Germany and the number five in Japan, and is a vulgar insult in Afghanistan, among other places (akin to holding up only the middle finger in the United States). Scuba divers universally acknowledge the clasping of the thumb and index finger into a circle (or "A-OK") as the buddy signal that "I'm OK." The same gesture is perceived as a vulgar insult in Russia and Italy, while it signifies "pay me" in Japan and displays a sense of "worthlessness" in France.

YES OR NO?

In the United States, shaking your head from side to side typically signifies "no" or "I'm not in agreement." However, it may signify "yes" or "no problem" in Bulgaria and elsewhere. The slight vertical nod of the head up and down signifies "I'm OK with it" in the United States but may signify "no" or "I don't see it" in Greece and elsewhere. As a friend of mine suggested, "Understanding these cultural differences is so critical for international business."

While nonverbal cues are intended to simplify understanding, they can complicate consensus in a multicultural setting. As with everything, context prevails. The role of the meeting facilitator requires you to police context on behalf of participants—so be careful.

Zen of the Experience

When seeking innovation and breakthrough during meetings or workshops, do not clone yourself. Keep your blend of participants highly diversified. I call it the "Zen of the experience"—speaking to all senses and perspectives to stimulate and maintain vibrancy.

Moods and judgments are profoundly influenced by experiences of sight and sound. For example, we feel happier on sunny days and more relaxed when listening to certain types of music. Negative environments produce contrary results. Research shows that heat and humidity provoke more fighting, violence, and even riots.

MUSIC HELPS A LOT

For my facilitation courses, I've created break timers that fuse musical memes that could be best described as eclectic—ranging from Frank Sinatra to Frank Zappa. My timers also include trivia questions for mental stimulation and some wonderful photography for visual stimulation.

TACTILE TRIGGERS

I have distributed chenille stems (also known as pipe cleaners) and foam stickers to meeting participants for years now, usually placing them beneath name tents. While some participants don't bother using them, research by Joshua Ackerman, Christopher Nocera, and John Bargh proves that the weight, texture, and hardness of the things we touch unconsciously factor into decisions we make that have nothing to do with what is being touched.[7]

Most people associate smoothness and roughness with ease and difficulty, respectively. Note the expressions "smooth sailing" and "rough seas ahead." According to Ackerman and colleagues, people who completed puzzles with pieces covered in sandpaper described their interaction as more difficult and awkward than those with smooth puzzles. Chenille stems offer both silky smoothness and flexibility, characteristics we seek from our participants and meetings. Chenille stems make everything seem better. They are effective, and research confirms why. Molding clay and Play-Doh are reasonable options, although some carry an odor you will want to avoid.

You will also find that the smell of citrus fruit and fresh air (along with alcohol-laden products like Purell) will alert and awaken participants who may be dozing off. Alternatively, consider using a 30-30, that is a 30-second "stand up and stretch" break every 30 minutes, to prevent doldrums.

USING VISUALS AND GRAPHICS

Nonnarrative or graphic methods provide an excellent alternative to words. Use matrices, tables, and diagrams to fuel basic information or hot innovative ideas. Graphic methods are highly supportive when . . .

- Agreeing on concepts

- Analyzing to be concise

---

[7] Joshua M. Ackerman, Christopher C. Nocera, and John A. Bargh, "Incidental Haptic Sensations Influence Social Judgments and Decisions" (2010).

Table 3.3. Seven Formats, from Most to Least Complex

Graphic Format	Defined	Example
Poster	**A central theme**	To announce the meeting, date, time, place, and purpose
List	**A sequenced list of ideas**	To list items that must be done before the meeting
Cluster	**An arranged collection of ideas**	To organize the items listed into appropriate groups
Matrix	**A forced comparison of ideas**	To associate a role with a specific assignment
Diagram	**A model of an idea**	To lay out the meeting room in two dimensions
Picture	**An analogy or image of the idea**	To illustrate a 3-dimensional view of the meeting room
Mandala	**A unifying, centered image**	To combine elements together showing how each relates to the core and to each other

- Exploring complex ideas

- Finding common ground during cross-cultural situations

- Scoping challenges

- Solving problems

- Strategically planning concepts for visions, missions, objectives

GRAPHIC IMPACT AND FORMATS

Complexity can be rendered more easily with charts than words. In 2008, Dr. Paul Krugman received the Nobel Prize for creating insight with his display of data, not for the originality of his ideas.[8] Arthur Young and David Sibbet developed seven graphic formats based on increasing complexity.[9] The formats engage people from conception through analysis and finally commitment to an idea. The seven formats are listed in table 3.3.

---

[8] Nobel Prize, "Paul Krugman," press release, October 13, 2008.
[9] See various works beginning with David Sibbet, "Encountering the Theory," n.d., ArthurYoung.com, https://arthuryoung.com/sibbet.html, and David Sibbet, "Standing Up to the Sixth Extinction," January 4, 2021, https://davidsibbet.com/category/process -theory/.

GRAPHICS IN MEETINGS

It is not enough to be comfortable drawing pictures. Knowing "which graphic format to use when" supports great meeting design. The graphic is the means to an end. Knowing the end and finding the appropriate means make for a more effective meeting. Realize that graphic formats help people think through problems and speed up the development of consensual solutions.

DOS AND DON'TS

The following are some basic guidelines for using graphics:

- Do build storyboards and other illustrations that link together concepts.

- Do worry about content. Do not worry about "artistry."

- Explain instructions clearly. Don't be vague or too restrictive.

- Learn if it doesn't work. Don't get worried. Fail with a bow.

- Let them know this is important and not "just fun stuff."

- Make graphics a means to an end, not the reason for the effort.

- Whenever possible, use icons, illustrations, and multiple colors to break up the monotony of a single-color hue or the monotony of all-narrative content.

A FUN EXAMPLE OF VISUAL IMPACT

To understand the sheer power of infographics and visual displays, consider that the back of the retina is made up of brain cells, not eye cells. It is where seeing and thinking occur simultaneously.

Treat yourself to an original demonstration in a short film by Charles and Ray Eames, *Powers of Ten* (https://www.eamesoffice.com/education/powers-of-ten-2). While modern versions such as the one narrated by Morgan Freeman provide superior sound and graphics, the original 1977 IBM-sponsored version remains hard to beat. This site provides an alternative soundtrack to play while viewing: https://mimirosenbush.com/powers-of-ten/.

Which Path? The Art of Questioning

For longer than the recorded history of humans, hikers and mountaineers have turned around, faced their group or partner, and asked, "Which way?" and as soon as someone says, "To the left," someone else asks, "Why?"[10]

As a climber, your decision or choice is a function of countless variables, including duration, distance, and elevation. Later in the journey, you will discover

---

[10] In my household, my significant other and our youngest child would ask, "Which left?"

the best path is also influenced by sun orientation and wind direction. As the decision about which path to take becomes a function of those primary variables, you will also realize that those variables are not equally valued.

As an example, for one person or group, ambient comfort (with their purpose being "experience") represents the highest importance, so sun exposure and wind chill are critical. Another group stresses elevation and distance (their purpose is "conditioning"). Both rationales are optimal for their respective groups. A neutral facilitator, armed with the appropriate *Tools*,[11] could help them both decide and agree on a path—and business decisions are usually far more complex than that.

A GUIDE ON THE SIDE, NOT A SAGE ON THE STAGE

Once you have confirmed that you accurately heard and understood what participants believe, use questions rather than edicts to advance the conversation. Use either prepared or impromptu questions that will:

- Build group cohesion

- Create receptiveness to change and development

- Direct teams to look for similarities—for example, apples and oranges are both fruit and similar in shape, size, and weight; they both bruise easily and rot as well

- Help maintain focus within scope

- Increase learning and innovative thinking

Questions are most effective when presented with an inquiring, probing, and neutral perspective. Effective questions are open-ended discoveries and not opinions disguised as questions.

- Questions that tend to shut down communication and turn off participants include these:
  - "Don't you think that . . . ?" (message: "Agree with me")
  - "Why don't you . . . ?" (message: "Do what I want you to do")
  - "You don't really believe that, do you?" (message: "You are stupid or naive")
- Questions that stimulate communication and creativity include these:
  - "In what ways might we . . . ?"

---

[11] When using the *italicized* term "*Tools*," the term refers to something specific in this book that might also be used as an individual *Agenda Step* or an entire *Meeting Approach*. For example, the procedure of using the *Root Cause Analysis Tool* frequently represents an entire meeting. When not italicized, the general term "tool" also refers to other tools or devices that are not included or discussed in this book.

- "What are the advantages (or disadvantages) of . . . ?"

- "What do you think about . . . ?"

- "What options do you see . . . ?"

Do not ask for permission to ask questions. "Tell us why" is preferred to "Would you like to explain?"

Prepare yourself to challenge participants and get them to think more clearly about causes rather than symptoms. For example, *why* they are fatigued is more important than the fatigue—get to the cause.

- Get comfortable with your word choice. I frequently, and quickly, follow up participant comments with the challenge "Because?"—forcing them to explain the reason behind their claim.

- Highly effective and spontaneous challenges include variants of "Why are you certain?"

- Remember, it is participants' responsibility to "speak clearly" and provide reasons to support their positions.

Superb questions convert subjective input into objective criteria, making it easier to build consensus:

- "What is the unit of measurement for _____?"

- "What proof have you discovered?"

- "What type of evidence can you provide?"

For precision, break questions into detailed pieces. As you know, it is not easy for an individual to respond to questions like "How do you solve global hunger?" While meaningful, the question is too broad to stimulate specific, actionable responses like "convert abandoned mine shafts in coastal Somalia to food storage areas."

We also tend to transition during meetings with questions like "Are we OK with this list?" or "Can you live with that?" Instead, apply precision and structure by adapting the following three questions to your situation, especially during transitions:

1. What do we need to clarify on this list?

2. What do we need to delete?

3. What needs to be added to this list?

These three transition questions make it easier for meeting participants to analyze, agree, and move on. The questions produce more powerful results than questions no one can answer, such as "Does everyone agree with . . . ?" (no one is able to read the minds of other participants).

HOW TO ASK

Follow a basic pattern when asking questions:

- Ask

- Long pause (three to five seconds)

- Invite

This pattern avoids placing participants on the spot. It allows the entire group to answer, yet enables you to nonverbally solicit an answer from a particular person should no one volunteer.

Remember that challenging participants to be clear and complete benefits everyone. Do not construe your challenges as stepping out of role, because clarification makes it easier for everyone to understand. Challenge whenever you sense nonverbal signals of fear, uncertainty, or doubt (FUD).

While we are interested in *what* participants think, consensus is built around *why* they think that way, and unanimity occurs when your challenges result in objective proof. Consider the following sequence that demonstrates increasing robustness:

1. *What* they know or believe to be true—good

2. *Why* they believe something to be true—better

3. *Proof* for their belief or claim—best

CAUTION

Questioning can represent your technique or obstacle, depending on how you use questions. Use questions to guide and stimulate your group, not to dominate or manipulate it. When fielding questions, you must be able to sort context questions from questions about content. Answer the context questions directly and act like Teflon to deflect all questions of content.

> **—Ryan Seacrest**
> *Talking is what I do, but listening is my job.*

For example, if you are asked by a meeting participant which option you favor (content), reflect the option back to other participants with: "It doesn't matter what I think. What do you folks think about _____?"

However, if asked by a meeting participant which tool you plan to use to prioritize a set of criteria, NEVER ask them which tool they would like to use (context). As their "process policeperson" step up and tell them exactly what *Tools* are anticipated to help them analyze their own content.

INTERACTIVE LISTENING QUESTIONS

The following questions have been "scrubbed" as solid, open-ended questions that demand more than a yes or no (or maybe) answer:

- "And then what?"
- "Because?"
- "Share with us . . ."

Avoid interrupting:

- Don't change the subject without announcing your intention to do so.
- Interrupt only to clarify questions or to increase momentum through a quick comment.

Clarify:

- "Explain how . . . ?"
- "How do you mean that . . . ?"
- "How will that impact . . . ?"
- "Huh?"
- Practice saying "Go ahead . . ."

Encourage without validating:

- "Hmmm . . ."
- "No kidding"
- "Really"
- "That's interesting"
- "Wow"

At the end of the comments, summarize important points and ask for confirmation that everyone understood the issue or interest:

- "To what extent have we captured your point of view correctly?"
- "Your position on the matter of _____ is . . ."

Leverage body language:

- Involved posture: lean forward, don't fold arms, and avoid cold shoulder.
- Use pleasant, encouraging facial expression—smile.

> **—Terrence Metz**
> *Dr. Max Bazerman claims the most powerful word in negotiations is "huh"—as in, tell me more. Listening, not speaking, makes you a more powerful negotiator. Likewise, silence can make you appear to be a warmer and more trustworthy person and facilitator.*

Maintain silence:

- A silence lasting three to five seconds encourages the other person to say more.

Restate and ask for confirmation:

- "Let's see if we understand that correctly. We heard that . . ."

FACILITATION'S DARK SECRET: LISTENING IS MORE PERSUASIVE THAN SPEAKING

A senior vice president at Honeywell once told me, "Selling is a series of well-thought-out questions." We know "facilitating" secures consensual answers to questions by "making it easier." Therefore, facilitating is a method of making it easier to sell and persuade by asking a series of well-thought-out questions. And it begins by listening to understand and not listening to reply.

NOTE: Dr. Amy Cuddy's research demonstrates that people answer two questions when they first meet someone:
- Can they TRUST the person?
- Can they RESPECT the person?

Others may refer to these two dimensions as "warmth" and "competence." Cuddy effectively asserts they clearly develop in the sequence shown. Trust always comes before respect. [12]

> *The biggest communication problem is that we don't listen to understand, rather we listen to reply.*

Silence generates trust when the persona exudes authenticity, compassion, and warmth. The tendency of most of us is to believe that competence comes first. However, belief in competence does not develop until trust is established.

Listening, not speaking, makes you a more powerful negotiator. Likewise, **silence can make you appear warmer and more trustworthy.**

Reducing errors helps reduce costs within products, projects, and processes, but preventing omissions may help even more. Groups recall and remember more than individuals and may use the input from individuals to create a response that integrates multiple viewpoints. Questions drive consensual understanding by minimizing errors, but more important, proper challenges help prevent costly omissions.

---

[12] Amy Cuddy, *Presence: Bringing Your Boldest Self to Your Biggest Challenges* (2018).

The Core Skill of Active Listening

For servant leadership and effective facilitation, active listening becomes indispensable. As a practitioner you will discover that feeding back (reflecting, restating) what the participant said never compares to the value of understanding and sharing *why* they said it.

NATURE PROVIDES TWO EARS YET ONLY ONE MOUTH

Active listening serves to benefit dyads, groups, teams, and tribes for these reasons:

- Arguments and evidence encourage everyone to comment.

- Often, participants formulate ideas spontaneously, and feedback helps refine their thoughts. The act of communicating affects what is being communicated.

- Participants value being heard—listened to.

- With an attitude of openness and listening, we can all learn something new.

In a conversation we make contact and absorb what the other person is saying. Then we move on to the next question. With active listening we need to feed back the reasons for what we have heard, confirm whether we got it right, and challenge them for anything substantive we may be missing (see table 3.4).

Conversations take less time. However, active listening prevents misunderstandings and helps generate options that were previously not considered, thus improving decision quality.

ACTIVE LISTENING PROCEDURE

People don't care what you know until they know that you care. Genuine active listening connotes empathy and requires four activities:

Table 3.4. It's Easier to Have a Conversation

Conversation	**Active Listening**
Make contact	Make contact
Absorb what is being said	Absorb what is being said
Move on to the next question	
	Feed back rationale supporting WHY it was said
	Confirm that your reflection is accurate and complete
	Move on to the next question

- Contact—Connect with the participant who is speaking. Make eye contact. Maintain an open posture.

- Absorb—Take in all aspects of what is being said. Do not judge or evaluate.

- Reflective feedback—Mirror, reflect, or give feedback about what you have heard and why the participant's claims are valid.

- Confirm—Obtain confirmation that you heard the participant's message accurately. If not, start the sequence over again at the beginning by having the participant restate his or her view.

THE FEEDBACK DIFFERENCE

Reflection distinguishes active listening from passive listening, in which people conversationally move from one statement to the next without verifying that content has been understood. Reflection may be oral or visual.

Capturing input verbatim is preferred, but at least provide feedback and confirm using one of three responses:

- Summarize—Much communication occurs without foresight. Often more words are used than necessary. When you summarize, boil input down to its essence or core message, ideally to the point of isolating the key verb and noun components first. Participants argue most frequently about adjectives and adverbs (modifiers), rarely about nouns or verbs.

- Synthesize—Shape fragments into a whole, integrate the stream of consciousness intended by group conversations.

- Paraphrase—Repeat what participants said using fewer words while preserving the original meaning and intent.

When reflecting feedback, depersonalize a participant's content with pluralistic rhetoric. Do *not* say "You said . . ." Rather, convert participants' expressions with integrative rhetoric such as "We heard . . ."

Strive for completeness when providing reflection. Try to avoid general expressions like "Does everyone agree with that?" (What was "that"?) Substitute specific content for impersonal pronouns such as "that," "these," "it," and so on. For example, "Does everyone agree that torture can be consciously objectionable because it is inhumane and opposed to the Geneva Convention?" works better than "Does everyone agree with that?" because participants understand precisely what is meant.

> **—Dalai Lama**
> *When you talk, you are only repeating what you already know; but when you listen, you may learn something new.*

THE WORD "LISTEN" USES THE SAME LETTERS AS "SILENT"

Active listening captures a powerful discipline that builds relationships among participants. Exercising active listening sets an example for your participants and lays the foundation for building clarity and shared understanding. Active listening makes it easier to see the world through others' eyes.

REFLECTING THEIR CONTENT WITH PAPER

Large Post-it presentation sheets provide immediate and visual feedback. Working with paper makes confirmation and editing faster and more thorough than trying to remember what someone said earlier. For me, working with paper is also faster than capturing content in electronic form, especially in group sessions, when participants are tempted to spell-check and edit anything being projected, blocking the creative flow.

—Dr. Carl R. Rogers

To listen with understanding means seeing the expressed idea and attitude from the other person's point of view, sensing how it feels to the person. . . . This may sound absurdly simple, but it is not.

Remember the following when reflecting participants' content with paper:

- Anticipate where sheets will be mounted. Be sensitive about everyone's sight lines. Save your prime real estate, front and center, for your work in progress (WiP).

- Banners and headlines provide a perfect opportunity to splash color and graphics. Create them in advance. When unveiled, your preparation connotes a sense of importance.

- Experts recommend a minimum of three colors per sheet. Use only black or dark blue for primary content. Use red for edits and scoring; use green for linking, or later edits (shows chronological shift). Use lighter colors for grid lines, underscores, and highlights.

- Predrawing illustrations (in pencil or light marker) enables you to draw over light or thin lines with broad markers, like tracing paper.

- Rip and mount your pages, never simply flip completed pages. Participants need to see their prior work. A bunch of flipped sticky pages nested in a clump becomes difficult to disentangle.

- Speed up content capture by using two scribes. Work this system out in advance, and if relying on another participant for documenter help, give them some time at the end to add their own content.

- Use hyphens and indent content four to six inches along the left-hand column to be further defined or scored during analysis, such as when using the *PowerBalls Tool* (chapter 7).

- Use flip chart graph paper with blue-line squares to keep the size of writing consistent. Test the size of your letters before the meeting to see whether the person farthest away can read them. Normally, capital letters should be two to three inches tall, and lowercase letters should be one to two inches in height.

PUNCTUATION

When capturing online or on paper, do not forget the power of tiny punctuation marks either.[13] Compare the potential distraction factor of an example like this: "Let's eat, grandma" versus "Let's eat grandma"!

Facilitation Power: Observing

Observation and remaining neutral fortify active listening. Use observation (for example, eye contact) to manage the collective dynamics and energies of the group.

Observation depends on both gazing and focusing. Improve your peripheral vision so that you can do both at the same time. Understandably, online meetings reduce the benefits of observation because we cannot see everything nor sense as much. However, observation remains critical.

GAZING

Gazing is the predominant form of looking around. Gazing is not judgmental, evaluative, visually prodding, or analytical. When gazing:

- Eyes are serene and unfocused.

- Eyes may move steadily from one participant to another.

- Online, in "gallery view" (with "no hiding" as a ground rule), continually scan participants.

- When you make transitions, step forward and smile, lower your voice and raise your eyebrows, open your hands, and scan the room—intuitively sense that everyone "can live with it" and "support it."

LASER FOCUSING

Laser focusing is more direct—almost staring, while sharply focused. The eyes do not move. When focusing:

---

[13] If you need to brush up on your punctuation, with a little humor, check out Lynne Truss's *Eats, Shoots & Leaves: The Zero Tolerance Approach to Punctuation* (New York: Avery Publishing, 2004).

- Make direct eye contact; do not glance away too quickly, and keep it comfortable by lingering two to three seconds.

- During online meetings, move your face closer to the camera, taking up about one-third of the screen. Don't be afraid to "cut off your head" so that the eyes are clearly dominant.

- Make use of single-pointedness. Use laser focusing when you require concentration to hear and understand participants. Also use laser focusing to manage people with problems—letting them know that you are aware of their distracting behavior.

STROLLING HELPS

Increase your friendliness further by avoiding podiums. Being conversational and natural increases likability. Get closer, measured in terms of physical proximity, to your participants. The easiest way to achieve closeness without violating personal space is to stroll toward participants. Moving closer to someone increases their feelings of warmth for you.[14]

Stroll forward during appropriate moments—particularly in these situations:

- As select personality types are inclined to become disruptive

- To display a stronger sense of engagement and active listening

- While making introductory remarks for both your meeting and for each *Agenda Step* (with online meetings, move your face closer to the camera if you are sitting; if you are standing, stroll directly to the camera)

Strolling is difficult when stuck in a small conference room with a big table or a huddle room with little perimeter, but walk around the table and the room anyway to keep people engaged. A U-shaped seating arrangement always makes it easier to stroll, positions you closer to participants, and enables you to be more conversational.

Use your space wisely. When participants are vibrant and need a scribe, stay at the easel as a documenter while their energy remains high. But as uncertainty or disagreement develop, slowly stroll forward to make it easier to vivify active listening and to demonstrate respect and value for the participant speaking.

During online workshops, I use three cameras: one for sitting and observing while others are facilitating; one for standing, while capturing participants' content on one of two easels, or pointing to wall space to the side and behind (standing and movement add to the feel and "texture" of an online experience); and a third camera for clear and detailed zooming and sharing of documents and artifacts.

---

[14] Harvey Black, "Stop Slouching!" (2010).

Staying neutral means keeping your opinions to yourself. You do not lose your opinions—but you learn to keep your mouth shut about content. Remember that an important part of your role is about keeping your opinions to yourself. Neutrality represents a discipline that does the following:

- Conveys acceptance of opposing views

- Draws out quiet people and perspectives

- Prevents facilitator alignment with "sides"

- Validates the *Meeting Approach*

KEEPING NEUTRAL

If you align yourself with a participant's point of view, you become another participant. You must learn to draw out others' perspectives without disclosing your own opinion. If you lose neutrality, stop the meeting, or simply ask the group to rein you in so that you can ask for forgiveness and move on. If your tendency is to violate neutrality, begin the meeting by telling the group that your role demands neutrality. If necessary, have participants police your actions, behaviors, and comments. Your candor will help a great deal.

STAYING HUMBLE

Neutrality is amplified by being perceived as humble. Remember, "Humble does not mean you think less of yourself. It simply means you think of yourself less often." (I wish I had said that first. C. S. Lewis is considered the original source.)[15]

"WE" AND NOT "I"

Speak in pluralistic terms, using "we" instead of "I." To make the group responsible for commitments and obligations, avoid expressions such as "I think," "I want," or "my plan."

Embrace pluralistic rhetoric with your questions. Instead of saying, "I wonder what would happen if we raised prices?," try saying, "What if we raised prices?"

- As the group makes progress, use "we."

- When claiming success, use "we."

- And when you are tempted to take credit, use "we."

NOTE: Notice the difference between the words "illness" and "wellness" (singular versus plural first person).

---

[15] C. S. Lewis was an Irish-born scholar, novelist, and author of about 40 books. See "C. S. Lewis: Quotes," *Goodreads*, https://www.goodreads.com/quotes/7288468-humility-is-not-thinking-less-of-yourself-it-s-thinking-of.

YOUR IDEA SUCKS

Dr. Thomas Gordon's seminal research confirmed that your judgment of their content will shut them down.[16] Counterintuitively, his research also revealed that it is better to tell someone in a group that he or she has a bad idea than to tell the participant that he or she has a promising idea. You should do neither, and here is why.

If you tell participants their ideas suck, they will disconnect, and you will lose them for the rest of the meeting. However, if you tell a participant that he or she had a great idea, chances are you shut that person down as well, because he or she can now go home a "winner" by not opening his or her mouth again in the meeting. Simultaneously, someone who does not agree with your judgment, and does not think the idea was great, will also disconnect from you and the meeting because that person's judgment is different from yours. Now you have lost two (or more) participants. **So stop cheerleading!**

IF ALL ELSE FAILS

If biting your tongue, candor, and conscious behavior fail you, consider the following ideas:

- Neutrality is not without passion. Share your passion about the *Meeting Approach* and its impact, but not about specific content.

- Dispense your expertise before a meeting (for example pre-read or *Participants' Package,* chapter 5).

- Present your knowledge as a discrete activity before the meeting when you assume a different role, as presenter.

- Integrate your expertise around questions: repeat *what* is needed and then solicit participants' recommendations about *how* they would respond.

- Bite your tongue—do *not* "switch hats" back and forth between being an expert (a consultant) and a facilitator. You will be viewed as potentially psychotic.

- Be painfully honest. Ask participants to object when you violate neutrality.

Neutrality is one of the few characteristics that are black-and-white. People will not view you as partly neutral any more than someone might say "I am partly pregnant." You are viewed as either neutral or not. When you are not neutral, you are leaving your participants without a facilitator because you have become another participant.

---

[16] See *Parent Effectiveness Training*, by Dr. Thomas Gordon (2000).

Quick Summary on Facilitating

Consensus is *not* compromise. By definition, a compromise is a lose-lose situation; both sides give in. Consensus is a win-win resolution, because everyone can live with it, support it, and not lose any sleep over it.

CONSENSUS, NOT COMPROMISE

Your meeting participants must also understand the difference between consensus and compromise, and it is your job to carefully clarify that consensus does not mean giving in or conceding. Rather, consensus means "I can live with it" or "I will not lose any sleep over it." Participants need to understand that, even though the deliverable (decision, final agreement, or whatever it is) may not be the "favorite" of any single participant, everyone has agreed that the deliverable is robust enough to support, making it the best deliverable for the group. Everyone can live with and support the deliverable, even if each preferred something else. Also, participants will not denigrate the deliverable in the hallway or subvert it when they get back to their office.

> NOTE: You cannot control a participant's integrity. If someone says one thing in the meeting and something else in the hallway, shame on them. As well-paid professional adults, participants have a duty and an obligation to speak up when they have pertinent content to share. Remember, your meeting is not an opportunity for them to contribute—rather, contributing is an *obligation*. And while it's your obligation to protect them, it is not your responsibility to reach down their throats and pull their contribution out of them.

A BALANCING ACT

As the meeting leader you are responsible to balance the following imperatives:

- Being a leader—and serving the group
- Challenging and probing—while remaining content neutral
- Focusing on your tasks—while also focusing on their tasks
- Forging consensus—while listening to outliers
- Policing context—while inspiring content
- Staying in the moment—yet anticipating what comes next
- Waiting for a response—yet urging participation

Anyone who thinks all this is easy is clueless. Moreover, we have not addressed two of the more difficult aspects of successful meeting leadership—namely, managing dysfunction (conflict) and completing your meeting design. Fortunately, we have the rest of the book to make both these tasks easier for you.

4

Collaborating

HOW YOU CAN MANAGE CONFLICT

Meeting conflict derives primarily from individual thinking styles, individual behavior, group dynamics, and other situational factors, including the facilitator and their environment. The meeting facilitator is *not* responsible for resolving conflict. However, they *must* have a procedure for (and therefore be confident about) managing arguments, conflicting claims, and contradictory evidence.

The Ways People Think

As a meeting facilitator, you empower participants by enhancing their ability to understand and communicate with one another. You also inspire them to think creatively about their business. But not all participants respond to messages the same way (figure 4.1).

PEOPLE PRINCIPLES

Participants in a meeting argue over an elementary issue. Two people hear the same thing and react as if they were in different meetings. Why? Because people interpret information differently.

PEOPLE THINK DIFFERENTLY

There are many theories about how people process information. One theory states that the two hemispheres of the brain govern our thinking with right brain or left brain bias. Another theory, explained in the book *Communicoding* and summarized in table 4.1, states that the two primary modes of processing information are vertical and horizon-

> **—William Shakespeare**
> *What we wish, we readily believe, and what we ourselves think, we imagine others think also.*

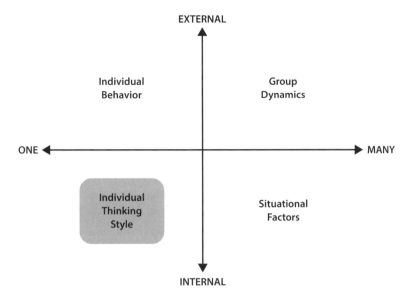

Figure 4.1. Individual Thinking Style

tal.[1] Either way, people with opposing modes of thinking have a tough time communicating with each other because each perceives the world differently.

VERTICAL THINKERS FIND DIFFERENCES (THINK ENGINEERING)

Vertical thinkers find differences, decompose issues, and design something new from the pieces (inductive reasoning). Vertical thinkers are logical, organized, and detail oriented. They will . . .

- Easily discern immediate dynamics of a problem

- Identify specific details and relate issues to reality

- Know what can be accomplished within a given time

- See barriers and obstacles to be removed

- Take the common path to reach results

HORIZONTAL THINKERS FIND SIMILARITIES (THINK MARKETING)

Horizontal thinkers find similarities and common threads, making new associations among unrelated items (deductive reasoning). Horizontal thinkers are far-sighted, innovative, and conceptual. They will . . .

---

[1] Susan Tynan and Ruth Feldman, *Communicoding* (1989).

Table 4.1. Critical Thinking Comparison

Vertical Thinking	Horizontal Thinking
Explains the "plot" when describing a book or movie	Explains the "message" when describing a book or movie
Finds differences	Finds similarities
Fits into structure	Prefers the unstructured
Looks for risks	Looks at the benefits
Processes language	Processes visually, sees patterns
Seems logical	Seems intuitive
Thinks sequentially	Thinks nonsequentially

- Easily discern the underlying dynamics of a problem

- Identify contextual details, relating issues to a larger perspective

- Know what impact can be achieved within a given context

- See possibilities and benefits

- Take an unlikely path to reach results

You cannot change the way people think—nor should you ever label participants. Your role is to help participants to hear one another and to better understand their communication challenges. Clues that thinking differences are causing problems include the following:

- One person is arguing about the problems, while another is focused on the benefits.

- One person is trying to get to the details, while the other is trying to focus on the ideas.

- People are using the same words yet meaning something different or arguing as if they are saying something different.

- People are using different words that seem to be saying the same thing.

THERE ARE NO SAFE PLACES, ONLY SAFE PEOPLE

As I begin to explain how to manage these and other differences, don't forget my Rosetta stone: *remove distractions*. Therefore, my cardinal rule will be to not embarrass people. I don't have this rule because we are professionals or compassionate. Rather, in the role of meeting facilitator, embarrassment is the single most powerful cause of a participant being distracted.

Thus, I encourage you to apply the following guiding principles when dealing with people (based on the golden rule of treating others as you wish to be treated):[2]

- *Never embarrass people*, especially in public.

- People are intrinsically reasonable.

- People do not like to be blamed.

- People have different goals in life.

- People prefer the positive to the negative.

- People share similar fears.

Evidence: Smart People Make Dumb Decisions

There is a fine line between embarrassing someone and challenging their thinking. Challenging meeting participants to provide objective proof, evidence, and examples is necessary to effective facilitation. All people are influenced by cognitive biases. Original writings by cognitive scientists like Daniel Kahneman[3] and Nassim Nicholas Taleb[4] should be consulted for a thorough, if not scary, treatment on this topic of biases, filters, and heuristics. Major errors, biases, and illusions they have identified, proven, and illustrated include these:

> **—Daniel Kahneman**
> *Smart people in extremely high-performing situations will consistently underestimate how much time it takes to complete certain tasks.*

- *Anchoring or availability error*— People seize on the first piece of information that makes an impression.

- *Attribution error*—People rely on stereotypes for judgment.

- *Control error*—People behave as if chance events are subject to their influence. Simply stated, people who believe that they have some control over their situation perceive "odds of success" that are much higher than they actually are. Numerous studies have proven the illusion of control. Money managers, for

---

[2] See the appendix for golden rule comparisons in 13 cultures or languages, as well as the silver rule: "Do *not* do to others what you do *not* want done to yourself."

[3] Daniel Kahneman, *Thinking, Fast and Slow* (2013).

[4] Nassim Taleb, *Incerto: Fooled by Randomness, The Black Swan, The Bed of Procrustes, Antifragile* (2016).

example, behave as if they can beat the market when, in fact, *no one* consistently outperforms the major indices.

- *Superiority error*—Most people consider themselves "above average" drivers. Likewise, most professionals place themselves in the top half of performers. Clearly, these judgments are absurd, because statistically at least one-half of drivers are "below average." People maintain an unrealistically positive view of themselves because not everyone can be above average. According to one large study, more than 80 percent of those surveyed considered themselves above average. Remarkably, and scarily too, the least capable people often have the largest gaps between their perception and reality. Those in the bottom quartile of assorted studies dramatically overstate their abilities. And everyone tends to dismiss his or her shortcomings as inconsequential.

—Michael J. Mauboussin, "Smart People, Dumb Decisions," ***Futurist* (2010)**
While people are very poor at guessing when they'll complete their own projects, they're pretty good at guessing when other people will finish.

According to the World Future Society, multiple studies over various periods of time and place consistently show that numerous factors bias group decision-making.[5] For example, *everyone* poorly estimates the time needed to complete a task. Psychologists call it the planning fallacy and the bias of overconfidence. Fallacies and biases put us all at increased risk of failing to reach our objectives and include these issues:

- Confusing desirability and familiarity with probability

- Distorting data through selection and repetition

- Forecasting with a preference toward change or biased by patterns

- Framing complex issues in a skewed fashion (selective perception)

- Homogenizing multiple data sources (for cost savings)

- Lacking clear confidence intervals (how clean the data are)

- Mistaking correlation for causation (a quite common error)

- Over-immersion in local social values or filtered perceptions

---

[5] World Future Society, home page, n.d., https://www.worldfuture.org.

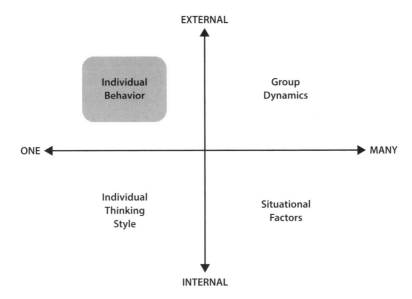

Figure 4.2. Individual Behavior

"Politikos": The Science of People

The term "politikos" translates as "the science of people." Find comfort in knowing that you will deal better with participants as you gain more experience and come to recognize common patterns of behavior that occur predictably (figure 4.2). In the meantime, keep one fact constant; participants cause problems for a finite period. Often a participant causing problems becomes productive in a different situation. Do not label people permanently. There are no "problem people," only "people with problems," and that means all of us at one time or another.

PRAISE IN PUBLIC, DISCIPLINE IN PRIVATE

The unit of measurement for assessing problems becomes the extent to which a participant's behavior is distracting. Assume that people have good intentions, and focus your energy on discovering what is causing the difficulty. In other words, identify the problem—do not highlight the person with the problem.

Learn to be kind, but at the same time don't be too nice. While the difference remains difficult to explain, here are two examples:

- *Nice* is volunteering to share responsibility with someone else. *Kind* is permitting one and only one person responsibility so that when others have questions, there is no finger-pointing between the two cochairs. Have you ever contacted a cochair only to have them tell you that they thought the other cochair was working on it—ad infinitum?

- *Nice* is donating money to an indigent "street person." *Kind* is taking a few moments to engage the person in a compassionate conversation about his or her actual well-being, showing that you care.

FIRM BUT FLEXIBLE

Empower your participants. The deliverable or decision must be theirs to own, not yours. Manage politics by removing ideas from the individual participant and turning them over to the entire group. It's not *who* is right, rather, *what* is right that we seek. Ideas belong to the group—never to an individual. But when erratic or distracting behavior occurs, be prepared to control it. *Ground Rules* (next section) will help manage much of the nonmalicious behavior.

> **—Aldous Huxley**
> *It isn't who is right, but what is right that counts.*

MANAGING SYMPTOMS

Here are the tactics I rely on, listed in order of priority and frequency of use for managing personalities:

- Conversations with your participants (detailed in chapter 5)
- *Ground Rules*
- Eye contact
- Body position
- Intervention tools
- Take a break

GROUND RULES

Ground Rules provide norms for the behavior of groups. Rules help you and the group establish decorum, keep conversations on track, and get DONE faster. *Ground Rules* apply to participants equally and, therefore, are unbiased. One popular facilitation method begins its workshops by building *Ground Rules* with the participants. Others call *Ground Rules* "working agreements" or "working assumptions" because the term "rule" feels too harsh.

Solicit and Present

When explaining *Ground Rules* during your meeting *Launch* (chapter 5), present the primary *Ground Rules* that will be used in every session. Do not skip or remove any of the first four *Ground Rules* (five when you add "no hiding" for online meetings). Provide additional *Ground Rules* when you realize they are needed. Do not use more than nine *Ground Rules* total or they will become burdensome rather than a device for getting done faster.

Primary Ground Rules

1. **Be Here Now:** The first *Ground Rule* addresses electronic leashes and punctuality. Encourage people to keep laptops down and phones on stun (vibrate only). Do not permit text messaging during the meeting.

Ask people to take calls and reply to messages in the hallway so as not to distract others. Studies have shown that participants who insist they can "multitask" display a meeting IQ that drops below that of a chimpanzee! So avoid facilitating a room full of monkeys.[6]

Since you won't be able to change an entire culture with only three words ("be here now") in your *Ground Rules*, meet with participants in advance and secure their permission and agreement to stay away from non-meeting-related material during the meeting.

Tardiness is often caused by "back-to-back" meetings, so schedule 50-minute meetings instead of one-hour meetings. Begin meetings at five minutes after the hour and finish by five minutes before the hour.

2. **Silence or Absence Implies Consensus:** As meeting facilitator, you must stress that each participant has a fiduciary responsibility. If participants have content relevant to the conversation, it is their duty and responsibility to mention it. Also, their contributions are not voluntary, optional, or an opportunity. Rather, they must be viewed as the obligation and fiduciary obligation of a well-paid professional adult.

> **—Marcus Tullius Cicero**
> *Qui tacet, consentire videtur. (Whoever remains silent, is taken to consent.)*

Your job is to protect participants and separate judgment of their contribution from their personae. However, if participants intentionally fail to contribute, they have violated integrity, something you cannot control. Again, you must stress fiduciary responsibility, since participants are not accustomed to having an *obligation* to speak up. Most participants treat meetings as an opportunity and therefore leave with much of their wisdom and their feelings "contained." You need to make it noticeably clear that their sharing is an obligation; if a participant cannot support that principle, he or she should be replaced or cancel the entire meeting. If participants have content that needs to be considered, shame on them if they do not share it openly.

Silence or absence indicates that participants have provided their assent. If they cannot support the responsibility and obligation to make content contributions about their subject matter expertise, then you have much bigger problems than the meeting (see also "How to Manage Quiet People," chapter 4).

---

[6] Apologies for the insult to my primate brothers and sisters.

3. **Consensus Means "I Can Live with It":** Carefully define consensus so that people know it does not necessarily mean that they will get their "favorite" outcome. However, consensus does imply that we are 100 percent in agreement to support the result, though it might not be everyone's or even anyone's personal favorite.

   As a group, you are seeking a resolution that is robust enough for everyone to support and not cause anyone to lose sleep over it. So rather than asking the unanswerable question, "Do we have consensus?," ask whether everyone will support the outcome or whether anyone will lose sleep over it. These are surrogate questions, implying consensus, that each individual *can* answer.

4. **Make Your Thinking Visible:** People do not think causally. They think symptomatically. Additionally, they rarely argue about verbs and nouns. Rather, they argue about modifiers (such as adjectives). For example, two people eating the same type of curry may argue over how "spicy" it is. To one, the curry is hot. To the other, it is not. They are both correct.

   A great meeting facilitator will get the two people to "objectify" their claims so that they both can agree that the curry rates 1,400 Scoville Heat Units. However, they are not predisposed to think about Scoville Heat Units. They think "hot." As meeting facilitator, you must challenge participants to make their thinking visible.

5. **No Hiding:** For video conferences, enforce a rule that prohibits people from turning off their live video stream. When hidden, no one has any idea what they are doing or if they are even listening. Dr. Tufte uses the term "flatland" to describe the two-dimensional view, such as the view of online participants on a screen. Working in flatland makes it difficult enough to observe nonverbal reactions. Culturally, you may need to get participants' permission to use this rule, but don't back down. Enforce "no hiding."

Optional Ground Rules

I refer to other *Ground Rules* as situational. Vary their use depending on the meeting type, participants, deliverable, and timing. Secondary *Ground Rules* I have found effective include these:

- Bring a problem, bring a solution.

- Chime in or chill out.

- Everyone will hear one another and be heard.

- Focus on "what" not "how."

- Hard on facts, soft on people.

- It's not *who* is right; it's *what* is right.

- No "yeah, but"—make it "yeah, *and . . .*"

- No big egos or war stories.

- Nobody is smarter than everybody.

- No praying underneath the table (texting).

- One conversation at a time (share airtime).

- Openly share relevant information.

- Players win games; teams win championships.

- Share reasons behind questions and answers—*because*?

- Speak for easy listening—headline first, background later.

- Topless meetings (laptops down).

- Ventilate undiscussable issues.

Audiovisual Support

In addition to the narrative *Ground Rules*, you may select some audiovisual recordings to support and reinforce the *Ground Rules*. I rely on public domain commercials that help emphasize these principles:

- Be here now.

- Speak clearly.

- Things are not the way they always appear to be.

- Trust one another.

GETTING FULL PARTICIPATION

What can you do to inspire participation, especially among quieter or socially reserved participants? I rely on five activities described under the "Quiet Person" (next section) that secure critical input from all participants. Additional suggestions proven to work include the following.

- Brain breaks: Stimulate the mental aspects with quick challenges, riddles, and other warm-up exercises. Keep your cadence energetic.

- Deepen your ice breakers and team-building exercises so that participants motivate one another with comments and deeper, personal, sharing.

- Go kinesthetic: Keep people active, not passive. Use *Breakout Teams* (chapter 6) for online meetings and distribute tactile props for in-person meetings such as modeling clay and chenille stems.

- Increase the fun level: Even serious topics should be treated loosely enough that participants don't tighten up too much. Remind people that deliverables serve the people and not the other way around.

- Texture: Continually stimulate the auditory, kinesthetic, and visual pathways with music, activities, and emphasis on graphic stimulation.

Table 4.2 covers different people's characteristics and useful suggestions for specific problems. These tips have proven highly effective with certain personality types.

Groups Evolve, Then Regress

As meeting facilitator, you may also witness conflict coming from the entire group. Internal and external conflict reflect emotions that, when harnessed, enable creative change.

DON'T RUN

It's your job to understand and manage group dynamics and conflict (figure 4.3). A meeting without conflict is a boring meeting, and I have seen truly little value derived from predictable and unexciting meetings and workshops.

Additionally, the International Association of Facilitators (IAF) aspires for you to do the following:

- "Help individuals identify and review underlying assumptions,

- Recognize conflict and its role within group learning / maturity,

- Provide a safe environment for conflict to surface,

- Manage disruptive group behavior, and

- Support the group through resolution of conflict."[7]

EVOLUTION

Facilitators manage groups, and groups are not stagnant. You need to understand how groups develop and appropriate ways to help them without getting in their way. The following sections outline the evolution of groups and two primary types of behavior to exhibit: relationship behaviors and task behaviors.

GROUP LIFE CYCLE

Groups, like people, develop and evolve. Groups can also regress. As meeting facilitator, you are responsible for moving a group through a developmental process. Every group goes through four stages as it evolves through its life cycle.

---

[7] International Association of Facilitators (IAF), home page, https://www.iaf-world.org/site/.

Table 4.2. People with Problems, or "Wait—Why Am I Talking?"

Title	Characteristics	What to Do
Can't Stay	Jeopardizes progress and damages morale by leaving meeting early	They may have a legitimate reason such as another meeting, day care pickup, or van pool departure. Understand constraints before the meeting begins and schedule accordingly.
Cliquer	Close friends who whisper during meetings and hold sidebar conversations	Standing close to Cliquers will stop their conversation. Enforce "one conversation at a time" *Ground Rule*. Also enforce this rule if you sense too much private online chatting.
Controller	Keeps telling the meeting facilitator what to do—or not do; attempts to control the meeting by changing the activities and procedures	Listen first; however, never turn over control. Talk to the Controller during breaks. Enforce scope carefully to avoid scope creep.
Disapprover	Actively expresses disapproval using body language and nonverbal cues such as rolling eyes, shaking head, crossing arms, and so on	Move near the Disapprover. Direct open hands in the person's direction, seeking viable counter-positions. Gently call on online participants by name, but always give online participants the option of saying "pass" whenever called upon.
Disengaged	Constantly engaged with their smart phones or laptop; ignores the facilitator; may read unrelated materials	Use laser focus so that the Disengaged person knows you see him or her. During breaks, talk to them. Do not publicly call out their name. Encourage your culture to embrace the "topless meetings" *Ground Rule* that prohibits laptops and handheld devices. For online violators, send a private chat.
Genius	Uses credentials, age, seniority, or stratospheric intelligence to argue his or her point	Writing down the Genius's input fully will satisfy him or her. Interrupt Geniuses who repeat themselves, reading back to them what you have. Carefully challenge them to explain how their contribution relates to the question at hand (to avoid scope creep).

(continued)

Table 4.2. (continued)

Title	Characteristics	What to Do
Impatient	Jumps into the conversation and cuts off someone else; acts impatient or concerned that his or her ideas will not be acknowledged	Interrupt Impatient participants immediately to protect the person interrupted, but do not forget to return to them later. Impatience is preferred over apathy.
Monopolizer or Randomizer	Talks often and loudly; dominates conversations and is difficult to shut up; may be someone who has a higher rank outside of the meeting than others	Record input if in scope of the question at hand. If not in scope, ask Monopolizers to write the question down so they don't forget it when you turn to them later. Use *Breakout Teams* (chapter 6) and round-robins to prevent the opportunity for them to dominate.
Quiet Person	We are not going to convert quiet people into extroverts, but five activities will transform the quantity of contributions from quieter participants	1. Interview your participants 2. *Breakout Teams* 3. Nonverbal solicitation 4. Reinforce during break 5. Round-robins and Post-it note techniques
Repeater	Brings up the same point repeatedly; tries to focus airtime on his or her issue	Repeaters need to understand that their point of view has been captured. Document their input. Show them visually that you "got it." When they begin to repeat themselves, interrupt them and read back what you have. Ask them, "What would you like to add?"
Skeptic	Voices skepticism shrouded with genuine concern; may degrade someone else's performance	Use the "What—So What—Now What" *Content Management Tool* (chapter 9). Skeptics may justify their skepticism with facts or examples. Through conversations in advance of the meeting, anticipate them speaking up and give them an optimal time to bring up their concerns. Skeptics offer more value than someone apathetic or quiet.

Table 4.2. (continued)

Title	Characteristics	What to Do
Snoozer	Challenged to stay awake, especially early morning or around 3 p.m.	Enforce the "no hiding" *Ground Rule* for online participants who must open their video windows. When in person, walk around the room or take a quick ergonomic break.
Spinner or Twister	Speaks for someone else; twists ideas or meanings and frequently distorts them when interpreting	First get the original speaker to confirm you received his or her input correctly and then offer the Spinner time to add his or her own point of view.
Tardy	Arrives late and may insist on catching up with what he or she missed	Use 50-minute meeting intervals to allow people some transition time between back-to-back meetings. Enforce "be here now" and "no hiding" *Ground Rules*. Do not interrupt the meeting. Review material during a break or after but not during the meeting—or pair participants off with someone else to give them a recap in the hallway or chat room.
Unexpected	Shows up without an invitation	Explain and enforce the role of observers, noting that they may speak during breaks or after the session has completed.
Verbal Attacker	Launches verbal, personal attacks on other group members or facilitator; ridicules a specific point of view	Stand between two people arguing. Immediately interrupt online attacks and mute the attacker if necessary. Make sure comments remain professional and not personal.
Workaholic	In and out of meetings; gives impression of being so important he or she is missed elsewhere	Treat the same way as someone who fits the Tardy or Can't Stay descriptions; enforce the "be here now" *Ground Rule*. Allow frequent bio-breaks, even when meetings are online, for people to respond to bodily needs and their electronic leash requests.

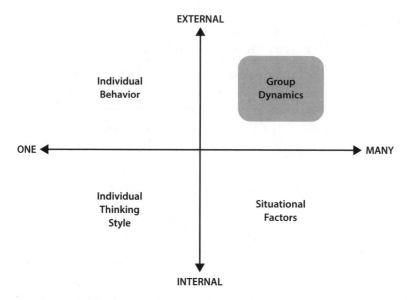

Figure 4.3. Group Dynamics

For any given group, you may see only the first two or three stages.

The following are stages and characteristics of group development (see figure 4.4):

- *Forming*—orientation, hesitant participation, search for meaning and purpose

- *Storming*—conflict, dominance, rebelliousness, power, and ignorance

- *Norming*—expression of opinions, development of group cohesion

- *Performing*—integrated solutions, formation of a cohesive "team," pluralistic rhetoric ("we" and "us"), telling you what to do ("write that down")

> **—Diane Coutu, "Why Teams Don't Work," *Harvard Business Review* (2009)**
> *Perversely, organizations with the best human resource departments sometimes have less effective teams. That's because HR tends to focus on improving individual rather than team behavior.*

Stage 1

Forming—State of Confusion

Key words: "I," "confusion," "why"

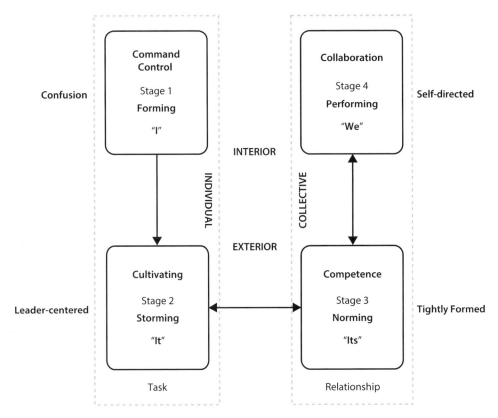

Figure 4.4. Four Stages of Group Performance and Individual Consciousness

Note: The four stages are adapted from B. W. Tuckman, "Development Sequence in Small Groups" (1965), 384–399. (Tuckman added a fifth stage, called adjourning, that we intentionally do not discuss.) These stages are overlaid with Ken Wilber's integral theory ("I") and Metz's facilitated meeting stages (Command). Osburn, Moran, Musselwhite, and Zenger (1990) added labels for the stages: (1) confusion, (2) leader-centered, (3) tightly formed, and (4) self-directed (Agile).

Facilitator response: command control (seven-activity **Launch** *in chapter 5)*

- Groups at this early stage are working on two primary areas—the reason they are attending (purpose) and social relationships. These are some typical landmarks:

  – Concern over purpose, relevance of meeting, "How does this help?"

  – Looking to the leader for structure, answers, approval, acceptance

  – Looking to the leader to prove that their time will be worthwhile

  – Quiet groups

- Participants meanwhile stay focused on "I" concerns, such as these:

  – "Why am I here?"

- "I wish I had eaten something before this meeting."

- "I wish I had that seat over there."

- "I wish I had gone to the bathroom first."

Stage 2

Storming—Leader-Centered

Key words: "what," "FUD (fear, uncertainty, doubt)," more "what"

Facilitator response: *cultivating, explaining, and redirecting*

- Some participants "get it" and some don't

- Participants begin to acknowledge differences in perspectives; conflict is characteristic between members or between members and leader. Some landmarks:

    - Hostility toward leader or others

    - Looking to or expecting the leader to be magical

    - Open expression of differences

    - Some members with strong needs to dominate

    - Struggle for control, potential for scope creep

- Participants get nudged to begin thinking about what "it" is that justifies our time together (namely, the deliverable), why the effort is important, and how much the effort is worth ($ or FTP).

Stage 3

Norming—Tightly Formed

Key words: "I can," "You should," "Who will?," "fear," "belief," "hope"

Facilitator response: *cadence, clarity, communications, creativity*

- The participants are more comfortable about expressing their opinions. Some landmarks:

    - Focus on the deliverable—getting done

    - More open communication and questions between participants

    - Selective intermember support

    - Some unwillingness to be fully responsible for outcome or ownership

- Individuals start thinking about how the deliverable impacts "its" people and resources throughout the organization.

Stage 4

Performing—Self-directed

> *Key words: "we" ("We can," "We should," "We might"), "us," "community," "collaboration," "confidence"*

Facilitator response: optimally becomes a scribe for the group ("Write that down")

- Participants recognize their commonalities, interdependencies, and shared interests. They form a cohesive team—they unite and collaborate. Some landmarks:
  - Creativity and exploration ("What if . . . ?")
  - Integrated team functioning—a community
  - Pride in the group's ability and contributions
  - Sense of urgency
- They are individuals no longer; they have become a collaborative team and view themselves as an integral unit, known as "we."

Unclear Boundaries

Boundaries between stages are not always clear, nor does a group permanently move from one stage to another. You guide the group through the earlier stages toward a high-performance mode, understanding the likelihood that even high-performance teams may regress.

Anticipate regression when something new enters the picture, whether a new team member, new *Agenda Step*, or even a new *Tool*. The group may return to "storming" with questions like, "Now why are we doing that?"

> NOTE: There is no law that groups must reach Stage 4 and become collaborative and high-performing. Most groups never make it past a basic level of competence (Stage 3) in the group life cycle. For groups that reach high-performance mode (Stage 4), your role changes from facilitator to documenter as they tell you what to do ("Write that down").

Facilitating Multiple Generations at the Same Time

Staying relevant and compelling when you facilitate multiple generations presents significant challenges. Problems develop when meetings include different mindsets, communication styles, and priorities. Scheduling, work patterns, and technology intensify friction. Teams are ever-changing and often cross time zones and cultural boundaries. An attitude of acceptance provides you with an effortless secret when you facilitate multiple generations—several types of people—because one trait, common to everyone, is that people would rather be asked than told.

Whether you prefer the Meyers-Briggs Type Indicator, the DiSC assessment, the E-Colors indicator, or something else, it is clear that not everyone thinks alike. Overgeneralizing should be avoided, but trends suggest the following:

- Baby boomers (born between 1946 and 1964) remain competitive

- Gen Xers (born between 1965 and 1977) exhibit skepticism

- Gen Yers (also known as millennials, born since 1978) prefer technology

In addition to projecting an attitude of acceptance, embrace the following:

- Anticipate a variety of personality types and learning styles

- Be careful not to stereotype based on appearances and comments

- Don't overgeneralize groups based on individual character traits

- Prepare as if every type of person plans to attend your meeting

Suggestions for all generations include these:

- Appeal to the Zen of the experience. Use break timers with music. Provide and build graphical support to enliven the narrative world. Remember, we facilitate "meaning," not words; nonnarrative evidence makes it easier to dispel fake news and misinformation.

- Because meaning can be captured with illustrations, icons, and numbers, use the *Creativity Tool* (chapter 8) or *Coat of Arms* (chapter 6) to drive nonnarrative input.

- Be flexible and willing to adjust and accommodate constraints such as timing and availability. When a participant runs into an unexpected personal "issue," let's do what we can as a group to show support and respect for that person, rather than charging ahead. Decision quality correlates with complete or comprehensive answers rather than quick answers; see Kahneman's *Thinking, Fast and Slow* (2013).

- Demand that participants leave their egos and titles in the hallway. If they cannot leave their titles behind, do not invite them or ask them to leave. If they are "senior" and already have an answer, do not have a meeting. *Meetings are an ineffective and expensive form of persuasion.*[8]

---

[8] One alumnus told us that the US Joint Chiefs of Staff on occasion wear sweaters over their uniforms to hide rank. They understand how important it is for everyone to have permission to speak freely, regardless of rank, during select facilitated sessions.

- Do not let one person or group dominate. Prevent Repeaters by writing down their contributions on a whiteboard or large format paper. Prevent scope creep by asking precise questions. Avoid DUMB questions (Dull, Ubiquitous, Myopic, and Broad) through rhetorical precision.

- Embrace *Icebreakers* or *Check-In* activities (chapter 5) to get everyone contributing sooner. Likewise, anticipate and plan for additional team-building activities as appropriate. Make it easier for your participants to enjoy and value one another. Similarly, prepare some quick exercises (such as "Lost on the Moon")[9] that prove "nobody is smarter than everybody."

- Keep people moving around. Supplement *Breakout Teams* (chapter 6) with ergonomic "stretching" every 30 minutes. Take longer breaks every 60 to 75 minutes so that participants have ample time to reply to their electronic mail and messages. Do *not* wait two hours between breaks.

- Spend some personal time with your participants and get to know them better. Meeting participants respond better to leaders they respect, and respect must be earned. Formally or informally conduct conversations with participants. Discern their core competencies, concerns, and unique talents—everyone has one.[10]

- Stay neutral and stress your content neutrality. Stop judging (or even cheerleading), don't make comments about content, and avoid using the deadly first person singular "I."

- Use breakout activities liberally by mixing up your *Breakout Teams* frequently. People become more conversational in small groups (two to five people) and develop a stronger appreciation for one another. As you sense dysfunction, intervene. Coach participants about how to treat one another in a public environment. You will discover that more conflict arises because of personality characteristics and toxicity than because of age, culture, or diversity factors.

---

[9] See the National Aeronautics and Space Administration (NASA) website for a public domain challenge of prioritizing 15 items that need to be carried a long distance by foot when stranded on the surface of the moon: https://www.nasa.gov/pdf/166504main _Survival.pdf.

[10] See Howard Gardner's "Theory of Multiple Intelligences," https://howardgardner.com.

Situational Causes of Conflict

Hopefully, you begin to see conflict as both challenge and opportunity. Meetings are expensive and mitigating conflict provides one of the absolute best reasons for meetings. However, conflict also comes from the situation, and from you (figure 4.5).

"THREE TROLLS WITH THE COURAGE OF ONE": INTERNAL CONFLICT

Internal conflict is fear, something everyone experiences.[11] All people have some fear. When we allow fear to control us, we lose our ability to perform. The first step is to understand our fears. Once we do, we can control them. Fears never go away—we simply learn to acknowledge or contain them. Below are some typical meeting facilitator fears:

- Challenges and attacks

- Equipment breakdowns and technology malfunctions, especially with online meetings

- Inability to persuade, motivate

- Looking like a beginner

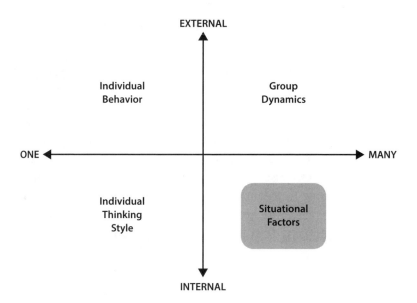

Figure 4.5. Situational Factors

---

[11] Nobody understands the title of this section, but I can't seem to let it go. Three trolls, in *The 10th Kingdom* (Mill Creek Ent.), an American fairytale fantasy miniseries, proudly call themselves "three trolls with the courage of one," oblivious to the line's meaning that each troll has only one-third the normal amount of courage.

- Losing control—asserting control

- Making mistakes or failing

- People with problems (managing conflict)

- Public speaking

- Wanting to be liked and to gain approval

- Wanting to give advice or ideas

- What to do about silence

FLY IN FORMATION

Once you identify your personal fears, you can make them work to your advantage. Adrenaline gives you an edge. Remember that the butterflies in your stomach will always be there. You don't want to eliminate them. You want to teach them to fly in formation.

A WHIFF OF PINE, A HINT OF SKUNK (EXTERNAL CONFLICT)

Conflict is natural and not necessarily bad, when responsibly managed. Managing conflict justifies the time and expense of face-to-face meetings because conflict cannot be resolved effectively by exchanging documents, email, and text messages.

Facilitative leaders can channel conflict into productivity. Look at the US Federal Mediation and Conciliation Service.[12] Managed well, conflict leads to expanded information exchange, surfaced rationales, more options, and higher-quality decisions. Managed poorly, conflict destroys. Effectively managed, conflict leads to transformation. If left festering in the hallways, conflict leads to chaos.

> NOTE: "A peaceful, harmonious place can be the worst thing possible for a business. Research shows that the biggest predictor of poor company performance is complacency. Conflict can shake things up and boost your staff's energy and creativity."[13]

Society places negative values on conflict at home and at school. We have not received formal instruction about collaborative problem-solving skills. The following sections on external sources of conflict, barriers you will encounter, and a four-activity *Argument Resolution* response show you how to manage meeting conflict.

Two leading indicators of external sources of conflict are tenure (how long somebody has been around) and reorganization—whenever participants' jobs,

---

[12] By the way, the penalty for a federal mediator who violates neutrality is prison.
[13] Joni Saj-nicole and Damon Beyer, "How to Pick a Good Fight" (2009), 50.

titles, or reporting situations are at risk or being changed. External sources of meeting conflict include the following:

- Habits—accustomed to disagreeing or arguing, cultural

- Misinformation—rumors, especially about change

- Participants' problems—out of control, unable to excel or bond

- Priorities—similar values, but varying priorities

- Semantics—understanding of words and intent

- Situations—business process improvement, restructuring

- Ways participants view others—biases, heuristics, prejudices

OTHER BARRIERS

Your ability to manage conflict is also inhibited by other barriers. Knowing about them in advance becomes the best way to overcome them. Once you are aware and prepared, you can adjust. When you are unaware or unconscious, all hell breaks loose. These other barriers include:

- Ability or willingness to listen—yours and theirs

- Copper or fiber (online meetings)—inability to challenge participants in person

- Image—inability to save face

- Lack of skill—a weak or poorly trained facilitator

- Time—consensus is seldom achieved quickly

Paradigm Challenges

Paradigms are established, accepted norms, patterns of behavior, or shared sets of assumptions. They are models that establish boundaries or rules for success. Paradigms may present structural barriers to creativity based on psychological, cultural, and environmental factors. Examples include:

- Flow charts, diagrams, and other conventions that people get comfortable with when presenting information that they rely on habitually (like swim lanes)

- Stereotypes about men and women and their roles in business, family, and society

- Where people sit in meetings, when in person—once they find a seat it becomes "their seat" for the rest of the meeting, or meetings, if the seat associates with their own desired level of position or power (could be high or low, a seat up front or far back)

GROUPTHINK

As creatures of habit, we blindly subscribe to our cultural paradigms, unknowingly allowing our biases and prejudices to affect our decision-making and readily falling prey to groupthink. There is power in large numbers but not necessarily an increase in quality. Voting reflects a method of groupthink decision-making. The winner is not necessarily a better decision; it just reflects a bigger number of supporters.

CHALLENGE BOTH

To cause groups to challenge their own paradigms or groupthink, try the following:

- Ask about "paradigm shift"—"What is impossible today, but if made possible . . . What would you do differently?"

- Force the group to look at a familiar idea or scenario in a new way by using the *Perspective Tool* in chapter 8. Shifting perspectives frequently helps "shake" paradigms.

- Consider using Dr. Edward de Bono's *Thinking Hats* (chapter 8) exercise, in which you impose a perspective, such as that of a monastery contrasted with that of an organized crime syndicate.[14]

Have a few tools in your hip pocket, usually visual or riddle-based. While thousands of such challenges may be found online or in books and libraries, my all-time favorite remains the "bookworm challenge" in figure 4.6. Provide a simple, mathematical answer to the problem before proceeding (*hint:* the answer has two digits).

This is not a trick question. The books are lined up in proper sequence from left to right, standing up vertically. Simply estimate the straight line distance from the first page in the set of four books to the last page in the set of four books.

I have conducted this challenge with thousands of people and barely a dozen have correctly answered the challenge. Nearly all participants—more than 95 percent—provide answers between 21 and 25 centimeters.

After you capture everyone's answer, you demonstrate statistical confidence by discarding the outliers, averaging the balance, and allowing a range of freedom of plus or minus 10 percent. The results yield a high confidence interval suggesting that the group should be 95 percent confident that the answer is between, for example, 21 and 25 centimeters, and everyone can go home confident.

---

[14] Edward De Bono, "Six Thinking Hats," n.d., https://www.debonogroup.com/services /core-programs/six-thinking-hats/.

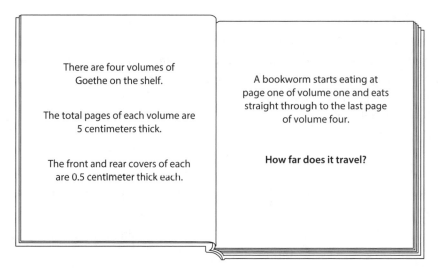

Figure 4.6. Bookworm Challenge

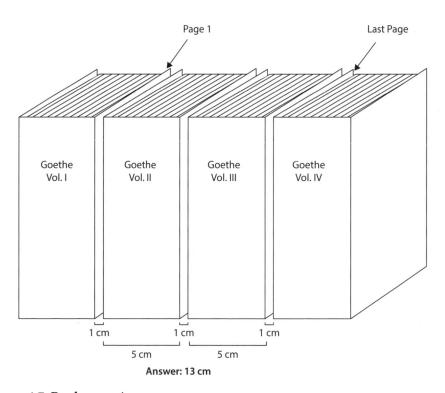

Figure 4.7. Bookworm Answer

Yet the correct answer is out of the range, by a factor of nearly 100 percent. You see, the correct answer is 13 centimeters. Few believe it until they see it, so I display the answer (see figure 4.7)—along with a clear message: voting sucks.

We may have even thrown away the closest answer because it deviated so much from the other answers that we assumed it had to be wrong. We're smart

Four Steps to Managing Arguments

Figure 4.8. Four Activities

people; we can't all be wrong by that much, right? Well, yes, we can, because we got caught up in groupthink, also known as the lemming solution, and we just fell off the cliff by agreeing to an answer somewhere around 23 centimeters.

Conflict as Challenge and Opportunity

There is no instructional class in the world that will teach you how to facilitate a resolution to all meeting conflict, especially arguments. Sometimes, people or parties refuse to agree simply because they do not like each other.

It is not your responsibility to resolve the conflict. However, you can rely on four steps to help you *manage* meeting conflict that frequently yield consensus (figure 4.8). Fortunately, the four steps are effective and repeatable:

1. CONFIRM OR CLARIFY PURPOSE

Begin to resolve conflict within a meeting by first understanding, clarifying, and confirming the purpose of the object[15] or topic being deliberated (figure 4.9). Effective conflict resolution depends on shared purpose. Competing purposes lead to competing solutions.

Your meeting design role demands that you build consensus around the purpose of the object the deliverable supports, the intent of the object, and why it is important. You cannot afford to have a moving target if you want to build consensus. Make the group's integrated purpose around the topic or object clear and visible. Document and display the purpose for everyone to confirm. Use the *Purpose Tool* (chapter 7) as a quick and effective means of writing a consensual expression of purpose. By visually displaying the narrative content, you make it easier to confirm whether everyone can support it or not.

Many analysts are surprised to discover that arguments around requirements and prioritization surfaced because participants could not agree on the purpose of some feature, object, or process. Some arguments are resolved by this clarification of purpose alone. Other arguments persist. If so, move on to the next activity.

---

[15] "Object" here means the person, place, thing, or event to be directly affected by the "objective" (deliverable) of the meeting.

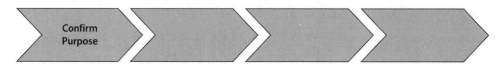

Figure 4.9. Confirm Purpose

Figure 4.10. Document Positions

2. DOCUMENT POSITIONS AND INTERESTS

Active listening demands that the facilitator provide reflection and confirmation of what the speaker said (figure 4.10).

When meeting conflict develops, participants may hear *what* was said, but they need to understand under what conditions the position holds true (and remains valid or not). My own experience has shown that it is critical to reflect *why* the speaker said something. Typically, speakers' first statements are about their position. Understanding the *why* behind their positioning requires additional challenge, leading to disclosure of their true interests.

For example, as a homeowner, I may not want a sewage treatment plant near my backyard. If I am challenged—"Why not?"—my position states, "Because it stinks." After further challenge we discover that the prevailing wind correlates strongly with the amount of stink and that my primary concern is that the treatment plant be located downwind from my residence. However, I become focused on my position. I don't think "prevailing wind"; rather, I think "stink."

Consensus is not built at the symptomatic level but at the causal level. Begin by getting everyone to understand under what conditions certain claims hold valid. Therefore, challenging the *why* behind *what* was said becomes critical. Solid facilitation effectively challenges participants to make their thinking visible by using one question: "because?"

Sometimes people who are in violent agreement with one another do a poor job of listening. So amplify your active listening during conflict. Remember that active listening comprises four separate activities:

- *Make contact* with the speaker; typically eye contact is leveraged to ensure the speaker is acknowledged, engaged, and valued.

- *Absorb* what is being said with serious intent so that you can provide the entire group an accurate and comprehensive reflection of what the speaker said.

- *Reflect* what was said to ensure the speaker understands what he or she said. But more important, reflect why the speaker made that statement.

Reflect how the speaker's position and interests relate to the question at hand (frequently it is best to show the reflection in writing on a large piece of Post-it paper).

- And always *confirm* that the speaker's content, as reflected, is correct—because sometimes we get it wrong.

At least one person in any given group does not listen or hear what another person says. Some people don't even listen to themselves. Reflection provides an essential activity of effective, active listening. However, you must *confirm* and not assume that your reflection is accurate.

Once two or more interests have been understood and documented well enough to satisfy the advocates, some arguments will drop by the wayside. Others will advance, so proceed with the third step.

3. APPEAL TO OBJECTIVES

Sometimes people understand each other and yet continue to disagree. Many arguments of this nature are about future conditions that cannot be proven one way or another. Participants may even rely on the same evidence-based support, such as facts, projections, and trends, but interpret this evidence differently in a future world.

To help resolve conflict, learn to sequentially appeal to objectives (figure 4.11), starting with the objectives of the product or project, and then proceeding with objectives of the department or program, of the business unit, and of the entire organization that your meeting supports. If the CEO were in the meeting, which argument would he or she say better supports organizational objectives—and, more important, *why*?

Carefully and fully document conflicting arguments with supporting claims, evidence, and examples. Have the group contrast their positions by asking them "to what extent" each interest supports the various objectives using the *Alignment Tool* (chapter 6). Specifically, ask these questions:

- *To what extent* does (each position or interest) support the overall project objectives?

- *To what extent* does (each position or interest) support the program objectives (the reasons for approving the project)?

- *To what extent* does (each position or interest) support the business unit objectives (what would the executive sponsor say)?

Figure 4.11. Appeal to Objectives

Figure 4.12. Escalate

- *To what extent* does (each position or interest) support the organizational objectives (what would the chief executive officer say)?

Appealing to the various objectives will reconcile some remaining meeting conflict, but not all of it. In some cultures, for example, safety is critical, and if one position can be viewed as "riskier," it will be rejected immediately. Consider using the holarchy (see figure 2.1 in chapter 2) for visually illustrating how competing interests should be compared to the various objectives.

So, what do you do, as meeting facilitator, if appealing to objectives fails?

4. ESCALATE

If the first three steps, in sequence, fail to drive consensual resolution, escalate decision-making by taking the documented positions back to the executive sponsor, steering team, or decision review board (figure 4.12). Show them the purpose and position documents and explain how you attempted to use them to arrive at consensual understanding.

Tell the executives that the group participants reached an impasse in the meeting and need help. Ask the executives to reach a decision and, more important, share the rationale behind it, so that this "because" can be brought back to the participants and make the group more effective with subsequent decision-making.

Sometimes participants fail to agree with one another based on irrational or irreconcilable terms. No meeting facilitator can build consensus around every issue, but having a method to manage the conflict provides confidence that you have performed professionally.

HERE'S WHAT HAPPENS

Executives absorb what you have provided. They review the documented statements of purpose and position and then go back and appeal to their own objectives, asking questions like:

- Why did we approve this project or initiative?

- Why was this important to my department or business unit?

- How does this initiative support the organization's forward-looking strategy and future?

Typically, executives have better line of site because they are more intimate with plans, shaping curves, and transitional and transformational efforts underway to ensure an organization reaches its vision than meeting participants will be. After the executives share their reasoning with you, take their rationale back to the group and empower participants to make higher-quality decisions in future meetings.

Surprisingly, when threatened with taking the decision out of the meeting room, many times participants acquiesce and suddenly become more flexible than ever before. Remember, no one likes to be told what to do.

Anger and Some Other Stuff

How well do you personally respond to conflict? To effectively facilitate conflict, you must keep the situation constructive:

- Build a toolkit for immediate help and prepare a hip-pocket set of *Tools* and procedures for the unexpected.

- Challenge—when people raise objectives, discover the cause of the objection. By challenging participants, you convert their "subject matter" bias into its objective nature. What causes the objection, and *what is the measurement of the cause*? "The chili is too spicy" (subjective) may be converted into "The chili's spiciness measures 1,400 Scoville units" (objective).

- Know how to communicate acceptance by promoting integral thinking—display a "Yes, *and . . .*" attitude, not a "Yes, *but . . .*" attitude.

ANGER—ONE LETTER SHORT OF DANGER

Realize that anger is as normal as any other emotion. We expect or want things to be different or better. Most people direct their anger at those who have some control over them. Anger can be healthy and is different from hostility, which is not healthy. Anger is often used to hide other feelings such as hurt or disappointment. Learn how to deal with anger in others and in yourself. Remain cautious, however, because the term "anger" is only one letter short of the term "danger."

When dealing with *others'* anger:

- Acknowledge and affirm the participant's beliefs.

- Encourage the participant to talk about the reasons for being angry. This helps diffuse the anger.

- Let the participant vent before trying to explain or apologize.

- Use nonjudgmental active listening. This lets the participant know that you care.

When dealing with *your own* anger:

- Acknowledge and accept the anger. Do not deny it, or it will resurface at the wrong time.

- Deal with the problem that caused the anger as quickly as is practical. However, do not make decisions when your anger is in control.

> **—Carl Gustav Jung**
> *Everything that irritates us about others can lead us to an understanding of ourselves.*

- Take a break, whether in person or online. Take a walk and reprogram yourself.

When you listen to participants, they become more prepared to listen to one another. Anger often dissipates, and trust begins to emerge. Make sure that both you and the participants avoid communicating rejection. Rejection incites defensiveness and blocks listening.

Quick Summary on Collaborating

All consensus-oriented meeting facilitators are responsible for maintaining balance:

- Avoid being the expert authority on the subject. You can be an authority figure, but your role is to listen, question, enforce the procedure, or offer optional methods.

- Avoid using participants' names; doing so may display favoritism or too much "friendliness."

- Challenge with follow-up inquiries such as "because . . . ?" *Why* people justify the way they feel is more powerful than *what* they feel.

- Do not let your personal prejudices interfere with your role as meeting leader. Let go of the need to win everyone over to your point of view. You are there to serve the group and seeking to understand their point of view by using impeccable listening skills.

- Don't talk too much. Let the group speak—you are seeking an answer they will own.

- If an overarching issue develops that affects the rest of the meeting and jeopardizes the deliverable, stop the meeting, and secure a resolution. Do not stick it in the *"Parking Lot"* (an area reserved for important yet unreconciled issues to be managed later; this is more fully explained in chapter 5).

- If you feel compelled to give them praise, commend them only for the quantity of work completed, not quality of work.

- Learn to expect hostility, but do not become hostile. Develop an attitude of acceptance. You may not agree with what is being said, but you can listen and record their answers and opinions. If you need to discount their content, do it after the meeting, privately.

- Recognize any contributions and encourage participation. Your ability to convey interest and enthusiasm about the importance of the deliverable will be critical to your success.

- Stay neutral (Did we say "stay neutral" yet?). *Do not lose your neutrality.* Allow me to repeat that statement: **Do not lose your neutrality.** The greatest facilitators in the world *exude* neutrality. The worst facilitators already have an answer.

- Stop a meeting if the group is sluggish and difficult to control, even if participants wish to continue. When people are burned-out, no progress occurs.

- You will be phenomenally successful if you *do just one thing to change your behavior*: do *not* use the singular first person "I" or "me"; be pluralistic, and use "us" or "we."

DON'T FORGET

It is not your job to resolve every piece of conflict and each argument. Rather, it is your responsibility to have a method for *managing* conflict and arguments. And when you follow the advice and sequence of the four steps in this chapter, you have a method for managing all types of conflict in business settings.

5

Structuring

MEETING DESIGN MADE EASY

No group wants the leader to ask group members how they want to proceed. They need a meeting leader prepared with the right approach and tools who will tell them how to proceed, keep them focused on the right questions, and explain how their responses support the deliverable (getting DONE).

Two Types of Agendas

Successful meetings demand a clear purpose (beginning), a meaningful *Meeting Approach* (middle), and a consensual review and wrap (end). Throwing together a *Basic Agenda* and then relying on your speaking skills and charm may let you skate by as a person, but do not qualify as exhibiting competent meeting leadership skills. Professionals require a fully *Annotated Agenda* to supplement the *Basic Agenda*.

> NOTE: Here's why most people would rather attend a movie than a meeting: even a lousy movie has a beginning, a middle, and an end.

This chapter describes how to build two complementary types of agenda: a *Basic Agenda*, which simply lists the *Agenda Steps* (topics to be covered) and is used by participants to track progress, and a detailed *Annotated Agenda*, which describes in detail *how* the facilitator will lead the group to get DONE. The *Basic Agenda* is a simple list, usually 6 to 18 items. The *Annotated Agenda*, a playscript for the facilitator, may run 20 pages or more for a lengthy workshop. For example, the annotation support for the *Planning Approach* in this book runs around 50 pages.

Each *Annotated Agenda* includes a *Basic Agenda* but more closely resembles a playscript because the *Annotated Agenda* details and explains the *Tools* used during each *Agenda Step*. Each *Tool* uses procedures that a meeting facilitator unveils at appropriate times as discrete activities, questions, tasks, and visual prompts.

- By using *Tools*, each *Agenda Step* produces its own deliverable, such as prioritized criteria or a decision or assignments.

- *Tools* are determined by the type of question or deliverable each *Agenda Step* demands.

- Some *Tools* require other *Tools*. For example, the *PowerBalls* (chapter 7) might rely on *Definition* (chapter 6) and *Bookend Rhetoric* (chapter 7) to deliver a clear set of priorities.

START WITH THE END IN MIND

Leadership consciousness begins by knowing what the end looks like. Yet describing the end of a successful meeting is not enough. The name for each *Agenda Step* needs to describe its result or deliverable. Remember, the objective for each *Agenda Step* is an object—a noun. You cannot deliver up a verb. *Agenda Steps* are best described by answering the question, "What does DONE look like?"

Describe your *Basic Agenda Steps* with nouns because verbs like "identify" and "define" add little value. Verbs involve work. Verbs only help facilitators, who need to know what they are going to do. So put the verbs (and everything else) in your *Annotated Agenda* and spare your participants the burden of doing your work. They simply want to get DONE.

THREE PHASES OF ALL MEETING AGENDAS

Meetings and workshops should have . . .

1. A beginning,

2. A middle, and

3. An end.

Have you ever been in a meeting without one of these phases? Of course, you have. Many meetings fail because the leader ignores the importance of a strong start and clear wrap-up. Because every meeting you ever lead must have a beginning, a middle, and an end, we begin by explaining seven activities that you should command for every *Launch (Introduction)* and then explaining four activities that you should command for every *Review and Wrap (Conclusion)*.

Then, the rest of this chapter will explain building an *Annotated Agenda*. The balance of the book will unveil various *Meeting Approaches, Agenda Steps,* and *Tools* for everything you need to facilitate the meeting between your *Launch* and *Wrap*.

Launch (Introduction) Agenda Step

Your beginning sets the tone, confirms the roles, clarifies the boundaries (scope), and describes what happens during the middle of the meeting. Your meeting launch should last no longer than 5 minutes—no longer than 10 minutes for workshops—excluding icebreakers or other special activities such as an executive kickoff or a product or project update.

SET-UP

Before you begin your meeting *Launch*, have a document or screen prepared or your room set up with visuals ready to share, in person or online. Somehow, visually display the meeting purpose, meeting scope, and meeting deliverable, preferably unveiling one display at a time. If you do not know what your meeting deliverable looks like, then you are not prepared to lead a working session.

If you cannot convert the meeting purpose, meeting scope, and meeting deliverable into 50 words or less (for each), then you are not ready yet to launch your meeting.

For in-person workshops, use large-format paper (see the example of four sheets in figure 5.1), mounted on a side or rear wall. For a 50-minute meeting, provide the same content printed on an 8.5-by-11-inch or A4 sheet of paper. Use an arrow or indicator (like "you are here") on your agenda to consistently show where the group is in the agenda.

For online meetings, consider writing "artifacts" by hand, such as 4-by-6-inch cards that have the same content.[1] As explained by online expert Daniel Mezick, the feel and sense of handwritten materials (artifacts) when brought closely into the camera adds to the texture of an online meeting, making it more vibrant.[2] You may use both sides of the cards and flip them over in front of the camera. Or use an even larger sheet and unfold it in front of the camera, revealing a separate item each time you flip or turn a page.

Use the following *Launch* procedure and follow the exact sequence of the seven activities to launch every session, even a 50-minute meeting. Your *Launch* is not an appropriate time to experiment. These seven activities, in this sequence, have been stress-tested and proven to be most effective.

1. ***Introduce*** yourself in the role of meeting facilitator as neutral and unbiased. Stress the roles of participants as equals. Remind them to leave egos and titles in the hallway. Stipulate how much money or time (FTP) is wasted or at risk if the meeting and thus the organization, product, or project fails. Complete this activity within 30 seconds (figure 5.2).

---

[1] As the term is used in this book, an artifact could be a printed poster, a screen-shared item, a digital wallpaper poster (like a weather person on television), a digital emoji, or preferably a handwritten or hand-drawn card held up closely to the camera.

[2] I am certified by Daniel Mezick's HTTO Level 1, Open Leadership Network, "Connect & Communicate: How to Teach Online," http://newtechusa.net/danielmezick/.

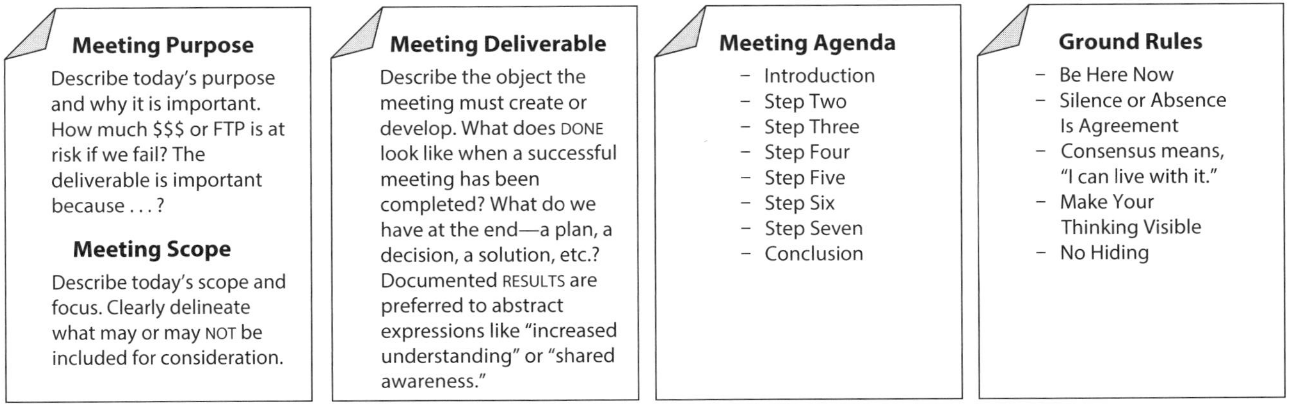

Meeting Purpose

Describe today's purpose and why it is important. How much $$$ or FTP is at risk if we fail? The deliverable is important because . . . ?

Meeting Scope

Describe today's scope and focus. Clearly delineate what may or may NOT be included for consideration.

Meeting Deliverable

Describe the object the meeting must create or develop. What does DONE look like when a successful meeting has been completed? What do we have at the end—a plan, a decision, a solution, etc.? Documented RESULTS are preferred to abstract expressions like "increased understanding" or "shared awareness."

Meeting Agenda

– Introduction
– Step Two
– Step Three
– Step Four
– Step Five
– Step Six
– Step Seven
– Conclusion

Ground Rules

– Be Here Now
– Silence or Absence Is Agreement
– Consensus means, "I can live with it."
– Make Your Thinking Visible
– No Hiding

Figure 5.1. Large-Format Paper or Screen—Always Make This Content Visually Accessible

My name is _____ and my purpose is to serve you. Our goal is to complete an *Approach* that will accelerate Product/Project _____ (or department or organization) with results that each of you can support.

If this meeting fails, we're jeopardizing the entire project (or, department or organization) that is worth an estimated $_____ and _____ FTP (one-time value or per year).

My role is to remain impartial about the content and your perspectives, but I am passionate about the session's importance. Leave your egos in the hallway because in this room, we will treat one another as equals.

Our time is short so let's begin.

Figure 5.2. Launching Script

2. ***Meeting purpose:*** Describe the meeting purpose, either on large-format paper, a handout, or a screen. Stress again that this session is important *because* . . . and seek audible assent from your participants. Frequently, for this first request, put hands to your ears while saying "I can't hear you" to force a louder audible response. Professional facilitators constantly strive to shift "airtime" to their participants, and participants' vocal affirmation transfers ownership.

3. ***Meeting scope:*** Describe the meeting scope, either on large-format paper, a handout, or a screen. The meeting scope is either the entire organization, department, product, or project, or part of them, but never more. Again, secure an audible assent from your participants that builds consensus and transfers ownership.

4. ***Meeting deliverables:*** Describe what DONE looks like by using your prepared statement. After securing audible assent here, you will have facilitated audible agreement three times within two minutes. If participants cannot agree on the meeting purpose, meeting scope, and meeting deliverable, then your *Agenda* is at risk, and you have even more serious problems to address.

NOTE: This meeting purpose, scope, and deliverable should be provided to participants before the meeting as part of an invitation, pre-read, or read ahead. Those statements should *not* change at this point. If they do, the meeting may be challenged, and the *Agenda* may no longer be valid. I have been asked to modify the scope a few times, but it was always sharpening and not broadening the prepared statement (I now know that Greenland and parts of Iceland are in North America).

5. ***Administrivia:*** Explain that "administrivia" is any noise that might be causing a distraction. You want to clear participants' heads from thinking about themselves, especially their creature comforts. For brief meetings, you might include where to locate emergency exits, fire extinguishers, lavatories, or coffee and tea. For workshops and longer

meetings, you would also cover the frequency of breaks, break times for responding to email, lunch arrangements, and any other "noise" that might prevent participants from staying focused. You may also conduct *Icebreakers* here, or after presenting the *Ground Rules* (chapter 4) in the seventh activity in this sequence.

6. ***Today's agenda:*** Describe each *Agenda Step*, including the reason for the sequence of the *Agenda Steps* and flow. Explain how the *Agenda Steps* relate to one another. Do not read them. Rather, explain *why* the *Agenda Steps* help us get DONE and why they are listed in the sequence provided. Link *Agenda Steps* back to the deliverable so that participants see how completing each *Agenda Step* helps us get DONE.

   Fully explaining the *Agenda Steps* helps groups move out of "storming," Stage 1 of the group life cycle. Again, do *not* read the *Agenda Steps*—explain them! Optimally, use a nonprofessional analogy to explain your *Agenda Steps* (chapter 6).[3] You have heard that a picture is worth a thousand words; well, an analogy is worth a thousand pictures (and a story is worth a thousand analogies).

7. ***Ground Rules:*** Share appropriate *Ground Rules* (chapter 4). Supplement your narrative posting of *Ground Rules* with audiovisual support, including humorous clips, but keep it brief. After presenting your essential *Ground Rules*, solicit any additional ones from the group, if desired.

OPTIONAL OR OCCASIONAL TOPICS

Have everyone introduce themselves by providing a structured *Icebreaker*. Complete *Icebreakers* before moving out of your *Launch Step*. If you expect *Icebreakers* or *Check-ins* to take up a significant amount of time, more than a half-hour, consider sequencing this activity sooner and move it up within the fifth activity ("administrivia"). Next you will find some *Icebreaker* examples that I have successfully used at least once.

Icebreakers Tool

WHY?

To get your subject matter experts participatory sooner by having them introduce themselves beyond names and titles. Always use *Icebreakers* during online meetings, providing participants with a way of connecting with one another.

---

[3] For an example, see the section "Explanation via Analogy" in the *Planning Approach* (chapter 6).

PROCEDURE

Have participants share their responses with the group.

- An undemanding yet effective method begins, "If I were a . . ."—for example, "If I were a gem, I would be a _____," or "If I were a bird, I would be a _____."

- Describe your dream career as a child.

- Explain how you got one of your scars (and where it is).

- If you could change anything about your childhood, what would it be?

- If you could wake up tomorrow having gained any one quality or ability, what would it be?

- If you were an animal, you would be a _____.

- If you had a yacht, what would you name it?

- "My hero is . . ."; "My collection is . . ."

- If limited to five items, what would you bring with you on a desert island?

- Name a talent that you have that no one here knows about.

- Name your favorite James Bond or Elizabeth Bennet actor and explain why.

- Tell two truths and a lie—participants guess the lie.

- What is the one word you would use to describe where you are at?

- What is your favorite sport to play? Why?

- What kitchen appliance or tool would you be and why?

- What was the first concert you attended?

- What was your strangest paying job or chore?

- What would be the title of your autobiography?

- What's on your reading list or nightstand?

- Who is your most fascinating person in history?

- "Would you rather?" questions: Would you rather be invisible or be able to read minds? Would you rather live without music or live without television? Would you rather be four feet tall or eight feet tall? (see http://www.teampedia.net/)

OR MEETING SPARKS

- Start with a "fun fact": everyone shares something previously unknown about themselves to all the others.

- Based on a project theme, create new surnames for participants—for example, Anna Aconcagua (highest mountain in South America).

- On a rotating basis, have participants bring in some fun trivia or jokes.

CHECK-IN: MAD, SAD, AND GLAD

Used commonly in frameworks supporting Agile, begin and end meetings with three questions that require participants to state they are checking in, along with sharing something about which they are mad, sad, or glad.

- "I am mad about . . ."

- "I am sad about . . ."

- "I am glad about . . ."

- "I am fully checked in."

Have participants pass the turn on to someone else by calling out his or her name.

Other Considerations

As your *Launch* sequence continues, you may need to address some particular situations.

EXECUTIVE KICKOFF

For a kickoff or significant event launch, have your executive sponsor explain the importance of the participants' contributions and what management intends to accomplish. Consider a quick program update. However, do not allow the update or executive sponsor to take more than five minutes. Your meeting is not a mini town hall (unless it is).

Do not modify the seven activities of the *Launch* sequence except for the executive sponsor activity. As soon as the sponsor enters the room, if the meeting has begun, stop and introduce that person. If the sponsor is present at the start, introduce him or her immediately. Have the sponsor up front and out of the room as soon as possible or practical, preferably without letting him or her sit down. If the sponsor insists on staying, seat him or her in the back or on the side as an observer, unless the sponsor is going to be an equal participant, like everyone else.

Script talking points for the executive sponsor. Provide him or her with a written paragraph that makes these points:

- What the session is about

- What management hopes to accomplish

- Why this time things are different (if a repeat effort)

- Why these people were chosen

- Executive support for the *Meeting Approach* and people in the room

NOTE: Kickoffs are rare compared with most meetings. The executive will not follow your script, but your scripting has set levels and managed expectations. The executive knows you are expecting 45 seconds from him or her, even 4 or 5 minutes, but *not* 45 minutes.

PROJECT TEAM

Product owners and project managers or sponsors may provide updates about progress or changes that have occurred since a prior session. Have them remain brief by sticking to the vital information affecting the participants. Do not let them go too far "into the weeds," providing details that bore everyone else. Keep them focused on *what* has transpired (abstract), not *how* it is being done (concrete).

OPEN ITEMS

You may need to conduct a review of open items from prior meetings. Preferably, have the product or project manager or sponsor read open items and share a status update while you document or record participants' comments, if needed.

DAILY LAUNCH DURING MULTIPLE SESSION WORKSHOPS

Each morning (or each week for a string of sessions), begin by reviewing and reconfirming the meeting purpose, scope, and deliverables, along with progress made and where the group is in the *Agenda*. Repeat and reinforce *Ground Rules* (chapter 4). This is an appropriate time for using audiovisual reinforcement, especially brief clips on safety moments or quick and humorous television advertisements with an appropriate message (such as "trust one another"). Quickly review output completed previously and *Agenda Steps* planned for the current session. Optimally, return to your analogy to link the *Agenda Steps* to one another and back to the deliverable.

> NOTE: During the *Launch* of multiple-day workshops, complete the same seven activities at the start of each day (except kickoff). Additionally, review content that was built or agreed on in prior session(s) and how it relates to the overall progress being made toward completing the deliverable.

TRANSITION REMINDER

As we learned with the group life cycle model, transitions are risky. You are more likely to cause confusion during a transition than during the middle of *Agenda Steps*. Therefore, take the following steps during transitions:

- Slow down.

- Move forward (lean forward for video).

- Lower your rate of speech and volume.

- Connect where you were to where you are going (connect the dots).

CAUTION: Have you been in a meeting when someone, usually an outlier, asks "Now why are we doing this?" Feel the oxygen get sucked out of the room? An effective meeting facilitator anticipates confusion and slows down during transitions. This approach is counterintuitive, because most say, "Let me review this quickly."

The group life cycle model (chapter 4) suggests that groups, even high-performance teams, are subject to regression when transitioning from one step in an agenda to another. Be forewarned: transitions are the best time to slow down and carefully explain the white space, the *why* behind the *what*.

As your meeting progresses beyond the *Launch*, continue to treat your transitions carefully:

- Why are the *Agenda Steps* in the sequence provided?

- Why did we need the output from the prior *Agenda Step*?

- How does this *Agenda Step* help us get out of this meeting faster—how does it support or partly fulfill the meeting deliverable?

- What are we going to do next? Why?

Carefully explain the white space by answering these questions. You will discover that, when you provide clear context, your meetings finish faster than ever, because participants trust that you know where you are going. It's easy to trust and follow a leader who has clear line of site.

Review and Wrap (Conclusion) Agenda Step

An effective *Review and Wrap* requires four activities. None of the following should ever be skipped, so expand and contract based on your situation and constraints:

1. Review and confirm what has been DONE.

2. Manage the *Parking Lot*.

3. Agree on a communications plan.

4. Assess the effectiveness of your leadership and the session.

Review and Wrap Activity 1: Review Deliverable

Do not relive the session, but do review the outputs, decisions, assignments, and so on. Focus on the results and deliverable from each *Agenda Step*, not on how you got there. Participants do not need a transcript. They need to be reminded about significant takeaways and offered the opportunity to ask for additional information or clarification before the session ends.

If possible and practical, use the documentation generated during the session to structure a quick walk-through. During the walk-through, include real-life examples for participants to see how well the deliverable performs.

REVIEW ACTIONS

Add an action review to planning or problem-solving meetings. Have the group confirm action items they have already agreed to or will undertake—starting with actions for the next day. List the actions, clarify them, have someone take responsibility, and have the group assign a deadline (month, day, year) for the action to have been completed. Consider applying the *RASI Tool* (chapter 6) to convert complex action items into assignments, called *Roles and Responsibilities.*

Absence or silence is unacceptable during assignments. Do not permit actions to be assigned to anyone not attending the session, either live or online.

Review and Wrap Activity 2: Manage Open Issues Using the Parking Lot Tool

Most organizations use the term "Parking Lot" to describe open issues. Regardless of the term or phrase embraced by your organization, open issues need to be managed properly and not left unattended. So, during your meetings, record open issues as they arise. During the *Review and Wrap*, use one of the following three *Tools* to manage them.

WHY?

There are numerous terms people use to describe open issues that develop during meetings. Besides "Parking Lot," other terms used include "Issue Bin," "Popcorn," and my favorite, "Refrigerator," a term used in the Middle East.[4] Here are three different procedures for facilitating standard, quick, and complex open issues.

STANDARD PARKING LOT PROCEDURE

During meetings, record open issues as they arise. Now review each open issue. First make sure the open issue remains valid.

> NOTE: Ever turn to a *Parking Lot* item and no one could remember what it meant? Ever look at your to-do list on a Saturday morning and draw the same blank? The secret to effectively capturing open issues and action items is to always include a verb-noun pairing, at minimum. Do not write down your open issue so quickly or illegibly that you will not remember what it was. For example, do not write down "Policy," write down "Update Inspection Policy."

---

[4] Vehicles rust while sitting in a parking lot, but open issues temporarily stored in a refrigerator can be preserved and even used later to cook up a whole new meal.

Over the course of meetings, some open issues are no longer "open" and can be deleted or marked accordingly (for example, "OBE" for "overcome by events," or taken care of). Append each valid open issue with the following:

- The issue status—along with a complete, coherent expression or description (consider using the *Definition Tool* (chapter 6).

- Who is responsible for communicating back to the group on the status of the open issue (frequently worded as who will do or complete the open issue)?

- When this group may expect a status update (frequently worded as when completion may be expected)? Confirm that the group can wait until the date requested for the update.

- How will progress or completion be communicated back to this group (for example, where the file will be located)? Consider email size limitations, file-naming conventions, SharePoint passwords, and file-server security restrictions.

NOTE: I carefully ask, "Who will be responsible for reporting back to the group on the status of this issue?" I do *not* ask "Who will do this?" Frequently, when they return to their office, the volunteer assigns the work to some of their employees.

We don't care who is going to do it. We need to know whom to call if there are questions. Be kind and allow one and only one volunteer. Do not be nice and allow two people to share the responsibility. If you are nice you risk having them point fingers at each other when asked for a progress report.

QUICK AND EASY 2-BY-4 PROCEDURE

An uncomplicated method for managing open issues is called the "2-by-4." Meant to connote a standard piece of lumber, the method suggests three quick questions—namely:

To . . . do what?

By . . . whom and when?

For . . . what purpose or benefit?

COMPLEX BHAG PROCEDURE

For complex open issues, or big hairy audacious goals (BHAG) that might constitute major or multiple new products or projects and cannot simply be assigned to someone, use the *Content Management Tool* (chapter 9). Use the output from this meeting (*what*) as input for a future meeting when the time, place, and people are available to conduct further analysis and make appropriate decisions or assignments. In that next meeting, begin with this open issue as input by asking "So what?" or "Why do we care?

CLOSED ITEMS

Separately capture "acorns" or other nuggets of value such as decision points and resolutions or assigned actions that are agreed upon. Acorns represent ideas that need to be nourished after the meeting before they grow into something substantial and sturdy, like an oak tree.

Review and Wrap Activity 3: Create a Communications Plan

Because it is a clever idea (in other words, *important*) to sound like we were all in the same meeting together, build a communications plan for the meeting results. The purpose is to get your participants to agree on what they will tell other stakeholders was accomplished during the meeting so that participants sound like they all attended the same meeting.

Minimally consider two audiences, such as superiors and other stakeholders, and record the bullets or sound bites for each. I normally use a simple T-Chart with two columns, for example for Superior and Stakeholders. Next, ask for participants' "elevator speech," "coffeepot" description, or "water cooler" summary.

For more complex riffs and variations, see the *Communications Plan* (chapter 6). You may be shocked how often participants argue about using specific words such as "complete" versus "progress." The more times you conduct a *Communications Plan*, the more you will come to realize what a powerful quality control activity it provides by ensuring that everyone agrees on the same messaging.

A communications plan for meeting results offers exceptional value when there are translation or transliteration issues because it helps everyone homogenize the rhetoric and specific terms that should or should not be used to describe meeting results.

Review and Wrap Activity 4: Assessment Tool, with Four Options

Evaluation at the conclusion of meetings provides insight about how well you performed and what you can do to be better. General areas to seek feedback about include these:

- Facilitator effectiveness (or not)

- Session success (or not)

- What else might you have changed for the better?

The following are four assessment procedures, ranging from simple through complex. Adapt one to your situation.

OPTION 1: PLUS-DELTA PROCEDURE

Gather participants' comments at the end of your meetings by building a T-Chart called *Plus-Delta*. On one side list what went well, a *Plus*. On the other side, list what could be improved, a *Delta* (the Greek letter Δ, which stands for "change").[5] When conducted openly, however, participants mostly mention "creature comfort" concerns and do not provide the substantive critique you need to improve your facilitation.

Therefore, Better Yet

Get feedback on the session context, including how well (or not) you did. Set up an easel or a whiteboard by the exit door, or provide a screen link that can be annotated. Have each participant contribute at least one thing he or she liked about the meeting (+) and one thing he or she would change (Δ). Ask participants to mount each note in its respective column before they depart.

Workshops

Use *Plus-Delta* at the end of each day of a multiple-day session to correct problems before the next day. Comments made during your meetings enable you to monitor context so that you can make quick fixes such as issues with picture quality, lighting, sound, and so on.

OPTION 2: SCALE IT

Scale It provides numerical feedback on a few questions along with some limited, anecdotal comments. Modify the questions shown in figure 5.3 for the specific feedback that you seek, using a scalable technique. With *Scale It*, print three or four per page, reducing the "visual burden" on your participants as you hand them a small slip of paper rather than a full-size sheet.

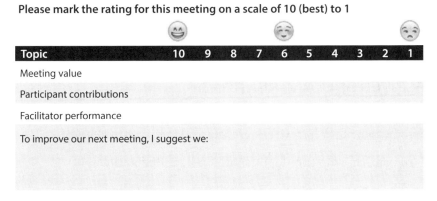

Figure 5.3. Scaled Assessment

---

[5] This method is also called "Benefits and Concerns (Bs and Cs)," "Star-Delta," and other names.

OPTION 3: WHERE ARE YOU NOW?

Have each participant offer one, two, or three words to describe "How do you feel right now?" or "Where are you at?" You might contrast the participant's response with the one provided in the *Launch* during the *Icebreaker*. Participants' responses provide leading indication about the level of ownership and follow-through the team might expect.

OPTION 4: DETAILED EVALUATION FORM

At the conclusion of noteworthy events and multiple-day workshops, obtain extensive feedback. Modify the eleven questions in figure 5.4. Note the importance and value of question 10, about improving your own performance.

Structuring with Mindful Conversations

Preparing the *Agenda Steps* between *Launch* and *Wrap* takes longer than the meeting itself. Plan on a ratio of preparation time to meeting time of 2:1 or 3:1 (or more) to thoroughly prepare yourself and others. For online meetings, experts are telling people to double that amount of time, because the planning must be detailed and explicit, sometimes down to the level of specific keystrokes. For standard 50-minute meetings, you would be wise to allow at least another 50 minutes to organize, invite, and prepare—although a few hours may be more prudent if you are seeking exceptional results.

CONVERSATIONS WITH PARTICIPANTS

Speak with participants in advance to learn about them, the people they work with, and their pain points. For workshops, allow 15 to 30 minutes for one-on-ones. Meet face-to-face when permitted, or at least by videoconference, so that you establish eye contact before facilitating the meeting.

SEQUENCE OF CONVERSATIONS

Optimally, meet the executive sponsor, business partners, project team, stakeholders, and meeting participants. Conduct conversations privately and assure participants that their responses will be kept *confidential.*

OBJECTIVES OF CONVERSATIONS

These conversations have the following aims:

- To become familiar with their role and their competencies

- To confirm who should, or should not, attend and why

- To help participants show up better prepared to contribute

- To identify potential issues, hidden agendas, and other obstacles

- To transfer ownership of the purpose, scope, and deliverables

MG Rush Facilitation
Training & Coaching
Richmond IN 47375-0054
+01.630.954.5880 tel
http://www.mgrush.com/

WORKSHOP EVALUATION

Instructions: You have just completed an *MG Rush* workshop. In order for us to continue improving, please take two minutes to answer seven questions fully and honestly.

1. To what extent did the workshop meet your expectations?

    _____ Not at all   _____ A little   _____ Mostly

    If not "mostly", why not? _____

    _____

    _____

2. How would you rate your overall experience?

    _____ Poor   _____ Fair   _____ Good   _____ Very Good   _____ Excellent

3. How effectively did the session leader explain the method?

    _____ Poor   _____ Fair   _____ Good   _____ Very Good   _____ Excellent

4. How effectively did the session leader control the group and keep you on track?

    _____ Poor   _____ Fair   _____ Good   _____ Very Good   _____ Excellent

5. How would you rate the overall performance of the session leader?

    _____ Poor   _____ Fair   _____ Good   _____ Very Good   _____ Excellent

6. What suggestions do you have for improving the performance of the session leader?

    _____

    _____

7. Other comments or suggestions? (also use reverse side): _____

    _____

    _____

Figure 5.4. Detailed Evaluation Form

MINDFUL QUESTIONS TO ASK

The questions below are structured, stress-tested, and well-sequenced. Begin by explaining your role and ask for permission to take notes.[6] Use the following open-ended questions, sit back, and listen—discover the participant's value and the value added by the participant to the initiative you are supporting.

Get to know participants' subject matter expertise and attitude toward workshops with openers like "Tell me, what do you do?" and "What has worked for you in the past?" Then continue with questions like these:

- What do you expect from the session?

- What will make the meeting a complete failure?

- What should the output look like?

- What problems do you foresee?

- Who should attend the meeting? Who should not? Why?

- What is going to be my biggest obstacle?

- Does the deliverable and agenda make sense to you?

- Is the "electronic leashes" ground rule acceptable?

- What questions do you think we should answer?

- What should I have asked that I didn't ask?

PARTICIPANTS' PACKAGE

After structured conversations, send participants a pre-read package, especially at the kickoff of major events. If you happen to provide printed packages, place the spiral edging across the top to make the package both unique and easier for left-handed notetakers. Try to include the first five items listed here in every package. The other suggestions are supplemental:

- An articulate workshop purpose, scope, and deliverables along with the *Basic Agenda Steps*

- Glossary for terms used in the workshop purpose, scope, deliverables, and *Basic Agenda Steps*

- Organizational and business unit strategic planning support— especially *Mission, Values, Vision*, and performance *Measures*

---

[6] Please do not tell someone that your conversation is confidential and then take copious notes without asking. I have only had two people say no, they would rather I not take any notes. I've had dozens compliment me on the question itself because rarely have others extended the courtesy to ask for permission to take notes.

- Product, project, or team charter and detail about the value supported by the session

- List of questions to be asked during the session

- Relevant reading materials gathered during conversations[7]

- Responsibilities of the participants, including any overnight assignments, reading, or exercises that may be included in a multiple-day workshop

- Sponsor's letter of invitation—organizational strategic plan

- Team members' contact information

COMPLETION

If you can answer yes to the following questions, you are ready to proceed:

- Can the participants answer the questions for each *Agenda Step*?

- Can you describe a potential deliverable from each *Agenda Step*?

- Does a walk-through of your *Annotated Agenda* provide the right deliverable?

- Have you had conversations with stakeholders?

- Is your *Annotated Agenda* comprehensive and printed?

Annotated Agenda Development

Methods such as strategic planning, decision-making, and problem solving determine the *Meeting Approach*. Each *Meeting Approach* requires clear and detailed *Agenda Steps*.

METHOD DICTATES *MEETING APPROACH* DICTATES *AGENDA STEPS* DICTATES *TOOLS* REQUIRED

For example, *Launch (Introduction)* represents one clear *Agenda Step*. Each *Agenda Step* requires a procedure that relies on answering questions and conducting activities that are supported through a variety of *Tools*. During the *Launch*, for example, we might use *Icebreakers*. Or, during a *Prioritization Agenda Step*, we might use *PowerBalls* (chapter 7). For most *Agenda Steps*, there is more than one *Tool* that might be used.

TOOLING FOR EACH *AGENDA STEP* REQUIRES SCRIPTING

Scripting furnishes an anchor during workshops by telling you precisely what to say to be clear, helping you when you forget where you are going, and providing

---

[7] The less important terms are "grayed out" because they signify or trigger meaning about the more important questions in black that should be the focus of the *Agenda Step*. This convention is also used elsewhere in this book.

additional support when you have trouble getting there. We all need help at one time or another. Therefore, for every *Agenda Step*, in every agenda, a well-scripted *Annotated Agenda* compels you to anticipate and visualize the tools, activities, and procedures you need.

An *Annotated Agenda* provides tremendous predictive power. From reviewing the rigor and thoroughness of an *Annotated Agenda*, I can easily predict how well your session will move forward, regardless of your talents and skills (or lack thereof, because someone not highly skilled but thoroughly scripted will *outperform* anyone not well-scripted but relying on their "natural" talent).

Annotated Agendas begin each *Agenda Step* on a new page. Printed versions are preferred, even for online meetings, because they are faster and more reliable. For each *Agenda Step* write down the following:

- Agenda Step *name:* Write down the name of each *Agenda Step* as shown exactly on the *Basic Agenda* that you distribute and post.

- *Estimated time:* Estimate a range for how much time this *Agenda Step* requires—consider best and worst case scenarios for your low and high estimates.

- *Purpose and closure:* Write down a one- or two-line description (to launch and wrap up each *Agenda Step*) describing the reason for the *Agenda Step* and how it contributes toward completing the deliverable. Never be afraid to read from your printed *Annotated Agenda*. Chances are, if you go rogue (extemporaneous), you will use more words and leave people a bit confused.

- *Procedure:* Stipulate precisely what activities, tools, and tasks will complete this *Agenda Step*. Include specific questions, examples, desired output format, and other notes. Detailing your procedure for each *Agenda Step* takes anywhere from one-half page to three pages or more of notes. An *Agenda Step* will frequently require more than one *Tool* at once, or in sequence. Script *how* you are going to facilitate each *Agenda Step*, what you are going to ask, and the precise words you will or will not use.

- *Document output:* Write down instructions to yourself about what to document (for example, list, paragraph, matrix) and perhaps where to post in the room or how to post online, including output title.

- *Media support:* Identify slides or posters for definitions, legends, tables, and other technological support for online meetings that you will need to complete the procedure for each *Agenda Step*.

Do not rush your effort. Skimping on the *Annotated Agenda* ensures suboptimal performance. Next—please use it. Do *not* build it, set it down, and forget about it. We prefer a leader who is holding a piece of paper, reading to us, and being clear over one who speaks extemporaneously and leaves us a bit confused.

NOTE—Some facilitators add information about real estate management (where they are mounting their large-format paper, legends, ground rules, and so on) and online technology instructions such as which type of screen share to use. The sequence of the items in the *Annotated Agenda* is arbitrary, so create a template that works for you.

Three phases convert your *Basic Agenda* into a fully *Annotated Agenda*.

PHASE 1: DEVELOP THE BASIS

NOTE: While reviewing details for each phase in this section, remember that you are also responsible for managing group dysfunction or problems. As you identify and modify *Agenda Steps*, think about what may need to be done to correct potential problems with people. Interventions (such as team-building activities and trust generators) may be needed during other activities or as *Agenda Steps* by themselves. Some activities are planned but not used. Always keep them in your "hip pocket," ready to use if required.

Procedure

1. Write down your deliverable and get examples! Deliverables illustrate the required documentation and needed information. What outputs are we producing? What do they look like in printed form?

2. Quantify the impact from the meeting, measured in local currency and FTP, and articulate the project or product scope for your meeting. Understand what might be excluded (because of scope), or what the purpose and scope of the session are *not*.

3. Identify the *Basic Agenda Steps* that enable the team to produce the deliverable. Apply your organization's glossary, life cycle, and methodology (if available). The best sources for identifying draft *Agenda Steps* are these (in order of preference):

   a. Your organization's own methodology or in-house meeting design, which may include cultural expectations, examples, and templates

   b. The three upcoming *Meeting Approaches* and numerous *Tools* in the next three chapters, adapted and modified for your purposes

   c. Experience—look at past meetings and note what specific questions need to be answered to deliver the meeting objectives

   d. The stakeholders—speak with the executive sponsor, product owner, program manager, project manager, and subject matter experts

   e. The team or product charter—look at them to identify gaps the meeting output needs to fill, and supplement with secondary research, but do *not* rely solely on Google or Wikipedia, because some of the best methods remain protected by intellectual property rights

4. Identify the subject matter experts. Understand what knowledge or expertise each needs to bring to the session. Understand the political atmosphere—do the experts need trust building? Ask them for questions that they would like to see answered during the session. Their questions will either fortify your *Meeting Approach* or help you manage expectations by letting the subject matter experts know that we will not have time to address some of the questions they want answered.

Walk through the *Basic Agenda Steps* to ensure you can produce the deliverable. Do the *Agenda Steps* allow the group to advance without jumping around? Are the *Agenda Steps* sequenced properly? Will the deliverable provide the necessary detail required?[8]

PHASE 2: DRAFT YOUR TOOLS AND PROCEDURES

Now convert the *Basic Agenda Steps* into scripted activities while socializing (that is, sharing) the meeting purpose, scope, and deliverable with your participants. Output from this phase should include a consensually agreed-on purpose, scope, and deliverables, and your draft *Annotated Agenda*, replete with scripted activities and transitions for the meeting.

5. With each *Basic Agenda Step* determine your primary and backup activities, tools, and procedures that will create the required information. Review each activity considering the capacity of your participants and the limitations of your online technology or time. Begin to script your *Annotated Agenda* around the following components:

   – Define terms used in the purpose, scope, deliverables, and *Basic Agenda*. Update your glossary that should be shared with others.

   – Identify the activities (think *Tools*) you deem appropriate for each *Agenda Step*. Time permitting, write down backup options as well.

   – Determine if you need to add team-building, creativity, or other "groupthink prevention" exercises. Insert as appropriate—each just in time (just before the effect is required).

   – Design *Breakout Team* (chapter 6) activities and the precise questions you will assign the teams. Create team names and appoint CEOs (chief easel officers) and team members for each. Rotate CEOs and members across the entire session.

---

[8] For a downloadable infographic, see https://mgrush.com/wp-content/uploads/2019/07/Meeting-Pathway_MGRush-Facilitation_Poster-11x17.pdf.

NOTE: The *Annotated Agenda* provides a script for you to hold and use. It details every activity and assignment. It provides contextual understanding of the entire session—where you are, what you are asking, and what you need to support your explanations (such as a legend).

Build a rigorous annotated agenda, and use it.

PHASE 3: PREPARE TO FACILITATE

Refine and "beautify" your handouts, legends, slides, posters, screens, and other visual or video support so that you are fully prepared. This output represents your final and fully scripted *Annotated Agenda* with all the print and screen support you need to lead your session.

6. Complete preparation, rehearsal, coordination, and any final conversations with stakeholders, especially participants. Create and distribute in advance (as appropriate) support materials such as the following:

   – Glossary

   – Organizational *Mission*, *Values*, and *Vision*

   – Participant pre-read package

   – Presentation slides and handouts

   – Video supplements and graphic support and legends

   NOTE: With these three phases complete, you are not guaranteed that your *Meeting Approach* will work. However, *Annotated Agendas* dramatically improve confidence, which influences competence.

Meeting or Workshop?

Sessions include meetings and workshops. The meaning behind the term "workshop" is similar to the meaning of the term "meeting." However, a few differences include the following:

- *Agenda Steps* in meetings are frequently boxed in time. Workshop procedures are not boxed in time, but front-end loading (getting more done sooner) makes it easier to complete the back-end activities and tasks.

- Leaders in meetings may not be expected to be entirely neutral. Some leaders learn to embrace the importance of meeting neutrality and active listening, but when required they must render an opinion or a decision. On the other hand, workshop facilitators risk total failure if they violate neutrality by offering up or evaluating content.

- Regularly held meetings (staff meetings or board meetings) conclude when time runs out, usually with an understanding that unfinished items will be picked up in the next meeting. When groups build toward a workshop deliverable, the sequence of the *Agenda Steps* is critical, and participants cannot leap ahead or advance until foundation work is completed.

- Roughly speaking, meetings deliver up outcomes or conditions, such as "increased awareness," while workshops document outputs such as strategic plans, decisions, and detailed solutions.

MEETINGS: WHERE MINUTES ARE KEPT, AND HOURS ARE LOST

As a result of timing, participant availability, and physical space constraints, many workshops may be spread across multiple weeks, turning full-day or multiple-day workshops into weekly "meetings." The main structural difference between contiguous-day and multiple-week workshops is that break periods between sessions are longer in duration.

Commonly, given the way the two terms "meeting" and "workshop" are used, the primary difference is duration. Sessions that last an hour or two are commonly called meetings, while sessions that run three hours through three days or more are commonly called workshops.

AGENDA STEP OPTIONS

For either, with each *Agenda Step*, you will be facing one of three conditions:

1. DONE—Content was developed before the session at a different time. Most of the group has previously indicated that the existing version of something appears acceptable. You need to review and confirm for consensual support. Carefully document any minor edits or word changes.

2. WIP (Work in progress)—A draft has been sketched or begun and needs to be completed. If you already started the effort and have built an initial framework, you should be able to complete your effort and surround the framework with supporting details.

3. BLANK—The procedures and activities I provide in upcoming chapters always assume that you are starting with a blank sheet of paper, and thus I explain procedures from start to finish.

Three Meeting Approaches

Some mindsets other than servant leadership do not need structure. For example, an autocrat may simply shout "do this" or "do that," and employees carry out that person's wishes.

BIAS TOWARD STRUCTURE

Today, however, especially since no one is as smart as everyone, we rely on groups for higher-quality, innovative solutions. Therefore, we should walk the talk and galvanize consensus by using structure to get DONE quicker.

My servant leadership mindset remains "technique agnostic." Servant leadership fully integrates across any consensus-based mindset such as board meetings and staff meetings, as well as more structured disciplines such as Agile and Waterfall, along with associated frameworks like Design Sprints, Failure Mode Effect Analysis, Lean Sigma, Organizational Design, Peer Review, Scrum, Strategic Planning, and so on.[9] But one thing is certain: you better have a *Meeting Approach* before your meeting starts.

WHAT IS A MEETING APPROACH?

My *Meeting Approaches* have integrated the *Agenda Steps*, *Tools*, and scripting for immediate use with your most significant or frequent meeting challenges. I have built, used, and refined more than 30 significant *Meeting Approaches* ranging from simple decision-making through complex organizational design. My annotated agendas on average run around 20 pages per *Meeting Approach*. I don't have time or space to explore them all, so I have selected the most frequent situations—those causing the most pain, yielding the most gain, and used most frequently. Specifically, chapters 6, 7, and 8 guide you through experiences about the following:

- Chapter 6—*planning* for any group

- Chapter 7—*deciding* on anything

- Chapter 8—creative *problem solving*

TOOL SELECTION

The *Meeting Approaches* provide you with *Tool* options. Select optimal *Tools* by understanding your desired output. Avoid becoming so comfortable with one or two *Tools* that they become the only *Tools* you use. To help decide on your *Meeting Approach*, *Agenda Steps*, and *Tools*:

- First define your desired output (or outcome).

- Engage in conversations with stakeholders to secure their input and begin to transfer ownership.

- Always apply the seven-activity *Launch* and four-activity *Review and Wrap* to *every* session, from 50-minute meetings through five-day workshops.

---

[9] Further details on other meeting types such as Organizational Design, FMEA (Failure Mode Effect Analysis), Peer Review, Risk Analysis, and so on may be found on my website: https://mgrush.com/.

- Review the forthcoming *planning, deciding,* and *problem solving* sections to determine which *Meeting Approach* best coordinates with your session's deliverable.

NOTE: The best way to learn my *Tools* is to use them. For a solution where everyone benefits, promote yourself among not-for-profit groups who desperately need facilitation help and better meeting design. They won't care in the least if you are using a *Tool* for the first time.

TOOL GUIDELINES

Detailed procedures for dozens of *Tools* are provided in the rest of this book. You will find *Tools* you knew about (such as *Brainstorming,* chapter 6) and *Tools* you never heard about before (for example, *Bookend Rhetoric,* chapter 7). When planning which *Tools* to use, consider the following:

- Build contingencies—plan to use a specific *Tool* but if something unexpected arises, do not be afraid to substitute something more appropriate.

- Do not ask your group for permission to use a *Tool.* You do not need participants' permission—so do it.

- Do not be afraid to use a new *Tool*—mine have all been field-tested, numerous times, and work well when used appropriately.

- Do not be inflexible like some gurus—there is more than one right answer.

- Explain the deliverable from each *Tool* and how using it supports getting DONE.

- For *Tools* designed to correct team dysfunction, remember that most groups did not become dysfunctional in 10 minutes, and their situation will not be corrected with a 10-minute exercise.

- *Never* present your *Tool* as a game or a gimmick.

- Scripting rigorous *Annotated Agendas* help you rehearse the *Tool* in your mind.

ADDITIONAL TOOLS

There are hundreds of team-building and trust-enhancing *Tools* not included in this book. Many are available from the Best Practices material available through my website at mgrush.com/blog. Continue to add to your arsenal. Build a Community of Practice (CoP) that archives activities, procedures, and graphical support so that you can make a quick decision about which *Tool* to use and rely on material that others have built.

I've taken a "just in time" approach to introduce *Tools* within agendas where you will need them. What if you're not deciding, planning, or solving and building something else? Figure 5.5 illustrates when and where the *Tools*

TOOL SELECTION GUIDE

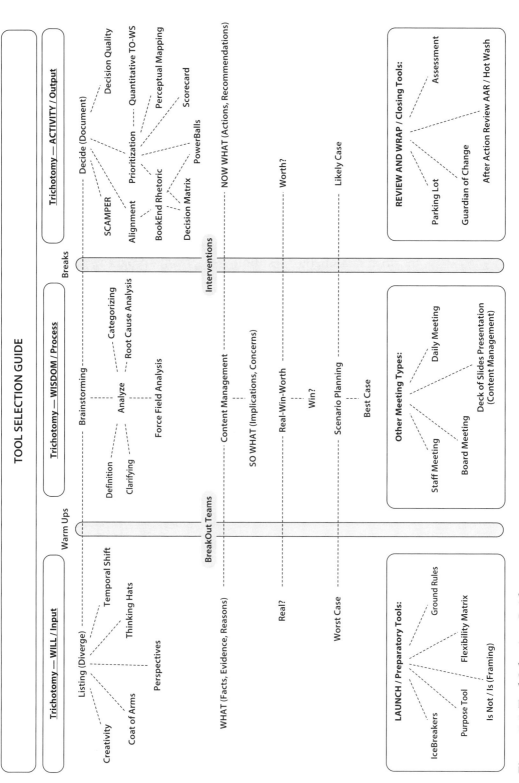

Figure 5.5. Tool Selection Guide

fit most frequently. Since "one size does fit all," please call or write about your situation and we can discuss your options.

Quick Summary on Structuring

Use the following guidelines for every significant meeting you lead.

1. **Codify the purpose and scope** of the meeting: What project or product are you supporting? Stipulate what it is worth in currency and FTP (*Why* is it important? How much is at risk if we fail?).

2. **Articulate the deliverables**: What specific content represents the output of the meeting and satisfies what DONE looks like. What is my analogy for explaining it? Who will use it after the meeting?

3. **Identify known and unknown information**: What is already known about the organization, business unit, department, program, product, or project? What information is needed to fill the gaps?

4. **Draft *Basic Agenda Steps***: Compose a series of steps from experience or other proven approaches that would be used by experts to build the plan, make the decision, solve the problem, or develop the information and consensus necessary to complete the deliverable and get DONE.

5. **Review *Basic Agenda*** for logical flow: Walk through the *Agenda Steps* with others to confirm that they will produce the desired results. Link your analogy to each of the *Agenda Steps*. Rehearse your explanation of the white space.

6. **Identify meeting participants**: Determine the optimal subject matter expertise you require or the meeting participants who can provide the information required.

7. **Detail the procedures** to capture information required: Gather and assemble specific questions that need to be addressed, even questions for which subject matter experts are seeking answers. Sequence the questions optimally. Build your *Annotated Agenda* including the appropriate *Tools* and activities to produce the information.

8. **Perform a walk-through** with business experts, the executive sponsor, project team members, and anyone else who will listen to you (grandmothers are good for this, and you might get a delicious, home-cooked meal in the bargain).

9. **Refine**: Make changes identified in the walk-through, edit your final *Annotated Agenda*, firm up your artifacts, fill out your glossary, complete your slides, distribute your handouts, and rehearse.

6

Planning Approach for Any Group

WHO DOES WHAT, BY WHEN?

Plan your work and work your plan. Let's begin your journey with planning (novel idea?).

For Strategies, Initiatives, Projects, Products, and Teams

What is the difference between a strategic plan, a department plan, a product plan, a project plan, a team plan, and so on? Primarily, scope. The word "plan" can be defined with three words (preferably five), namely "who does what" (by when)—that's a plan. The same logic extends throughout an organization. Every business group needs answers to the nine questions listed in the "Basic Planning Agenda" section that follows. This chapter shows you how to facilitate consensual agreement around those answers for any group.

> **—General Dwight D. Eisenhower**
> *In preparing for battle I have always found that plans are useless, but planning is indispensable.*

Modify the following *Planning Approach* to define organizational direction when your group needs to build consensus around its priorities and initiatives. A robust *Planning Approach* defines vision factors, success measures, actions, and responsibilities. Further, the *Planning Approach* also does the following:

- It becomes a compelling road map for future decision-making. The *Mission* anchors decisions, the *Vision* inspires decisions, the *Values* discipline decisions, and the strategic plan articulates decisions, highlighting *Actions* that need to be promoted.

- The *Planning Approach* describes a group's intent: *who* it is, *where* it is going, *what* to do to get there, and *when* the *Actions* will be accomplished.

- The *Planning Approach* may describe a situation, including problems or opportunities, *what* to do about them, and consideration about associated assumptions and constraints.

- The *Planning Approach* may describe the strategy, tactics, or activities along with roles and responsibilities for fulfilling products, projects, and other initiatives.

- The *Planning Approach* requires you to modify and reinforce your session with team-building exercises, creativity exercises, or both, as necessary.

- The *Planning Approach* suggests that preparatory conversations should focus on the people, personalities, and conflict issues, more than focusing on products, process, or technology content.

PLANNING DELIVERABLE

While a planning session's input begins with *why* a group exists, the output documents *what* team members agree to do. A primarily narrative document, plans may be augmented with . . .

- Supporting graphics or illustrations that represent the *Mission* and *Vision* (chapter 6),

- A numerical matrix for *Quantitative TO-WS Analysis* (chapter 6),

- An iconic or numeric *Alignment* matrix (chapter 6), and

- An *Assignment* matrix (chapter 6).

BASIC PLANNING AGENDA

1. Launch (chapter 5)

2. Mission (**why are we here?**)

3. Values (**who are we?**)

4. Vision (**where are we going? How do we know if we got there or not?**)

5. Success Measures (**what are our measurements of progress?**)

6. Current Situation (**where are we now?**)

7. Actions (**what should we do?—from strategy through tasks**)

8. Alignment (**is this the right stuff to do?**)

9. Roles and Responsibilities (*who* **does** *what,* **by** *when?*)

10. Communications Plan (*what* **should we tell our stakeholders?**)

11. Review and Wrap (chapter 5)

VISUAL AIDS TO ANTICIPATE

- Meeting purpose, scope, and deliverable in writing—handouts or large-format paper for in-person meetings and handwritten or handheld artifacts for online meetings

- *Basic Agenda*, easily accessible and preferably included in the pre-read, as well as additional handheld artifacts for online meetings, such as definitions or legends

- Definitions for each of the key terms, especially *Mission, Values, Vision,* and *Key Measures*—perfect for a slide or screen share because slides are good for transitory material that comes and goes, as with definitions or legends

- *Quantitative TO-WS Analysis* spreadsheet (Excel) (chapter 6)

- *PowerBalls* (chapter 7) and *Prioritization* (chapter 7) legends, posters, or handheld artifacts for online meetings[1]

- *Ground Rules* (chapter 4), readily available as posters or handheld artifacts

- Blank Refrigerator (*Parking Lot*) and *Plus-Delta* (chapter 5)

COMMENTS

Planning workshops require more facilitation skills because of personality challenges and other biases. Carefully control your operational definitions for critical terms (*Mission* versus *Vision,* goals versus objectives, and so on) and how they fit together to form a strategic or other type of plan *before* launching your planning session.

Observe that in the *Basic Agenda* I have used a lighter gray type for traditional terms like *Mission* and used black type to emphasize the critical words (**why do we show up?**)—the primary questions being answered during each *Agenda Step.*

NOTE: **Much confusion exists about the difference between *Mission* and *Vision*. Here's why.** Academic textbooks typically follow the sequence

---

[1] Artifacts describe a collection of handheld notices that may be used with online meetings by simply pushing them in from the camera. Rather than turning to another slide or screen, artifacts add texture to online meetings and are more fully explained in chapter 9.

I use, including defining the terms by the questions being answered. The military-industrial complex also sequences the questions in the same order I use but defines the associated terms differently.

For example, the US Armed Forces define *Vision* as the answer to the question, "Why do we show up?," and they define *Mission* as the answer to the question, "Where are we going?" Professional meeting designers remain agnostic and may use either sequence based on what is normally used by the culture being served. Keep in mind that the sequence of the questions *does not change* for either group. Both cultures need to know *why* they show up before they talk about *where* they are going.

For purposes of this book, **Mission will be defined as "why we are here,"** and **Vision will be defined as "where we are going."** I leave it up to you to make the necessary adjustments based on the culture of the organization for which you are facilitating.

This *Basic Planning Agenda* can be used at any level in the holarchy—anytime a group of people needs to define *who* does *what*. If you are facilitating strategic plans for organizations, business units, and significant departments, proceed with the agenda as shown, including *Mission*, *Values*, and *Vision*.

For other types of teams, including team charters for products and projects, substitute the *Purpose Tool* (chapter 7) instead of using *Mission*, *Values*, and *Vision*. Either tactic creates a sense of direction upon which you build the *Key Measures* such as objectives and goals. After completing either the *Mission*, *Values*, and *Vision* or the *Purpose Tool*, every team needs answers to questions from the other *Agenda Steps*, namely:

- *What* are our measurements of progress to know we are reaching our vision?

- *Where* are we now?

- *What* actions should we promote to ensure reaching our goals and objectives?

- Is that the right stuff to do?

- *Who* does *what*, by *when*?

- *What* should we tell our stakeholders?

RIFFS AND VARIATIONS

The detailed instructions and procedures that follow may be easily modified to accommodate your culture and preferences. There is more than one right way to facilitate any *Planning Approach*. More important, however, there is a wrong way. The wrong way surfaces when you don't know how to use or have not fully prepared a procedure.

NOTE: I will illustrate the *Planning Approach Agenda Steps* using a fictitious greenfield company called THRIVE LLC. THRIVE provides for-profit products and services to residential households, intending to make household and family activities and resources easier to manage. Occasionally, I will also reference the sport of mountaineering. Either may be used as an analogy to illustrate deliverables from the *Agenda Steps* covered over the next few dozen pages.

Explanation by Analogy

When explaining the agenda during the meeting *Launch*, provide a parallel path of change via analogy. Analogies help protect your neutrality while bringing to life the sequence and connections of *Agenda Steps*.

The *Mission Agenda Step* contains a unique challenge because *Mission* addresses *why* we show up. We could show up for any reason we want. The reason for showing up establishes the foundation for your analogy, helping you link each *Agenda Step* back to the meeting deliverable. I encourage you to work with an analogy around which you have a personal passion.

For example, if you love baking, the analogy could be a designer cake. If you love scrapbooking, the analogy could be an award-winning scrapbook. Or, in the analogy chosen for table 6.1, we love mountaineering, and therefore reaching the summit.

Refer to your analogy to help explain the purpose of each *Agenda Step*. The analogy guides smoother transitions as to why the *Agenda Steps* are listed in the sequence shown. Although I picked a sport (some people are turned off by sports), I selected a gender-neutral, generic sport with a clear deliverable, reaching the summit.

Please accept my apologies in advance for the upcoming "mixed metaphor" because I will also use THRIVE LLC for examples, to provide analogous explanations with "business-like" conditions.

Pre-session Survey or Online Poll—for Strategic Planning Only

For strategic planning especially, assess a composite view of answers to the following six questions (see table 6.2). Gauge your group in advance so that you can better estimate how much you might get done, how quickly (or not), and how much resistance you will encounter.

Liberally modify the questions yourself and add others that establish a feeling for the culture. I strongly encourage you to keep participant contributions anonymous. Aggregate results and display them in a chart when sharing your findings.

1. Launch (Introduction) Agenda Step

Use the seven-activity sequence for *Launch* (chapter 5). Remember that the *Launch* is the "preachy" part for a meeting facilitator. My own *Annotated*

Table 6.1. Mountaineering Analogy

Agenda Step	Corresponding Analogy
Mission *Why* do we show up?	We choose to show up because we love mountaineering.
Values *Who* are we, and how do we treat one another?	We could be young and vibrant with no cash, or more mature and experienced with lots of money. What do we carry with us? Young people have ropes and value rappelling. More mature people have Sherpas who carry ladders, among other stuff.
Vision *Where* are we going?	Which peak are we going to ascend? Young people may choose the south peak because they don't have much time. Mature people may choose the north side with switchbacks that enable them to use their ladders and stop for comfortable breaks.
Key Measures *What* are our measures or indicators of progress in reaching the *Vision*?	There are three types of criteria: *SMART*—Be at 5,000 meters suspended in our sleeping bags before the storm blows in at 3 p.m. (objective). *Fuzzy*—Get some nice photographs when we reach the summit (subjective or aspirational such as a goal). *Binary*—Did we reach the summit or not (critical consideration)?
Current Situation *What* is our current situation of things we control and do not control?	TO-WS analysis (showing the youthful mountaineers): EXTERNALLY CONTROLLED External *Threat*—avalanche External *Opportunity*—a "break" in the weather INTERNALLY CONTROLLED Internal *Weakness*—few supplies Internal *Strength*—stamina and flexibility
Actions—*What* to Do Given our *Current Situation, what* do we agree to do to reach our *Key Measures* placed as milestones to ensure we reach our *Vision*?	Young people—They are going to rappel up the south side of the face of the mountain to quickly reach the summit so that they can return to base camp before they run out of supplies.
Alignment Are those the right *Actions* and enough *Actions* to ensure we reach or exceed our *Key Measures*?	Do they have enough rope? If the young people are rappelling 100 meters but only have 50 meters of rope, let's find out before they take off so we can adjust either the path or the amount of rope.

Table 6.1. continued

Agenda Step	Corresponding Analogy
Assignments *Who* is doing *What*?	Who is carrying the rope?
Communications Plan *What* do we tell the world about what we completed here?	Phone home before they make their ascent in the morning when the weather is predicted to be calm.

Table 6.2. Pre-session Survey for Strategic Planning

Among employees, what is the balance between anxiety and hope?

Mostly   •   •   •   •   •   •   •   Mostly
anxiety   hope

How does senior management's point of view about the future compare to that of competitors and other industry experts?

Conventional •   •   •   •   •   •   •   Distinctive
and reactive   and far-sighted

To what extent are we engineering the present or designing the future?

Mostly an   •   •   •   •   •   •   •   Mostly an
engineer   architect or a designer

What amount of our efforts focus on catching up versus setting up our own future vision?

Mostly a   •   •   •   •   •   •   •   Mostly a
rule-taker   rule-maker

What amount of our efforts focus on catching up with competitors versus building new industry advantages?

Mostly   •   •   •   •   •   •   •   Mostly
catch-up   new stuff

Which issues absorb senior management's attention?

Re-engineering   •   •   •   •   •   Regenerating
core processes   core strategies

Note: If your marks lean to the left or in the middle, your organization may be spending too much time preserving the past and not enough time and energy strategizing a new future.

Agenda for a *Launch* is always around three pages. If you want to rehearse anything, try explaining the white space behind your *Agenda Steps*—why are they there? Contextual control provides a terrific opportunity to develop confidence among your participants.

NOTE: For multiple-day workshops, cover the same items at the start of the subsequent day. Additionally, review content that was built the preceding day or days and reinforce how that relates to the progress being made completing the deliverable.

Before you begin your meeting *Launch*, have your physical or virtual room set up to provide a visual display of the meeting purpose, scope, and deliverable. Let me repeat that if you do not know what the deliverable looks like, then you do not know what success looks like.

INTRODUCTION PROCEDURE

Follow these activities in this sequence for a robust start:

- Introduce yourself and stress the importance of meeting roles. Stipulate how much money or time is at risk if the session fails.

- Unveil your meeting purpose, scope, and deliverable. Seek audible assent from all. Ensure that all the participants can support them.

- Cover "administrivia" to clear participants' heads from thinking about themselves, especially their creature comforts. Explain where to locate lavatories, fire extinguishers, emergency exits, and other stuff they may be thinking about. Provide a check-in activity or *Icebreaker*, especially for online meetings and workshops.

- Carefully explain the logic behind the sequence of your *Agenda Steps*. Explain how *Agenda Steps* relate to one another. Link *Agenda Steps* back to the deliverable so that participants see how completing each *Agenda Step* provides content that helps complete the deliverable.

- Share *Ground Rules* (chapter 4). Supplement your narrative posting of *Ground Rules* with audiovisual support, including humorous clips, but keep them brief.

- For a kickoff, have your executive sponsor explain the importance of participants' contributions and what management intends to accomplish. Do not allow the executive sponsor to take more than five minutes.

2. Mission or Charter (Why Are We Here?)

Mission defines the *why* of any business area or organizational scope. For me, the definition is brief, like a slogan, so that it is never forgotten, *Mission* represents an action-oriented expression of an organization's reason for existence. When explaining, link back to your analogy.

> *Mission* expresses *why* the participants, or group, or organization show up—the purpose and reason for their existence.

The *Mission* expression provides the foundation upon which other *Planning Approach Agenda Steps* are built. Each subsequent *Agenda Step* refers to the *Mission* expression (as purpose), ensuring harmony with the *Mission* of the group and organization. *Mission* documents *why* an organization exists, vitally linking it to subsequent *Agenda Steps*.

HINT: *Mission* expresses *why*. *Why* are we here? *Why* are we doing this? I recommend a concise expression that could fit on a bumper sticker or T-shirt. Servant leaders strive to ensure that *Mission* balances both the head (will), the heart (wisdom), and the hands (activity).

WHAT DOES A *MISSION* EXPRESSION LOOK LIKE?
YOU DECIDE

You need to carefully determine what does your deliverable look like when you are DONE. Will it be a sentence, a paragraph, or a bumper sticker? Will it be brief and snappy like an axiom, or fully described? There is no single right answer; the wrong answer is not to know.

The following lists aggregate comments made by dozens of "experts" on strategic planning. Clearly, the characteristics of *Mission* expressions vary tremendously. Use the following and embrace what resonates with you:

Characteristics

– Connected to deepest interests

– Inspires commitment

– Stirs up passion

– Uniquely a description of *why* they show up *now* (*Vision* deals with the future, or *where*)

Clarity

– Not fuzzy (avoid words that mean different things to different people such as "excellent" or "best")

– Sufficiently clear to guide people in day-to-day decision-making

– Capable of being understood by a 12 year old

A Mission expression is **not** . . .

– *What* the organization does

– *How* the organization does that

– *Where* the organization is going

Length (if people can't remember a Mission expression, it serves only as a wall decoration)

- No more than one sentence long

- Short, clear, and usually less than 14 words

- Short and sharply focused

- If possible, 10 words or less

Ease of recall

- Easy to remember

- Easily recalled and recited, even if one is held at gunpoint

- What the organization wants to be remembered for

STANDARD MBA QUESTIONS TO CONSIDER

Next determine the questions you deem most appropriate to have your group answer. The *Mission* expression traditionally distills answers to the following, textbook MBA prompts:

1. Who the organization is and its role in the market environment

2. Scope (boundaries) of operations

3. Distinctive or unique characteristics—core competencies

4. The organization's customers or stakeholders

5. The organization's products or services

Other academic styles apply similar logic:

- Who are the targeted customers

- Need of the customers or opportunities being fulfilled

- By the primary products, services, or other value-add activities performed

- That serve a clear purpose and generate specific benefits

- Unlike competitor or competitive alternative being displaced

- Unique characteristics and differentiators include . . . [2]

FOR AN EXTRAORDINARY *MISSION* EXPRESSION

Building a *Mission* expression can also be fun because you can use any questions that you think will benefit your group. Think about what you want your

---

[2] See Geoffrey Moore's *Crossing the Chasm* (1995) for a baseline that many others have modified.

group members to know about one another, their situation, their conditions, and their stakeholders.

To avoid the "common deliverable" that makes many companies sound exactly like their competitors, consider the alternative questions that follow. Especially for team charters and other planning efforts, find the passion, rather than using the textbook MBA questions (everyone wants to grow and provide quality service). What truly makes your group unique? *Why* do they really show up?

Find the passion:

- Nothing else can _____.

- We are famous for _____?

- What allows us to take market share away from them?

- What are we most proud of about _____?

- What do you want others to say about _____?

- What is it about our competitors that allows them to take market share away from us?

- When the lights go out at night, people know _____?

- Whom do we aspire to be in terms of the market? In terms of performance?

- Why would the world be a less rich place if _____ disappeared?

You can modify questions to work with any group. Michael Barrett, of Resonance LLC, uses the following questions with boards of directors of nonprofits. He emphasizes that in one meeting, when directors shared their illustrations with one another, some were moved to tears.

- What do you *bring* to this organization?

- What do you *need* from this team?

- What is one event that *fundamentally* shaped your life?

- What *legacy* do you want to help create through this organization?

Other topical areas you might explore include these:

- Defining moment

- Greatest challenge for this group

- Greatest success for this group

- Moment of pride

- Worst fear

To facilitate a *Mission*, I use *Brainstorming, Coat of Arms*, and *Breakout Teams Tools*, whose explanations follow. After the next *Agenda Step* (*Values*), we will look at the *Scrubbing, Defining*, and *Categorizing Tools*.

DETAILED PROCEDURE

Display, distribute, or post the questions that you have selected.

- Use *Brainstorming* (next section) to build input for the group's *Mission* expression.

- Use *Breakout Teams* during the Listing activity (explained after *Brainstorming*).

- Have each team use the *Coat of Arms* (explained after *Breakout Teams*) to answer each of your questions.

- Pull the teams together using the *Categorizing Tool* (explained in the next *Agenda Step—Values*) to analyze input and converge upon consensually agreeable output.

- Assign the output to two or three volunteers who take time after the meeting to write down candidate *Mission* expressions that can be reviewed by the entire team at another session.

- Allow time and gestation for the draft inputs to grow into a final expression everyone supports.

SAY WHAT?

Begin to appreciate the circuitous challenge of meeting design. It would be much easier to forget structure, sit around, and have a discussion. But how's that working out for you?

- I am suggesting that you use a *Tool* nested within a *Tool* that is nested within a *Tool* that relies on an additional *Tool* . . . Huh?

- *Coat of Arms* is nested within *Breakout Teams*, which is nested within the Listing activity of *Brainstorming*.

- Output from Listing provides input for the Analysis activity, such as the *Categorizing Tool*.

- *Categorizing* may rely on *Scrubbing, Defining*, and *Prioritizing*—all nested within the Analysis activity of *Brainstorming*.[3]

- Say what?

The meeting designer's life is never easy. I could go even further and use *PowerBalls* or *Perceptual Mapping* (*Tools* for prioritization) to prioritize input

---

[3] *Scrubbing* and *Prioritizing Tools* are explained in chapter 7.

for the *Mission* expression, but for now, let's keep it painless; *PowerBalls* and *Perceptual Mapping* are explained in chapter 7.

FOR MISSION EXPRESSIONS ONLY

The *Coat of Arms Tool* may be used for the Listing activity of *Brainstorming* when there is more than one question to answer. However, while especially useful for *Mission* expressions, time box (set a time limit) a *Mission* expression. *Mission* expressions can be highly emotional—so do not expect them to conclude smoothly or quickly.

Ask for volunteers to take time after this session concludes and return at some future time or date to share some expressions for all participants to consider. When reconvening, try to post the original *Coats of Arms* to stimulate and remind participants about their original answers.

COMMERCIAL EXAMPLES OF MISSION EXPRESSIONS

It's difficult to distill the passion and verve of any group, organization, or team into very few words. However, by my standards, the following (at some point in time) reflected *Mission* quite well:

- Caribou Coffee (seven words): To be the best neighborhood gathering place.

- Cirque du Soleil (nine words): Invoke the imagination. Provoke the senses. Evoke the emotions.

- Dunn's Local Newspapers (one word, three times): Names, names, names.

- Ritz-Carlton (seven words): Ladies and gentlemen serving ladies and gentlemen.

- United States Marine Corps (six words): The few, the proud, the Marines.

- Noncommercial examples:

  - The golden rule is expressed with only 10 words (see the epilogue to this book for 13 versions).

  - The Peace symbol (nuclear disarmament; see figure 6.1) is nonnarrative and yet communicates universal intent about peaceful protest and mission.

Figure 6.1. Nuclear Disarmament Symbol

CAUTION: *Mission* expressions should be time-boxed. There are horror stories of groups that went off-site for a few days and never completed the first step of their agenda, *Mission*. Crafting the perfect *Mission* expression is not easy. Nor should it be expected during the first attempt.

Don't hesitate to ask for two or three volunteers to take output from the initial exercise as an assignment when the session has completed. Have them go away and craft candidate *Mission* expressions to bring back to the group at a future session for consideration. Allow the power of gestation to work for your group. Their final *Mission* expression may take a few months, or longer, but continue to revisit the updated drafts until one version resonates with everyone.

CLOSURE

When you have assigned, documented, or drafted a *Mission* expression, and with the group's assent, apply your analogy and move the agenda indicator[4] for a smooth transition to the next *Agenda Step*, *Values*—answering the question, "*who* are we?"

COMMENTS

Effective meeting design is clearly *not* effortless—but the rest of this book will make it much easier for you. I will recommend using *Brainstorming*, *Coat of Arms*, *Breakout Teams*, and so on dozens of times throughout the book, so . . .

- I am not going to repeat the procedure for each *Tool* every time it is referenced. That would require hundreds of pages of redundant material.

- You will find an alphabetically sorted *Table of Contents* for *Tools* at the end of the book, making it easier to find the detailed explanations and procedures for each *Tool*.

Brainstorming Tool

A frequently abused and nebulous term, "brainstorming" is right up there with "process," "system," and "user experience." *Brainstorming* is the means to an end. It is not a verb. You cannot "brainstorm" something if you are using the technique of the creator, Alex Osborn.[5] You can, however, list, analyze, and then decide—or, using terms preferred by academics, diverge, analyze, and converge. Therefore, the trichotomous term (sorry) "brainstorming" should

---

[4] The agenda indicator is simply a mobile arrow, tab, highlight, or some indicator of where we are in the agenda.

[5] For the source of the term "brainstorming," see *Applied Imagination*, by Alex Faickney Osborn (1963).

Table 6.3. Trichotomy of Will, Wisdom, and Activity

Trichotomy	Will	Wisdom	Activity
Brainstorming	List	**Analyze**	Decide
Transformation	Thought	Word	Deed
Reflectionist	WHAT	SO WHAT	NOW WHAT

never be listed as an *Agenda Step*. To be successful, you must clearly envision the output from your *Agenda Step* before you apply *Brainstorming* activities.

> NOTE: The trichotomy unfolds transformation from the abstract to the concrete. Note the similarities of three different *Tools* in table 6.3. Brainstorming may be used to develop anything. Brainstorming intends to give us more information to use in a shorter amount of time by leveraging the power of groups. However, lists by themselves can be frustrating, since consensual answers never simply "pop out" of the wall or screen (flatland).

Successful *Brainstorming* depends on thorough analysis. Creating, typing, or writing down lists is the easy part. The hard part is understanding what you are going to do with the list—the hard part is the analysis.

When facilitating, the Analysis and Decide activities provide significant challenges. Yet most people equate the term "brainstorming" with the Listing activity alone, and that is not Osborn's definition, intent, or meaning.[6] Osborn created the term in 1953, describing it as "a structured way of breaking out of structure."

A THREE-ACTIVITY PROCEDURE

Brainstorming requires three discrete activities. Each could represent separate *Agenda Steps*:

1. Listing or diverge (describe *Agenda Step* by title of the list)

2. Analyze (describe *Agenda Step* by the outputs, such as prioritization)

3. Decide or converge (describe the *Agenda Step* by the deliverable, such as a "decision")

---

[6] "While brainstorming became a tool for creative problem solving in this general way, it is very different from the fundamentals of the original description of the brainstorming process designed by Alex Osborn." Hanisha Besant, "The Journey of Brainstorming" (2016).

1. LISTING ACTIVITY (ALSO KNOWN AS "DIVERGE")

Quickly list candidate items—do not talk about the merits of them or, in fact, have any discussion at all. Keep the energy high. Select from the following ideation rules as appropriate. Do not, as most facilitators do, become the first violator by asking for more information about an item, requiring further definition, mentioning that "we already have that," or starting any inquiry. As the expression goes, "Is there any part of the word 'no' in the rule '*no* discussion' that you don't understand?"

Special Rules for Listing

The first two rules specific to Listing are sacrosanct. If you monitor these two closely, you don't need any other Listing rules. The other Listing rules below may be helpful but are only supplemental. Remember, if you start or allow any comments or discussion during the Listing activity, you are *not* doing *Brainstorming*.

- No discussion

- Fast pacing, high energy

- Supplemental:
  - All ideas allowed

  - Be creative—experiment

  - Build on the ideas of others

  - Everyone participates

  - No wordsmithing

  - Passion is good

  - Suspend judgment, evaluation, and criticism

  - Five-minute limit rule (ELMO: Enough, Let's Move On)

Ideation Riffs and Variations

There are various activities for Listing and gathering input, such as the following:

- *Breakout Teams*—use separate teams to provide ideas simultaneously. Using *Breakout Teams* remains my clear preference since you can get more done faster. With *Breakout Teams,* participants provide narrative or illustrative answers to your questions.

- Surprisingly, it is easier to illustrate than narrate answers to complex questions. In person and online, groups are refreshed by breaking into smaller teams to have conversations. Plus, as you begin to Analyze, where two or more teams have offered the same or similar content, consensus arises immediately.

- Facilitator-led questions—keep in mind that you can use a support scribe(s), but if so, remind them of the importance of neutrality and capturing complete verbatim inputs.

- Pass the marker—again having prepared the online template or easel title/banner, have participants contribute in the order of an assigned round-robin sequence to list their ideas.[7] When in person, passing the marker after lunch or when participants' energy ebbs helps get participants up and moving around. Help them with their penmanship if necessary by telling them to write larger and encourage the use of more white space.

- Pass a sheet or post a digital template—particularly appropriate if time is short, the group is large, or you have many questions requiring input (distribute a separate sheet for each question). Write the question or title on individual large cards or pieces of card stock, and either sitting or standing, have the participants pass them around until each person has had the opportunity to contribute to each question. This activity helps reduce redundant answers, since participants can see what prior people have written.

- Post-it notes—Have individuals write one idea per note, as many notes as they want, and mount them on the appropriate easel, whiteboard, Mural, or Miro.[8]

- Round-robin—having prepared an online template or in-person easel title or banner, and in consort with a scribe or scribes, create an assigned order in which the participants offer ideas, one at a time, permitting anyone to say "pass" at any time. Consider one last round-robin for any missed or final contributions, again allowing participants to say "pass" if they have nothing to add.

NOTE: Consider time-boxing your ideation activity if necessary, typically in the range of 5–10 minutes. However, if you fastidiously enforce the "high-energy" rule, you will discover that most groups cannot maintain high energy around a single question for more than 6–8 minutes.

---

[7] Round-robin is a name used by seamen for some promise or agreement on which they sign their names "round a circle" to prevent the ringleader from being discovered if the agreement is found. In this context, a round-robin is a method of giving participants an opportunity to contribute or say "pass," which normally proceeds in the form of a circle or some rotation around the room, either in person or using a virtual seating arrangement for online meetings.

[8] As of this writing, Mural and Miro are popular online technology platforms.

2. ANALYZING ACTIVITY

Consensual understanding provides the foundation for all analysis. *Analyzing* comprises 80 percent of the *Brainstorming* effort. Listing is quick, as we just saw. Therefore, first "scrub" the lists and validate the clarity. Challenge participants as to why they contributed an item. *Scrubbing* may be quick or demand analyzing each item to determine

- what it means—define it (*Defining Tool*);

- whether it should be combined with another item or items (*Categorizing Tool*);

- the merits of each item (*Prioritizing Tool*); and

- whether it should be deleted as inappropriate, redundant, or superfluous.

To analyze successfully, you must first know what you are building. Know in advance what you are going to do with the list—what questions to ask and how you are going to clean up and document the final list.

Thorough analysis frequently requires input from more than one Listing activity. For example, *Deciding* and *Alignment* require purpose, options, and criteria. *Assigning* requires *who* and *what*. *Situation Analysis* requires understanding the resources that we control and factors we don't control.

Rely on the *Analyzing* activity (and all other *Tools)* to do the work for you. Rely on and trust the procedure, not your content knowledge. Participants may never arrive at your answer, but they will create a solution they can all understand and will support.

3. DECIDING ACTIVITY (ALSO KNOWN AS "DOCUMENT" OR "CONVERGE")

Thorough and complete analysis frequently relies on building some type of matrix. The Analysis activity sets up the matrix. The *Deciding* or converging activities document consensual findings resulting from the analysis your group set up by completing the matrix.

While I always remain hesitant about letting any tool make our decision for us, tools will frequently enhance focus by getting a group to agree on what *not* to consider or what *not* to talk about anymore. **Tools help groups deselect.** After deselection, most decisions are win-win because the remaining options may all be robust enough to secure everyone's support. We have rid ourselves of the weak options and the noise they generate that causes distractions in meetings.

At this point, your definition of consensus becomes critical. We may not be able to find a solution that is everyone's favorite. In fact, we usually won't. We may even develop a solution that is not anyone's favorite. But we have facilitated consensus by building an agreement, decision, or solution that everyone will support while not causing anyone to lose any sleep or withdraw their support.

Therefore, on a separate screen or sheet of paper, document the final list, output, or choice depending on what type of deliverable you have built. Confirm buy-in with your participants, securing an audible response from each participant as an outward sign of agreement and support. In highly contentious and politically charged situations, I've even circulated an 8.5-by-11-inch or A4-sized sheet of paper and required each participant to sign or initial.

COMMON PITFALLS TO AVOID

Plan *Brainstorming* ahead of time. Write down your precise question or questions before starting. Have a clear understanding of what you are building (a list of options, criteria, or whatever it is) before you start. Other cautions to heed include avoiding these pitfalls:

- Asking a question that is too broad or vague (such as "How do you solve global hunger?," "How do you boil the ocean?" = "What should we do about it?"); always remember that $Y = (f)\ X$'s, so ask about the X's and do not ask directly for the Y

- Asking the group "How should we categorize the list?"; if you do not know how, then prepare more thoroughly—groups frequently over-categorize and make things too general when they should head in the opposite direction and more fully articulate the attributes, characteristics, and specificity that describe their items

> **—David Allen, *Getting Things Done***
> *The problem with digitizing brainstorming is that we don't need to save what we brainstorm. . . . The critical thing is the conclusion. . . . The slick brainstorming capture tools . . . will probably not be as successful as hoped. There are significant differences among collecting and processing and organizing, and different tools are usually required for them.*

- Being the first to start a conversation by not waiting until everyone's input has been gathered and confirmed

- Cadence—not knowing when to stop or stopping too soon

- Not enforcing that everyone, including the meeting facilitator, must avoid *any* conversation while listing

- Not having an activity or tool prepared to analyze the list

- Not writing soon enough, waiting for speakers to finish, and then asking them to repeat themselves (to avoid this pitfall, write while they are speaking—it is easier to correct something wrong than to go back and remember something that was "right")

Breakout Teams Tool

Using *Breakout Teams* captures more information in less time and helps you overcome the monotony of relying too much on group Listings. Consider *Breakout Teams* whenever you are gathering information and ideas, typically where more is better.

NOTE: When building consensus, it is frequently best, however, to defer your Analysis activity until all teams have returned and assembled as one integrated group.

PROCEDURE

- In advance, have *Breakout Teams* assigned, predetermined, and provide reasons for how you determined who is assigned to which group.

- Provide something more creative and appropriate than relying on seating arrangements (such as "this half of the room"). Consider quick yet creative methods, such as alphabetically sorting participants' names, birthplaces, birthdates, clothing colors, favorite ice cream flavors, and so on. You might even use a deck of playing cards, and everyone drawing the same suit forms a team.

- Appoint a CEO for each team, telling them after the appointments have been made that CEO stands for the chief easel operator (with laughter as a response).[9] Assign their workspace (northwest corner of the room, or Room 3, for example), and have their workspace set up and provisioned with supplies such as an easel, paper, and markers. The CEO is not responsible for scribing but does provide a single point of contact when you ask that team for a status update. Ignore the loudest person or the person who speaks first, enforcing the status of the CEO role.

- Visibly post your assignment and questions to be addressed on a screen or handout. Be clear and explicit with instructions and the format you

[9] Never discount the power of laughter as "medicine," because groups that laugh together perform better together. Laughter positively affects group communication and group dynamics—even when there's nothing funny going on. See research from North Carolina State University that examined the role of laughter in jury deliberations during a capital murder case: "No Laughing Matter" (2010).

expect each team to follow (such as listing or illustrating). Keep the questions or instructions posted and available. Print and distribute copies for each CEO if teams gather outside the main meeting room.

- Remind team scribes to capture verbatim inputs and to use black or dark blue markers that are easier to read when they present their findings to the other teams. Also tell team scribes to contribute their own ideas toward the conclusion only if those ideas have not already been mentioned.

- When capturing content online, remind team scribes to shrug off any criticism about spelling. I show the symbol ☑ and tell them that this is a spell-check button for large easel paper and online note-capturing tools that will fix all the errors when the meeting has completed.

- Give teams a precise amount of time or a deadline and monitor them closely for functionality, progress, and questions that arise. You will be shocked how much teams can get done in three minutes with clear instructions.

NOTE: Be creative. Other ways to assign teams include birth order position, latitude of birthplace, mountain peaks, rivers, constellations, land features, mythical gods, historical icons, hobby or game themes (for example, sports), places, emotional categories, entertainment icons, and hobbies. If you want them to be creative, then walk the talk. For larger groups, consider using the day of the week you were born (making sure it can be looked up if they don't know), name of their first pet, first concert they attended, and so on.

Coat of Arms Tool

Any time you seek answers to more than one question, *Coat of Arms* can be used during the Listing activity of *Brainstorming*. Use *Coat of Arms* whenever you have multiple questions. The *Coat of Arms* is especially helpful when developing input for brief *Mission* or *Vision* expressions for any group or business. Always use in conjunction with *Breakout Teams*, thus creating more than one *Coat of Arms*.

PROCEDURE

Provide participants or teams with written and posted questions along with pre-drawn templates for their *Coats of Arms*. Partition each *Coat of Arms* into the same quantity of sections as you have questions. Typically carve out three to seven sections with a discrete corresponding question for each section.

- Use with *Breakout Teams* described on the previous page.

- Allow each team 3–10 minutes to draw answers to the questions, using illustrations in their respective sections, without using any words on their illustrations.

- Monitor teams closely and be flexible enough to extend the amount of time if required. When completed (if in person), have them mount their drawings in the front or center of the room.

- After the teams reassemble as one group, write down the interpretations by each CEO-appointed spokesperson (CEOs can always delegate). Do *not* wait until they are done speaking, forcing them to repeat as you write down their explanations; begin writing *as they speak*.

- Never cross out or write on their drawings, and do not interpret the drawings yourself. Always shift as much airtime as possible to your participants.

- Once the teams have completed their interpretations, ask for volunteers to integrate the list of sentiments that you wrote down into final expressions that everyone can support.

HELPFUL HINTS

- Maintain cadence. At quick intervals, prod the group to see whether the core concepts have been written down. If so, summarize and move on.

- After converting the drawings to narrative, reread entire expressions from the very beginning to see whether there are any modifications. Groups need to hear full expressions in final form.

3. Values (Who Are We?)

Values define the principles or internal rules, laws, policies, and philosophies of their conduct—the "stuff" we carry with us and value. To me they answer simply, "Who are we?" Weave your analogy into your introductory remarks.

You will also see *Values* labeled with different terms by organizations, such as "credo," "professional code," and "tenets of operation." Completed *Values* may be displayed as lists, paragraphs, sentences, and so on.

> DEFINED: *Values* describe who we are by defining "how we will work together" for the business, in support of our *Mission*. Some consider *Values* as ideals that lend significance to our lives, that are reflected through the priorities we choose, and that we act on consistently and repeatedly.[10]

Values may support:

- How participants manage the organization

- How participants treat one another

---

[10] For example, Brian Hall, PhD, author of the Hall-Tonna Values Inventory; see Brian Hall and Barbara Ledig, *Lifestyle Workbook: A Guide for Understanding the Hall-Tonna Inventory of Values* (1986).

- Importance of upholding participants' ethics

- Product and product quality

- Relationship to stakeholders, employees, and community

- Responsibility toward the environment

- The things to which we stay true

- What distinguishes us from others

DELIVERABLE

Values may be narrative descriptions of policies or philosophies. They may be full-sentence descriptions or phrases. Keep in mind that groups can identify both descriptive values (we are this way and walk the talk) and prescriptive values (hopes and aspirations). The former is associated with traditional management, while the latter is more associated with servant leadership.

> NOTE: Ken Blanchard asserts that an organization should limit itself to three values. Employees will not remember more than three. And if employees cannot remember their *Values*, then why build them?[11]

Values define "who we are" or "the things to which we stay true." *Values* provide foundation for all *Agenda Steps*. Eventually, we will review and validate output from the remaining *Agenda Steps* as harmonizing and supporting the *Mission* and *Values*, sometimes referred to collectively as the *Guiding Principles*.

PROCEDURE

- Define *Values* using the definitions given earlier or your own derivative.

- Use *Breakout Teams* and any *Brainstorming* Listing activity such as *Coat of Arms*, *Creativity* (chapter 8), or a straightforward narrative listing.

- After teams reassemble, use the logic of *Bookend Rhetoric* (chapter 7) to first document items that are identical or similar across teams—instant consensus. Next rotate to the most unique, and so on.

- Roll up the list by looking for common purpose as explained in the *Categorizing Tool* that follows on the next page.

- When the group seems to have exhausted their most important ideas, review the final *Values*.

---

[11] See Ken Blanchard and Jesse Stoner, "The Vision Thing: Without It You'll Never Be a World-Class Organization," *Leader to Leader*, no. 31 (Winter 2004), http://www.partner swithnonprofits.org/uploads/1/0/7/3/10733039/the_vision_thing.ken_blanchard.pdf.

Values do not have to be short statements, but what is easier to remember? *Values* may be full sentences (as the examples below), but they should always capture an articulate sense of "*how* we will work together."

NOTE: *Values* are best remembered as bullet points or brief sentences. When combined as paragraph expressions, they are much more difficult to remember.

ILLUSTRATIVE ORGANIZATIONAL VALUES USING THRIVE LLC

- We don't say "no"—we say, "How?"

- We foster risk-taking without reprisal.

- We strive to balance family life with professional responsibilities.

- We understand the importance of CREAM—Cash Rules Everything Around Me.

COMMERCIAL EXAMPLES

- "The Ritz-Carlton experience enlivens the senses, instills well-being, and fulfills even the unexpressed wishes and needs of our guests."

- "No compromise over guest accommodation which excites the senses. No replacement of intuitive, emotionally attuned service which cherishes each and every guest."—Regent Ball

- Donald Miller's Storybrand organization:
  - "Be the guide (help the customer win),
  - Be ambitious (go for it),
  - Be positive."

CLOSURE

At this point, when you have documented *Values* with the group's assent, apply your analogy and move the agenda indicator for a smooth transition to *Vision*— an explanation about *where* we are headed.

Categorizing Tool

Categorizing creates clusters or chunks of related items so that groups can sharpen their focus. Similar terms describing the same logic include "affinity," "chunking," "clustering," "distilling," "grouping," and so on. To roll up or distill any list or group of Mural or Miro items, Post-its, or other forms of multiple items, *Categorizing* provides both detailed procedure and the logic behind the rationale for categorizing most things: common purpose.

Categorizing eliminates redundancies by collapsing related items into chunks (scientific term). Labels or triggers that represent the titles for your chunks can be easily reused in flow diagrams, matrices, or other visual displays, making it easier for groups to analyze complex relationships.

> NOTE: Never ask the group *how* to categorize. They don't know how. That is why they engaged you. Explain the tool and teach them the logic of common purpose when it becomes necessary to group items.

PROCEDURE

Categorizing can take little or much time, depending on how much precision is required, how much time is available, and relative importance. After ideas have been gathered, preferably using *Breakout Teams*, do the following:

Underscore

Take the lists created during your ideation activity and underscore the <u>common nouns</u> (typically the object in a sentence that is preceded by a predicate or a verb). Use a distinct color marker or shape[12] for each group of nouns, and have the team add any synonyms or similar expressions that capture the intent for each group of items underscored.

Transpose

Ask a volunteer to take one grouping of underscored items (at a time) and provide a term or phrase (category) that combines, integrates, and reflects the sentiment of all the items underscored in that specific color (or shape).

Write the new term or phrase (category) on a separate page or screen. Use the *Definition Tool* to reinforce clarity if participants require better understanding.

Scrub for Clarity

Return to the original list—ask, confirm, and then delete items that now collapse into the new expression that you rewrote during the *Transpose* activity above.

The Don't Forget Question

After each new category, before moving on, *don't forget* to ask, "Which other items *not* underscored also belong to this category?" If so, delete those items or parts of them as well.

Remaining Orphans

Allow your group to focus on remaining items that have not been eliminated and decide whether they require unique expressions, need further explanation, or can be deleted.

---

[12] With only a few colors, or to provide enhanced accessibility to people who have difficulty distinguishing colors, use shapes such as dotted lines, dashed lines, boxes, ovals, and so on to distinguish probable clusters.

For each item not underscored or remaining, consider asking "Why _____?" Items that share common purpose may be categorized together. Create a new category if they remain unique or delete them if they are inconsequential.

Everyone witnesses building the final list, which now belongs to everyone, rather than being associated with one team or another. The original team contributions should be discarded once the group confirms that the sentiment has been effectively captured with the newly written term or phrase.

> NOTE: Always cross out and rewrite listed items so that there is one final list when you are complete. Everyone should witness the rewrite and now become an owner. Ideas should not belong to the contributor, and if you keep the original version, it will always belong to the person or team who wrote it.

Review

Before transitioning, review the new expressions (categories) and confirm that team members understand and will support them. Let team members know that they can add to the categories later, but if they are comfortable as is, move on, since the new categories may be reused later.

You are helping your group move raw input into a refined output on a new sheet or screen. Deleting their raw input when rewritten makes it easier to focus on the items not yet deleted. When the new categories are documented, with everyone present, it also transfers ownership because everyone witnesses and participates in creating the new categories (expressions).

LOCK INTO THE LOGIC OF CATEGORIZATION

The primary reason for categories of things is common purpose. Look at how we organize in businesses. Walk around an office building and you will see that people are grouped together, organized around "things." They are not organized around verbs.

Treasury personnel are organized around financial assets. Human resources are organized around human capital. Sales and marketing are organized around customers. Everybody performs the same verbs. They all plan, acquire resources, do their work, and control for the work they've done. What gives rise to the separation or categorization is symptomatic of the nouns or resources but the driving force behind the categories of most things is simply common purpose. Engineering has common purpose around products. The Enterprise Project / Program Management Office (EPMO) has common purpose around projects—and so on.

If there are arguments or uncertainty about which category something belongs, simply challenge the group with "Which purpose does it best support?"

LESS COMMON CATEGORIZING PATTERNS

People visually perceive items, not in isolation, but as part of a larger whole. These principles include human tendencies toward common purpose. Other, less common reasons for the "categories of things" may include these:

- *Continuity*—an identifiable pattern

- *Proximity*—physical closeness to one another

- *Sizing*—using a common unit of measurement

- *Timing*—based on duration, time of occurrence, or sometimes frequency

4. Vision (Where Are We Going? How Do We Know If We Got There or Not?)

It is hard enough to get a family of four to agree on where to go out to eat, much less getting a group of directors, executives, and managers to agree on where they want to drive their organization.

Vision defines the direction of an organization by providing details about where the organization wants to go. *Vision* should appeal to both the head and the heart, supporting the question, "Why change?" A clear expression of the future helps to gain genuine commitment. Illustrate your definition with your analogy.

> A *Vision* is a desired position specified in sufficient detail so that an organization knows when they reach the *Vision*. A consensual *Vision* provides direction and motivation for change. Optimally, a *Vision* should be specific enough to differentiate your organization from competitors.

DELIVERABLE

A few clearly defined expressions or a brief paragraph 25–75 words in length. Consider beginning with "We aspire . . ."

RELATIONSHIPS

Vision anchors the forthcoming *Measures Agenda Step* by expressing where your organization is headed. When thoroughly constructed, *Visions*:

- Provide a picture of what the organization aspires to become

- Motivate and energize members to focus on priorities

- Enable individuals and teams to make trade-offs or eliminate options for consideration

- Sanction *Measures* whereby individual and organizational performance can be evaluated

BASIC PROCEDURES

- Use *Breakout Teams* (chapter 6).[13]

- Use *Temporal Shift Tool* (chapter 6).

- Apply *Categorizing* (chapter 6) to distill their various aspirations into a common *Vision* expression they all support.

RIFFS AND VARIATIONS

Asking "Where have you been?" is too broad to effectively stimulate. Consider the dozens of *Perspectives* (chapter 8) to provide additional input that aggregates into a broader, overreaching *Vision,* a view that considers the evidence and facts arising from answers to questions such as these:

- Where are the thrust and focus for future business development and growth? Which products and services? Which customers?

- What channels, markets, products, and services should be minimized or excluded in a future vision?

- What core competencies are sought to take us into "tomorrow"?

- What does our business look like "tomorrow" if we do not change?

- What product or service mix or decision criteria will change over time, enabling us to get ahead of customer and market expectations?

- Which financial parameters drive the likelihood for growth and returns on investments?

The following is an example for the organizational *Vision* at THRIVE LLC:

We aspire that contractors, developers, and homeowners will order THRIVE products and services before their new home construction or renovation begins. Residential families will begin to THRIVE before they take occupancy of their property. They will view us as a trustworthy partner as they begin their new life, in a place they may consider foreign, but we will help them occupy as familiar so that they THRIVE and feel like home.

CLOSURE

This *Agenda Step* concludes when you have an expression or paragraph that the group believes captures the target or *Vision* of where they want to go. Confirm enough detail that they can recognize the target, and would all agree when

---

[13] Please remember to be more creative with team names than the Zoom default of Room 1, Room 2, and so on.

they get there. Use your analogy and move the agenda indicator for a smooth transition to *Key Measures*, setting goals and objectives (milestones) along the path toward reaching the *Vision*.

Temporal Shift Tool

Temporal Shift helps groups agree on where to go or be at some point in the future. It is much easier to ask and build consensus around "Where have you been?" or "What type of legacy have you left behind?" than to ask, "Where would you like to go?"

PROCEDURE

Temporal Shift defines a specific forward-looking view (*Vision*) of a group or organization in sufficient detail so that a group or organization can easily agree when they reach it (or not). Subsequent planning efforts direct attention toward reaching the *Vision*. Looking forward, shaping curves, or *Vision* help determine the optimal goals, objectives, and measures.

- Use *Breakout Teams* (chapter 6). Put each team and all the participants on a warm island with a beautiful beach and a cool breeze.

- Have a newspaper or industry magazine preselected for your participants to read.

- Hand out recent copies of an appropriate industry or trade magazine or periodical familiar to the participants. Decide which part of the paper or magazine will display a headline based on the success of the group (could be a column or specific section).

- Remind everyone that they are on the island at some point in the future. Calculate the point in the future as a date by when this team will have disbanded. For a project team, only 2–3 years. For executives, 5–25 years. Some Asian organizations look ahead 50 years; but it's frankly tough to get most North American organizations to look past 5 years.

- Have participants turn to a specific page (could also be the front cover or front page) or column that is frequently read. The *Wall Street Journal* serves as a default publication.

- Have each *Breakout Team* first develop a newspaper headline that they would like to see when reading this paper while sitting on that beach in the future—for example, "What would the headline read on January 15, 20__?"

- After they complete their headlines, instruct them to draft the story behind the headline, in the form of a 250-word article. Their headlines and stories become the foundation for integrating their final *Vision* expression.

- Bring the teams together to compare and analyze. Use the *Bookend Rhetoric* (chapter 7) to look for substantive similarities and differences. Rely on common purpose (*Categorizing*, chapter 6) to distill their input into final expressions or statements.

- Remember, first create the headline. The story augments the headline with details. Consider a final written expression starting with "We aspire . . ."

- Surprisingly, the article takes them less time to write than the headline, as the article becomes the "meeting minutes" of the conversation and "arguments" leading into the headline.

NOTE: When you have them pretend they are on a beautiful beach sometime in the future and pick up a periodical displaying a headline about their efforts, what you are really asking them is "What is the legacy you have left behind as a result of the effort you began back in this meeting?" See the following website for today's headlines worldwide, which could also be printed and given to team members, thus providing tactile stimulation: https://www.freedomforum.org/todaysfrontpages/.

5. Key Measures Agenda Step and Tool (What Are the CTQs, KPIs, and OKRs?)

This *Agenda Step* defines *what* the organization will *Measure* to determine its progress reaching its *Vision*. Relate each of the three measurement types explained here back to your analogy.

KEY PERFORMANCE INDICATORS OR CRITICAL SUCCESS FACTORS

The deliverable from this *Agenda Step* may be called by many names:

- Considerations

- Criteria

- CSF (Critical Success Factors)

- CTQ (Critical to Quality)[14]

- FMA (Future Measurement Acronyms)

- Goals

- Key Results ("OKR" stands for Objectives and Key Results)

---

[14] CTQ would substitute the following questions for the SMART test: Is it specifically stated with upper and lower specification limits? Is it directional so that we can objectively determine whether it is increasing, decreasing, or staying the same? To what extent is it linked to specific customer needs connected to the objectives of the project?

- KPI (Key Performance Indicators)

- Leading indicators

- NCT (New Consulting Terms)

- Objectives

There are three general types of criteria: (1) SMART (specific, measurable, adjustable, relevant, time-based), (2) fuzzy, and (3) binary. In the most common vernacular, these three types correspond with objectives, goals, and considerations. An objective "measure" is a standard unit used to express the size, amount, or degree of something.

An *objective* is a desired position reached by *Actions* within a specified time. Objectives provide measurable performance indication [≡] and are commonly made SMART.[15] With shorter duration than goals, they may be viewed as milestones en route to reaching goals.

A *goal* is a directional expression that may remain fuzzy or subjective to each observer [△]. Although a goal may not be technically SMART, it is directional and on a long-term basis, a deep-reaching, fuzzy criterion, or a measurement that might decompose into multiple objectives (or key results).

A *consideration* is a binary (yes or no) management issue, constraint, or concern that will affect reaching the *Vision* [✚].

DELIVERABLE

Clearly defined *Measures* or success criteria including a range of objectives, goals, and other considerations.

RELATIONSHIPS

Key Measures enable using measurements to calculate progress and the distance from reaching the *Vision*. *Measures* provide milestones that enable your group to better shape and define the most appropriate strategies, activities, or tactics (*what* to do to reach the vision).

BASIC PROCEDURES

Use the ideation activity of *Brainstorming* to draft and specify candidate *Key Measures*. See the *Scorecard Tool* (chapter 7) for additional detailed analytical support and scripting when analyzing *Measures*.

---

[15] Please be careful. Some consulting firms propagate definitions contrary to mine. Some claim that "goals" are SMART while "objectives" are fuzzy. While I remain agnostic and defer to the cultural preference, there is no universal standard or answer. Therefore, please ensure that participants within your culture apply consistent definitions. Facilitating *Measures* is not the time or place for contextual argument.

- First obtain rough ideas using the rules of ideation found in *Brainstorming*.

- Then explain the three measurement types (*Objectives* [SMART], *Goals* [fuzzy], and *Considerations* [binary]).

- Use the logic and rhetoric of the *Scorecard Tool* (chapter 7) to analyze the input and convert ideas into final and calculable *Measures*.

- To ensure clarity and consensual understanding, be prepared to use the *Definition Tool* (chapter 6).

- Review the fully defined *Measures* and assign *Measures* to a category by coding them as shown: *Objectives* [≣], *Goals* [⌂], or *Considerations* [✚].

- Analyze each objective [≣], one at a time, and make them SMART. Do not show the SMART definition until after you have completed writing down the initial input during Listing. Use *Breakout Teams* (chapter 6) to convert draft *Measures* into final form, making sure they are SMART:

  - **S**pecific

  - **M**easurable

  - **A**djustable (and challenging)

  - **R**elevant (and achievable)

  - **T**ime-based

- Remember to challenge SMART objectives by first identifying the **unit of measurement**. The unit of *Measure* is *what* we need first, *not how* we measure it (more on this later).

- Eventually, detail the precise calculation or formula and stipulate the source for obtaining the data to be used (including report name and line item from a spreadsheet if applicable).

- Separately list and fully define the remaining subjective goals (fuzzy and not SMART) and other important considerations (if any).

CAUTION: When purchasing a new vehicle, you may seek ample legroom in the back seat. What is the unit of measurement for ample legroom? If someone says "inches," are we talking about linear inches, square inches, cubic inches, or a tesseract?

If linear inches, measured from what point to what point? For this exercise we need to know "linear inches measured from rear middle of the parallel seat in row one when fully upright to the front of seat where the knees bend in the second row" (or whatever we are told the measurement is). We do not need to know how it is measured, whether using a tape measure or a laser scope.

Be careful in your organization to document the source of the data. For example, if the unit of measure is "barrels of oil," where are we obtaining the data? Which report? Which line item? We do not want participants to argue later over dissimilar sources of data.

The following discussion uses both THRIVE LLC and mountaineering as examples. Draw upon your own analogy for illustrative support.

THRIVE LLC objectives (SMART):

- Produce a detailed month-end analysis of sales from distribution channels within two hours, compared with 72 hours with the existing technique, using Report ABCD and line item 34 and have the sales total accessible for use by EOD (end of day) April 15, 20__.

- Accelerate organic growth beyond industry average of 7 percent per year, targeting 10 percent cumulative annual growth rate, by end of year, December 31, 20__, using Report ABCD and line item 73.

THRIVE LLC goals (fuzzy):

- Build leadership in the industry and become a go-to organization when others are seeking advice.

- Be feared by our competitors and other competitive options.

- Concurrent development and commitment of business units, including the determination and balance of dashboard success measures.

THRIVE LLC considerations (binary):

- Given current macroeconomic conditions that drive the new housing market, retire US$50 million in existing long-term debt by July 1, 20__.

- If Competitor X launches a new product line in widgets, leverage our analysis of other widget manufacturers to explore mergers or acquisitions.

ICONIC SUPPORT (MOUNTAINEERING ANALOGY)

Provide a legend that explains the icons you will use to code their input (using mountaineering to illustrate). You will also need a legend or artifact that defines SMART:

- Objectives [≡]: Be at 5,000 meters by 17:00 hours UTC Friday, April 15, 20__.

- Goals [◠]: Take some nice photos when we reach the summit.

- Binary considerations [✚]: Did we reach the summit, or not?

Keep a *Key Measures* legend visible and easily accessible until you complete the *Actions* (such as strategies, projects, and activities) and *Alignment* activities later. The team will need to refer to *Key Measures* to justify proposed *Actions* and to clarify, add, or delete *Actions*.

Script your analogy by relating your analog to the three types of *Key Measures*. What measurements indicate progress toward reaching the *Vision?* *Measures* are appealed to continuously when analyzing the *Current Situation* to determine the most optimal *Actions*.

CLOSURE

When the SMART measures have been fully built, and the non-SMART measures have been defined, close this *Agenda Step*. Move the agenda indicator to the next *Agenda Step*, *Current Situation* (also known as *Situation Analysis*). Emphasize that *Key Measures* are created to provide indication of progress toward reaching the *Vision*.

Definition Tool

Keep this *Definition Tool* in your hip pocket and be prepared to use it whenever you encounter discord over the meaning of something. You may also need this *Tool* when you manage open issues (*Parking Lot,* chapter 5) and during your *Review and Wrap* if your participants do not agree or cannot remember what something meant.

WHY?

Facilitators need a robust and objective *Tool* for defining terms, phrases, and other "things" mentioned by subject(ive) matter experts. The standards listed are demanding and include five separate activities.

I created this unique *Tool* to quickly build consensual agreement around words, terms, and phrases. However, for concepts like processes, a more extensive and illustrative *Meeting Approach* like *Activity Flows* (*Process Decomposition*)[16] might be required.

PROCEDURE

When a term or phrase requires further definition or understanding, never rely exclusively on dictionary definitions.[17] Instead, facilitate the group's definition with the following five questions or activities:

---

[16] Removed from this book to reduce bulk but available at https://mgrush.com/.

[17] We are not fans of dictionary definitions because none of us participated in the writing. Dictionaries do not agree among themselves on definitions. If you do use dictionary definitions, use them after the definition has been first built by the participants. Use the comparison to see whether anything critical is missing.

1. First identify what the term or phrase is *not*. For example, as a highly appreciative gift idea, a camera is *not* something disposable or pre-used.

2. Compile a narrative sentence or paragraph that describes it. For example, the camera is a handheld device for recording photographic images. If you must use a dictionary or other professional definition, use it to compare with something the group has already built to identify something important that is missing.

3. List the detailed bullets that capture specific attributes, characteristics, or specifications of the term or phrase as intended by the participants. For example, with a camera, we might detail requirements for the quantity of mega pixels, digital zoom range, and so on.

4. Get or secure a picture of concrete items or create an illustration of the item if it is abstract or dynamic (such as a process flow diagram).

5. Provide at least two actual, real-life examples from the participants' experience that brings the term or phrase to life. For example, a gift camera might be a Canon EOS Rebel T7 or a Nikon D3500.

6. Quantitative TO-WS Analysis Agenda Step (What Is Our Current Situation?)

Quantitative TO-WS (Threats, Opportunities, Weaknesses, and Strengths) *Analysis* reviews the *Current Situation* and is more frequently referred to as SWOT Analysis. While rare in use, I find *TO-WS* more appropriate, for these reasons:

1. Evidence indicates the best sequence for *Situation Analysis* begins with the external and uncontrollable threats and opportunities before moving to internal and controllable weaknesses and strengths.

2. I will introduce you to a quantitative *Tool* that I built to help groups generate consensus when prioritizing hundreds of options. Being unique, *TO-WS* brings a fresh sense to invigorate a stale tool (SWOT) that is poorly facilitated in most organizations.

3. SWOT has left a bad taste in people's mouths because they create four lists, hang them on a wall, stand back, and ask: "What should we do differently?" While some answers pop out of "flatland," rarely can you drive consensual answers with an unstructured style that uses a "global hunger" question like "What should we do differently?"

I developed my *Quantitative TO-WS Analysis* in 1994 while attending Northwestern's Kellogg Graduate School of Management because, unlike the four-list style, *Quantitative TO-WS Analysis . . .*

- develops shared understanding,

- making it easier to build consensual *Actions,*

- that ensure achieving or exceeding the *Key Measures,*

- established to reach the *Vision.*

As this *Agenda Step* develops you will see how easy it should be to apply your personal analogy.

NOTE: Time and time again, my students with MBAs and PhDs have commented that for them, two "lightbulbs" turned on with my structured planning that had never been clear in school:

1. The difference between *Mission* and *Vision* and why people are so often confused (chapter 6)

2. How to effectively use the logic and precise rhetoric of *TO-WS* to help build consensus

DELIVERABLE

A numerical analysis that describes the *Current Situation, Quantitative TO-WS* makes it possible to prioritize hundreds of options (*Actions*). *TO-WS Analysis* helps groups visualize their current situation and prioritize hundreds of potential *Actions* on a single page or screen.

NOTE: Previously we have relied on words (narrative), icons (symbols), and drawings (illustrations). Because we confront hundreds of potential strategies, initiatives, products, or projects, the numeric *Tool* that I use here makes it easy to deselect weak options and focus energies on the best options.

Quantitative TO-WS Analysis Tool: Current Situation or Situation Analysis

This *Tool* describes the *Current Situation* by developing shared understanding that supports *what Actions* a group should embrace so that they reach their *Key Measures* (chapter 6), such as objectives (SMART), goals (fuzzy), and considerations (binary).

A quantitative view of the *Current Situation* displays the foundation for justifying *Actions. Actions* that currently work well are potentially reinforced and renewed alongside new *Actions* that get approved and developed.

The term used to describe *Actions* will change depending on your level in the holarchy. For example, an organization will refer to *Actions* as strategies, a business unit may call them initiatives, a department or program office may call their *Actions* new products or new projects, and a product or project team may call them activities or tasks. For each group respectively, the term used represents *what* the group is going to do to reach its *Key Measures* that were established to ensure that the group achieves its *Vision* (chapter 6).

The *Current Situation* provides consensual descriptions of the following:

- Current environment (*TO-WS*)

  - Threats (externally uncontrollable, frequently trends)

  - Opportunities (externally uncontrollable, frequently trends)

  - Weaknesses (internally controlled, as viewed by competitors or competitive forces)

  - Strengths (internally controlled, as viewed by competitors or competitive forces)

- Assumptions made in developing analysis

- Model representing how stakeholders view the business or organization

- Input for determining *what Actions* the group foresees, given their *Current Situation*, to help reach or exceed their *Measures* in support of achieving their *Vision*

GENERAL QUESTIONS

- Which threats are most worrisome and justify defense?

- Which opportunities provide a real chance of success?

- Which weaknesses need the most correction?

- Which core competencies or strengths should be leveraged?

ALTERNATIVES

This *Agenda Step* may be completed one of two ways:

1. Traditionally, *Situation Analysis* may be mandated for a department, project, or work area and completed in advance. Once that effort has been explained and clarified, summarize, and move on to the next *Agenda Step*, developing *Actions* to reach the *Key Measures*.

2. Alternatively, use my proprietary *Quantitative TO-WS Analysis* (figure 6.2). Separate the external things we have no control over (threats and opportunities) and the internal things we control (weaknesses and strengths). Then use my numerical *Tool* for analysis that helps develop group comprehension and understanding about *what Actions* will have the greatest impact, given the group's *Current Situation*, to reach the *Key Measures* (akin to identifying *what* we should do different tomorrow).

		Situational Threats (–)						Threats Subtotals	Situation Opportunities (+)						Opportunities Subtotals	Totals
		Competition	Loyalty	Macroeconomic	Price	Suppliers	Trends		Acquisition	Channels	Development	Licensing	Sourcing	Speed		
Situational Strengths (+)	Ethics							0							0	
	Flexibility							0							0	
	Infrastructure							0							0	
	Reputation							0							0	
	Resourcefulness							0							0	
	Responsiveness							0							0	
	Strengths Subtotals	0	0	0	0	0	0	0	0	0	0	0	0	0	0	*0*
Situation Weaknesses (–)	Accountability							0							0	
	Communications							0							0	
	Costs							0							0	
	Operations							0							0	
	Product							0							0	
	Targeting							0							0	
	Weaknesses Subtotals	0	0	0	0	0	0	0	0	0	0	0	0	0	0	*0*
	Totals	**0**	**0**	**0**	**0**	**0**	**0**	**0**	**0**	**0**	**0**	**0**	**0**	**0**	**0**	**0**

Figure 6.2. Blank *TO-WS* Worksheet

PROCEDURE

I call this analysis *TO-WS* because most experts agree this is the best sequence to consider:

1. External **T**hreats: It's easy to imagine what could go wrong.

2. External **O**pportunities: Since threats come easier, remind participants to refer to their personal list of prepared factors.

3. Internal **W**eaknesses: Participants are usually more sensitive about things going wrong than with what is positive.

4. Internal **S**trengths: Begin by referring to participants' personal notes.

To conduct this analysis, do the following:

- Have participants prepared to share their *TO-WS* factors in advance but keep them private. Let participants reference their personal notes as we proceed.

- Develop consensual lists and complete definitions (*Definition Tool*, chapter 6) for each threat, opportunity, weakness, and strength. If necessary, reduce each list to the top four to six factors; see *Categorizing* logic (chapter 6) and then use *PowerBalls* (chapter 7) for prioritizing, along with *Bookend Rhetoric* (chapter 7) to prevent wasting time.

  – As you build four different lists, describe each entry clearly and carefully. Threats and opportunities are externally uncontrolled and frequently represent trends. Weaknesses and strengths are internally controlled as viewed by competitors and outsiders.

– Build and enforce strong definitions and potential measurements behind each *TO-WS* item. For example, strength of "brand" could be measured as market share among target customers, or the threat of "transportation costs" could be indexed to the cost of a barrel of oil or price for a liter of diesel.

NOTE: While the four-list style for *Situation Analysis* is normally called SWOT, technically, there are only two lists, both with a positive and a negative end of their continuum. If the factor is external and you do not control it, by definition it must be a threat or an opportunity (TO). If the factor is internal and you control it, by definition it must be a weakness or a strength (WS).

REMEMBER: **NEVER** allow a group to define an internally controllable weakness as an opportunity for improvement. If it is controllable, by definition it is a weakness and not an opportunity.

- Create a definition package so that each of the characteristics scored is based upon agreed "operational definitions."

- Transfer your four lists into a matrix (usually a spreadsheet), with Threats (–) and Opportunities (+) on the horizontal axis and Strengths (+) and Weaknesses (–) on the vertical axis (because it is easier to visually focus with columns rather than rows).

- Remind participants that they are on the inside looking out and have them score, using instructions that follow.

- Aggregate the individual scores into a collective score. If you are using the spreadsheet, it will automatically calculate a group total.

- Review with the group to identify the most impactful *Actions*—strategies, initiatives, products, projects, or activities.

CRITICAL NOTE: Carefully enforce the operational level in your holarchy and meeting scope, because the strengths and weaknesses *must be* within control of *this group*, not simply the company or organization. For example, a department may not control its budget, so financial resources may be viewed as a threat to the group because they do not control the budget or financial assets.

Some questions to generate threats include these:

- What is your competition doing much better than you?

- What regulatory issues could stop or hinder progress?

- Which trends are a real threat to your organization or project?

NOTE: Some factors might include new or existing competitors, competitive alternatives, slowing market growth, adverse government policies, vulnerability to recession and macroeconomic factors, changing buyer needs or tastes, adverse demographic changes, and so on—but do not bias participants with content.

Some questions to generate opportunities include these:

- What opportunities are you not seizing yet but could see yourself doing with the right dedication?

- What changes on the horizon in political policy might help?

- Which trends provide a new opportunity for you?

NOTE: Some candidates might include new market opportunities, complacency among rivals, market growth, exogenous economic factors, regulatory trends, supply channel technology, vertical integration, and so on—but do not bias participants with content.

Some questions to generate weaknesses:

- What could you improve?

- What doesn't work so well?

- What do others outside do poorly and so do you?

- What should you stop doing?

NOTE: Some candidates might include lack of strategic direction, obsolete facilities, lack of management depth, operating issues, underperforming R&D, narrow product line, brand image, distribution network, marketing, financial prowess, excessive cost basis, and so on—but do not bias participants with content.

Some questions to generate strengths:

- How do you currently achieve success?

- What do you do better than others?

- What do you know works well?

- What do others outside view as your strengths?

NOTE: Some candidate strengths might include financial resources, purchasing power, economies of scale, patents, proprietary technology, cost advantage, brand image, marketing, product innovation, experience, and so on—but do not bias participants with content.

PARTICIPANT SCORING INSTRUCTIONS

- Working within each column (one external factor), *one at a time* ask: "What am I suggesting we do (to defend us against this specific threat or take advantage of this specific opportunity)?"

- As you decide on *what* to do, write down your most important ideas on a separate piece of paper to bring with you to the next meeting.

- You have nine points to be used in each column. Within each column, distribute the nine points according to the impact or perceived value of each proposed *Action* (*what* we should do to defend ourselves against a threat or seize an opportunity).

- The total for each column should equal nine points (see figure 6.3).

- Avoid assigning one point to multiple items by awarding the most significant items three, four, or more points.

- Strive to assign all nine points among not more than three cells in each column. Assigning nine points to only one cell is absolutely A-OK. Another tactic might be to assign five points to the most important, three points to the next important, and one point to the third most important cell, with the balance of the cells kept blank.

		Situational Threats (–)							Situation Opportunities (+)							
		Competition	Loyalty	Macroeconomic	Price	Suppliers	Trends	Threats Subtotals	Acquisition	Channels	Development	Licensing	Sourcing	Speed	Opportunities Subtotals	Totals
Situational Strengths (+)	Ethics					2		2							0	2
	Flexibility					2		2	1	4					5	7
	Infrastructure			1				1			1	3			4	5
	Reputation	1	5					6							0	6
	Resourcefulness	4					1	5		2	1		2		5	10
	Responsiveness		4				5	9			1		2	5	8	17
	Strengths Subtotals	5	9	1	0	4	6	25	1	6	3	3	4	5	22	47
Situation Weaknesses (–)	Accountability				1			1			2				2	3
	Communications							0			2			4	6	6
	Costs	4		6	3	5		18	4				5		9	27
	Operations			1	2			3							0	3
	Product			1	3		3	7	4			3			7	14
	Targeting							0		3	2	3			8	8
	Weaknesses Subtotals	4	0	8	9	5	3	29	8	3	6	6	5	4	32	61
	Totals	9	9	9	9	9	9	54	9	9	9	9	9	9	54	108

Figure 6.3. Illustrative One-Person *TO-WS* Worksheet

- Use your business understanding—a blank cell does not mean it is unimportant. Rather, it means it is less important than others that offer more impact or leverage. If you are compelled to assign similar values to everything, the results will be watered down and provide less value for developing *Actions* than if you focus on the most compelling *Actions*.

NOTE: Participants should think about each cell in a column carefully when asking "What do we need to do to defend against this threat?" or "What can we do to seize this opportunity?" They might write their thoughts on a separate sheet of paper and when they have completely analyzed a column, go to the cells that represent the most important ideas and put the most points in those cells.

Scoring Tabulation

- Collect the scoring. Using a spreadsheet, compute the final scores for each cell intersection, each column, each row, and each quadrant.[18]

- Review the scores with the group and highlight the rows and quadrants with the most significant (highest) scores.

- Immediately move to the next *Agenda Step* to convert the results into narrative *Actions*. Anticipate the "law of large numbers" as people speaking early will defend themselves with the "large numbers" from the aggregated spreadsheet (see figure 6.4).

NOTE: In quadrant analysis, proactive organizations will find most of their points allocated to the upper right quadrant, leveraging strengths to take advantage of opportunities. Reactive organizations will find most of their points in the lower left quadrant, shoring up their weaknesses to defend themselves against threats.

RIFFS AND VARIATIONS

1. Using *Bookend Rhetoric* (chapter 7), force-rank each strength or weakness specific to each external factor. For example, if there are 12 combined strengths and weaknesses, do the following for each column:

   - Instruct each participant to ask, "Of these 12 controllable factors, which has the greatest impact on (taking advantage of this opportunity) or (defending us against this threat)?" More is better, so assign the answer a 12.

---

[18] Time for technology. It once took a chief financial officer and me around 90 minutes to manually add up a dozen handwritten sheets with 169 cells each and come up with an aggregate scoring sheet.

		Situational Threats (–)							Situation Opportunities (+)							
		Competition	Loyalty	Macroeconomic	Price	Suppliers	Trends	Threats Subtotals	Acquisition	Channels	Development	Licensing	Sourcing	Speed	Opportunities Subtotals	Totals
Situational Strengths (+)	Responsiveness	11	20	7	3	5	20	66	0	11	6	3	10	27	57	123
	Resourcefulness	20	5	0	5	12	13	55	0	13	11	11	12	7	54	109
	Flexibility	9	3	13	2	11	13	51	11	20	8	1	2	10	52	103
	Reputation	15	23	3	0	8	2	51	0	2	5	13	6	1	27	78
	Infrastructure	0	1	11	1	0	1	14	8	7	10	0	2	4	31	45
	Ethics	0	19	0	0	12	1	32	0	0	0	2	5	0	7	39
	Strengths Subtotals	55	71	34	11	48	50	269	19	53	40	30	37	49	228	497
Situation Weaknesses (–)	Operations	5	2	10	13	3	0	33	13	8	5	0	1	8	35	68
	Accountability	3	3	5	14	6	6	37	7	0	12	12	10	8	49	86
	Targeting	4	6	2	5	6	7	30	8	18	14	21	0	0	61	91
	Communications	2	3	5	1	4	13	28	10	7	10	4	9	27	67	95
	Product	8	4	11	26	9	18	76	20	13	9	20	16	3	81	157
	Costs	22	10	32	29	23	5	121	22	0	9	12	26	4	73	194
	Weaknesses Subtotals	44	28	65	88	51	49	325	80	46	59	69	62	50	366	691
	Totals	99	99	99	99	99	99	594	99	99	99	99	99	99	594	1188

Figure 6.4. Illustrative 11-Person *TO-WS* Worksheet

- – Now instruct each participant to ask: "Of the remaining 11 factors, which has the least impact on . . . ?" Assign that factor a 1.

- – Continue using *Bookend Rhetoric* (chapter 7), which is next most, next least, and so on, until all have been assigned a rank.

- – Aggregate scores and continue to convert into *Actions* described in the next *Agenda Step*.

2. You might conduct *Quantitative TO-WS* for the current date and situation and then conduct another *Quantitative TO-WS* for some agreed-on date in the future. If forward-looking projections are reasonable, then the strategy can be unveiled by determining what *Actions* will get us from the current date to the future date.

3. To support change management, you could also conduct *Quantitative TO-WS* at varying levels within the organization. Contrasting the *Current Situation* at the C-suite, director, and supervisory levels provides interesting and compelling evidence as to *what Actions* need to occur that will get us from where we are to where we would like to be in the future.

TIMING

The *Quantitative TO-WS Analysis Agenda Step* takes from a few hours to a couple of days to complete, depending on the level in the holarchy being facilitated. To maintain cadence, limit the scoring grid to the top six of each category of strengths, weaknesses, opportunities, and threats. *PowerBalls* (chapter 7) can be used to complete quick prioritization within each of the four *TO-WS* categories.

CLOSURE

Technically, when the quantitative matrix is complete, this *Agenda Step* is also complete. The *Current Situation* is available immediately, albeit in numerical rather than narrative form. Therefore, the next *Agenda Step* called *Actions* converts the numbers into narrative expressions and follows seamlessly once the *Quantitative TO-WS Analysis* is complete. Move your agenda indicator to the next *Agenda Step—Actions* that result when translating the *Quantitative TO-WS Analysis* matrix.

7. Actions Agenda Step (What Are We Going to Do to Reach Our Measures?)

Actions articulate the *what* (needs to be done) portion of any plan; they constitute a segue, from human beings to human doings. Keep in mind that the term used to describe *Actions* changes depending on your level in the holarchy. For example, an organization will refer to its *Actions* as strategies, a business unit may use the term initiatives, a business department or program office may call its *Actions* products or projects, and a project team may call its *Actions* activities or tasks.

> NOTE: Be careful to distinguish the operational definitions of terms. "*The* strategy," "a strategy," and "a strategic plan" are not the same thing. The word "strategy" is like "quality" and has a life of its own. The term can, however, be used intelligently if it is used with clear perspective.
>
> Henry Mintzberg wisely differentiates between strategy *formation* ("strategies") and strategy *formulation* ("the Strategy"). The results of strategies are frequently used to shape the overall Strategy.

DELIVERABLE

A concise description and plan of *Actions*—what we will need to do to meet or exceed the *Key Measures* and thus ensure we reach our *Vision*. Each proposed *Action* indicates some level of priority and criticality.

> Any strategy, initiative, or project represents a program of action for reaching *Key Measures*. *Quantitative TO-WS Analysis* allows us to interpret what to do at any level in the holarchy, whether strategies, initiatives, projects, or activities—what needs to be done. I will refer to them collectively as *Actions*.

RELATIONSHIPS

Actions (or, *what*) are the core of any plan. The rest of the plan is meaningless without *Actions* to achieve results. *Actions* require revisiting the *Key Measures* (chapter 6) and *Quantitative TO-WS Analysis* (chapter 6). Each *Key Measure* should have at least one proposed *Action* in support of it. Each proposed *Action* should support at least one *Key Measure*.

> NOTE: Fortunately, we have the holarchy to keep this all straight. Regardless, whatever you call a strategy, it represents an *Action* that *must* support reaching at least one *Measure* (objective or goal) or else remain impotent and dormant—hardly a strategy.

TIMING

The numeric conversion from *Quantitative TO-WS Analysis* into *Actions* takes a few hours. People know what they had in mind when they completed their assessment of the *Current Situation*. The question now is straightforward: What should we do differently tomorrow to reach our goals and objectives, which have been lined up to ensure that we get to our *Vision* (chapter 6)? It also takes longer to develop consensual agreement around organizational strategies than equivocal *Actions* for product or project teams.

CLOSURE

Since executing *Actions* will consume resources, mostly time and money, advocates are sensitive to the amount of investment required. Additionally, since responsibility for the *Actions* will be assigned to participants in the room, advocates will not recommend *Actions* they are incapable of leading successfully. So when participants appear satisfied, move immediately on to *Alignment* (next section). We can always return later for ideas about other *Actions*. Remember your analogy and move the agenda indicator for a smooth transition.

ILLUSTRATIVE ACTIONS

In the example in figure 6.5, without going into too much detail, this group might have recommended a dozen or more strategies. Referring to "large numbers" for support, translation might have resulted in something like the following:

1. (32) "Given our excessive cost basis, we could reduce the cost of our working capital by retiring our expensive, long-term debt."

2. (26) "Our excessive costs are a problem. Additionally, we need to get closer to the source of our manufacturing. We are sitting here in North America while all our product is being produced in China. We need to get closer to the source of our product and open an office in China."

		Situational Threats (–)							Situation Opportunities (+)							
		Competition	Loyalty	Macroeconomic	Price	Suppliers	Trends	Threats Subtotals	Acquisition	Channels	Development	Licensing	Sourcing	Speed	Opportunities Subtotals	Totals
Situational Strengths (+)	Responsiveness	11	20	7	3	5	20	66	0	11	6	3	10	27	57	123
	Resourcefulness	20	5	0	5	12	13	55	0	13	11	11	12	7	54	109
	Flexibility	9	3	13	2	11	13	51	11	20	8	1	2	10	52	103
	Reputation	15	23	3	0	8	2	51	0	2	5	13	6	1	27	78
	Infrastructure	0	1	11	1	0	1	14	8	7	10	0	2	4	31	45
	Ethics	0	19	0	0	12	1	32	0	0	0	2	5	0	7	39
	Strengths Subtotals	55	71	34	11	48	50	269	19	53	40	30	37	49	228	497
Situation Weaknesses (–)	Operations	5	2	10	13	3	0	33	13	8	5	0	1	8	35	68
	Accountability	3	3	5	14	6	6	37	7	0	12	12	10	8	49	86
	Targeting	4	6	2	5	6	7	30	8	18	14	21	0	0	61	91
	Communications	2	3	5	1	4	13	28	10	7	10	4	9	27	67	95
	Product	8	4	11	26	9	18	76	20	13	9	20	16	3	81	157
	Costs	22	10	32	29	23	5	121	22	0	9	12	26	4	73	194
	Weaknesses Subtotals	44	28	65	88	51	49	325	80	46	59	69	62	50	366	691
	Totals	99	99	99	99	99	99	594	99	99	99	99	99	99	594	1188

Figure 6.5. Highlighted *TO-WS* Worksheet

3. (27) "Customers value our responsiveness, and we could do an even better job by installing a new Radio Frequency Identification (RFID) Warehouse Management System (WMS)."

4. And so on!

Actions Tool

Using the law of large numbers, participants convert numerical scores from their *Quantitative TO-WS Analysis* into the *what* (needs to be done) portion of any plan.

PROCEDURE

- Using their *Quantitative TO-WS Analysis* (have participants convert their numeric values into narrative *Actions (what).*

- Initially write down candidate *Actions* without discussion—for example, "retire long-term debt" or "open up an office in China." Apply the logic of *Brainstorming* (chapter 6), and do *not* allow discussion or additional details until the initial listing is complete.

- Now return to the list and fully define each *Action*—considering *Key Measures* (chapter 6) and SMART standards—for example, "retire 100 percent of 20_____ issued Senior Unsecured Class B Convertible Bonds by July 1, 20_____"; or "rappel up the northern face of the mountain to be at 5,000 meters protected in our tents when the storm erupts at 4:00 UDT."

NOTE: You may also look at the totals in each row of your *Situation Analysis* to see which strengths or weaknesses provide the greatest impact on reaching the *Key Measures.*

- Be prepared to use *Definitions* (chapter 6) to fully define terms and make proposed *Actions* truly SMART.

- There is no need to prioritize the *Actions*, because the next *Agenda Step* will confirm *Alignment* and display the priorities.

ALTERNATIVE SOURCES FOR PROPOSED ACTIONS

Alternatively, or additionally, you may ask the participants to describe *what Actions* they plan to perform—for example:

- Presentations to explain and/or request funding

- Completing details on their portion of the drafted plan

- Follow-up meetings, with smaller teams

- Revisions contingent on securing additional information

RIFFS AND VARIATIONS

The more thoroughly you have developed answers to the following questions, the quicker and easier *Actions* will proceed. Answers to the following questions stimulate conversations by clarifying intent when participants convert scores from the *Quantitative TO-WS Analysis* back into narrative expressions.

Business Definition

- What customer needs do you satisfy, or pains do you focus on?

- What customer segments are not being served?

- What market characteristics change with time?

- Where do you (or this product) add the most amount of value?

Key Success Factors (KSFs) (or CSFs or KPIs)

- What core competencies (skills and abilities) does your group control well enough to distinguish itself from competitors?

- What changes do you expect in your KSFs over the next five years?

- What key factors differentiate between the winners and the losers?

- What makes the difference between success or failure in your business?

- What new competencies must you develop in the next few years to align with the changing KSFs?

- To what extent do your current competencies support the current KSFs?

COMPETITIVE ANALYSIS

Consider including or building competitive analysis to predict competitors' future behaviors.

- Compare KSFs to each significant competitor, scoring or ranking.

- For each, note what are their significant strengths and weaknesses, so that you can become competitive with their strengths and take advantage of their weaknesses.

- Identify unique core competencies for your competitors that could lead to competitive advantages and set up actions to alleviate that from occurring.

- What future competitive maneuvers are projected in the next few years (consider *Scenario Planning*, chapter 8)?

8. Alignment Agenda Step (Is This the Right Stuff?)

Alignment compares each proposed *Action* (chapter 6) against each *Key Measure* (chapter 6). Building consensus around *Alignment* helps groups identify gaps, omissions, and overkill (wasted resources) to confirm appropriateness and balance from the proposed *Actions*.

> DEFINED: *Alignment* induces the judgment that the proposed *Actions* are the right things to do—there are no gaps or redundancies to calibrate or fix.

DELIVERABLE

Identification of any missing *Actions*, deletion of *Actions* that cause unnecessary overlap, or modifications of *Actions* required to establish proper balance among proposed *Actions* and resource allocations.

RELATIONSHIPS

Alignment ensures that there are enough *Actions* (strategies, programs, projects, or activities) to reach every *Key Measure* and that none of the proposed *Actions* are consuming too many resources for the benefits to be realized.

PROCEDURE

Use the *Alignment Tool* in the next section. There you will find the intersection of each criterion (*Key Measure*) with each strategy (proposed *Action*) fully explained, resulting in a diagram (see table 6.4).

CLOSURE

Alignment may cause additional or deleted *Actions*. Once the group is comfortable that the final list of proposed *Actions* provides them with the confidence

Table 6.4. Illustrative Alignment

Criteria / Strategy	Profit	Revenue	Customer Satisfaction	. . .
Retire debt	◑	◯	◯	~~~
Office in China	◑	◯	◑	~~~
RFID WMS	◯	◑	●	~~~
. . .	~~~	~~~	~~~	~~~

that they will indeed reach the *Key Measures* (specified to ensure reaching the *Vision*), move on to *Roles and Responsibilities* (chapter 6). Remember your analogy, and move the agenda indicator for a smooth transition.

Alignment Tool

Alignment compares your options to your decision criteria. For our purposes, in what follows, the *Actions* (chapter 6) represent options, and the *Measures* (chapter 6) represent decision criteria. Normally, building consensus around *Alignment* can be challenging, especially relying on narrative analysis. Here, *PowerBall* icons (figure 6.6) are appropriate and powerful.

PROCEDURE

Proposed *Actions* (options) are aligned against *Key Measures* (criteria):

- Create a matrix of the *Actions* and the *Measures*.

- Analyze the matrix, cell by cell, but always be precise when asking the open-ended question "To what extent does X (*Action*—option or strategy) support Y (*Measure*—target, goal, or objective)?"

- Having defined *PowerBalls* (preferably with a wall-mounted or media-projected legend), label each cell with either a high, low, or moderate *PowerBall* symbol, indicating the extent to which the *Action* supports the *Measure*.

- After the grid is filled, look at each column, one at a time, and use the following verbatim for each *Key Measure*: "Do we have enough *Actions* going on to ensure we will reach or exceed *Key Measure* _____?"

- Ask the group to confirm completeness. Add any missing *Actions* or modify as required (for example, change or calibrate an *Action*).

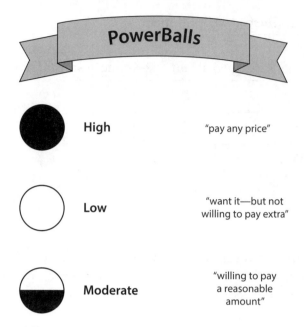

Figure 6.6. PowerBalls

- If there is any uncertainty, consider adding a new *Action*. To identify the next best available *Action*, return to your *Quantitative TO-WS Analysis* (chapter 6).

NOTE: Each *Action* must support at least one *Key Measure*. Each *Key Measure* must have sufficient *Actions* to enable success.

ALIGNMENT INTERPRETATION

We learn from the *Alignment* matrix (in table 6.5) that the mentoring strategy (option) will have the greatest impact supporting the goals (criteria). Facility expansion has the least impact. We also see that the expansion criterion is receiving the greatest support, while the confidence criterion is receiving the least support. The impact of marketing and fundraising is comparable while the support behind the knowledge and leadership goals is also comparable.

If confidence was our most important goal, we would need to add an additional strategy. If expansion is not that important, we would kill the infrastructure strategy and redeploy the financial resources to more important strategies.

9. Responsibility Matrix (Who Does What by When?)

Define the roles and responsibilities for any project, plan, or group using a *Responsibility Matrix*.

Table 6.5. Alignment Illustration

Goal/ *Strategy*	Confidence	Leadership	Relations	Knowledge	Expansion
Mentoring, community involvement	◑	●	●	●	○
Community awareness, marketing	◑	◑	◑	◑	●
Fundraising	◑	◑	◑	◑	●
Facility expansion, infrastructure	○	○	◑	○	●

RASI—RESPONSIBLE, AUTHORIZES, SUPPORTS, INFORMED

In the *Responsibility Matrix*, you develop assignments for making the *Actions* (chapter 6) come to life. Remember, begin by importing the *Actions* confirmed in the prior *Agenda Step* along with the business units, departments, functions, roles, or titles to be represented during the session.

> NOTE: Avoid using participants' names or making assignments to some person or position not in attendance or being represented. Rather, assign to business units, organizations, departments, or positions. If an individual departs or is reassigned, that person's replacement will inherit the assignments.
>
> Some organizations use a C for Consults instead of an S. Because "consults" can be a nebulous term (contronym), avoid using it. With Consult, it is never clear whether I am giving them something or they are giving me something. If both, then the code should be an "S," because Supporters both give and receive.

DELIVERABLE

RASI completes the plan by assigning "*who* does *what*, by *when*" and develops consensual understanding about each participant's *Roles and Responsibilities*.

PROCEDURE

Use the *Roles and Responsibilities Tool* that follows.

CLOSURE

The *Responsibility Matrix* ensures that we leave the meeting with our deliverable, consensual understanding about *who* does *what*. The assignments provide confidence that the plan the group developed will be implemented. Remember your analogy, and move the agenda indicator for a smooth transition.

Roles and Responsibilities Tool

PROCEDURE

Build the following matrix at any level of the holarchy. Your *what* (*Actions*, chapter 6) or assignments may take the form of different terms including strategies, initiatives, programs, projects, activities, or tasks (see figure 6.7).

As you increase the resolution from the abstract (for example, strategy) to the concrete (for example, task), expect to increase the resolution of the role or title of the responsible party. For example, strategies may get assigned to business units, while tasks get assigned to individual roles such as business analyst or product owner.

The *who* dimension might include business units, departments, roles, or people but must be consistent across the board and match closely to the appropriate level of responsibility for the nature of *what* needs to be done. For each *Action* item, define one of five areas of support:

- **R** = Responsible—is held responsible for successful completion—should be *one and only one*

- **A** = Authorizes—pays for the assignment—could be more than one

- **S** = Supports—assists in completing the assignment—could be many

- **I** = Informed—is kept informed of the progress or results—could be many

- **Blank**—if irrelevant, simply leave it blank

WHO/WHAT	Finance	Distribution	Marketing	Human Resources	etc.
Retire Debt	R			I	
Office in China	S	S	I	R	
RFID WMS	S	R			
etc.					

In the example, the A in RASI is the Board of Directors. They will authorize all the strategies.

Figure 6.7. Basic Roles and Responsibilities Illustration

In portrait view, when using an easel or flip chart, write the *who* (units, job names, and so on) across the top and the tasks, jobs, projects, and so on down the left-hand side (the *what*). In landscape view, build a matrix on a whiteboard or other large writing area with the *what* across the top and the *who* down the left-hand side.

> CAUTION: The biggest challenge facilitating a RASI chart remains the mechanics. You must plan the mechanics of building the matrix well in advance. Large whiteboards, flip charts, or electronic spreadsheets or templates are the most conventional means to capture the information. You can always make it pretty after the session is completed.

First, consider footnoting the *A* since it is likely that the person or group with authority has authority for the entire scope of work. If not, record unique or shared *A*'s as appropriate.[19]

Next, and most important, is the **Big Bold *R***—one and only one per assignment. For each *Action*, determine who will be responsible to ensure that you have enough time to complete. Whether you use paper, whiteboard, or electronic means, use a bright **Big Bold *R*** to document responsibility for each *Action*.

> NOTE: Remember, one and only one Big BOLD *R*. Do not allow people to be "nice" and share responsibility. If you do, you risk finger-pointing later: "I thought he was working on this," and "I thought she was working on this." Confusion arises because we were too nice.

Time permitting, consider capturing the deadline, resource request (for example, FTP or currency value to complete the assignment) so that you can convert your RASI chart into a project planning tool such as a Program Evaluation Review Technique (PERT) chart, a Gantt chart,[20] a value stream diagram, and so on (see next section). Time permitting, go back and work horizontally across each *Action* to complete the other relationships (cells) as appropriate with an *S* or an *I* or leave it blank.

Follow these rules:

- At least one *A* who is not the *R*—may be more than one

- One and only one *R* per assignment (that is, for each *Action*)

> NOTE: I call this the "power of a cell" (figure 6.8). Rather than using all of the available space for one letter, break the cell into four sections. When the information is available or can be approximated, also capture the approximate financial resources required to support the action, an estimated due date, and approximately how much time or labor is

---

[19] For figure 6.7, *A = Board of Directors since they are Authorizing the proposed *Actions*.
[20] A Gantt chart illustrates a project schedule and is named after its creator, Henry Gantt.

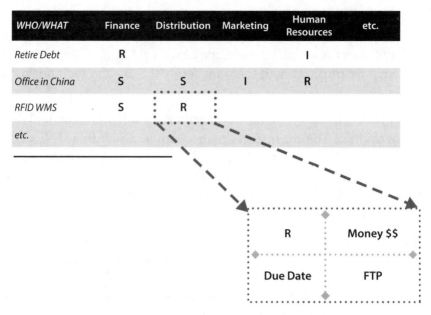

WHO/WHAT	Finance	Distribution	Marketing	Human Resources	etc.
Retire Debt	R			I	
Office in China	S	S	I	R	
RFID WMS	S	R			
etc.					

R	Money $$
Due Date	FTP

Figure 6.8. Enhanced Roles and Responsibilities Illustration

estimated to be consumed (FTP). Allow subject matter experts a range of freedom, such as plus or minus 50 or even 100 percent. Each cell captures an estimate, not a budget.

Here are some, but not all, real-life variations of the *Responsibility Matrix* being used today:

- AERI (Endorsement)
- ALRIC
- ARCI
- CAIRO
- CARS (Communicate, Approve, Responsible, and Support)
- DACI (Driver, Approver, Consulted, and Informed)
- DRACI (Drives)
- DRAM (Deliverables Review and Approval Matrix)
- LACTI (Lead, Tasked)
- PACSI (Performed, Accountable, Control, Suggested, and Informed)
- PARIS
- RACI (Responsible, Accountable, Consult, Informed)

- RACI-V

- RACI+F (F = Facilitator)

- RACIA (+Approve)

- RACIB (+Blame)

- RASCI

- RASCIO (+Omitted)

- RASI (Supports NOT Consults)

- RASIC

10. Communications Plan (What Do We Agree to Tell Others?)

It's a clever idea to sound like we were all in the same meeting together. The *Communications Plan* may also be referred to as the *Guardian of Change*.

DELIVERABLE

Here you build a communications plan to report back to others on what was accomplished during the session. The *Communications Plan* adds extraordinary value, especially when there are translation or transliteration challenges as well.

PROCEDURE

Use the *Communications Plan Tool* that follows.

> NOTE: Empirical research shows that it is better to guard and protect messages than to simply shout out. Different audiences may need distinct messages and may react differently to descriptive terms used and the media or form used to communicate the messages.

PROJECT REPORTING

Consider a *3*30 Report*, a written summary of results that should take no longer than 30 minutes to write and no longer than three minutes to read and reply. The *3*30 Report* may be ideal to direct at executives and other team members who are interested but not fully invested.

EASY VARIATION

At the very least identify a consensually agreed-on message that answers one or both of the following questions:

- "The most important thing we should do tomorrow is _____ ."

- "If we do nothing else tomorrow, we must _____ ."

CLOSURE

This *Agenda Step* nearly concludes your *Planning Meeting*. Final review occurs in the next *Review and Wrap Agenda Step*. When your *Communications Plan* is complete, immediately move on to your *Review and Wrap*.

Communications Plan Tool

At minimum, team members need an "elevator speech" that can deliver an effective synopsis of the meeting results. At the other extreme, if the meeting is strategic, there could be numerous audience types such as the investment community, regulators, trade personnel, and so on. If so, identify the key audience members before determining the message, medium of communication, and frequency of communication for each.

PROCEDURE

When it is important that it sounds like the participants attended the same meeting together, consider agreeing on the rhetoric and specific terms used (or *not* used) to describe meeting results. Typically, at least two major audiences are intended:

- What do we tell our bosses or superiors we got done in here today?

- What do we tell stakeholders or other people dependent on our output if they ask?

I use a basic T-Chart with two column headings, such as "Superiors" and "Stakeholders." Next, ask the group for their "elevator speech" or "coffeepot" description or "water cooler" messages for each column.

COMPLEX VARIATION

After identifying multiple target audiences, ask for each, "What are we going to tell _____?" List the messages as bullet points intended to homogenize (create consistency) the meeting participants' messages as they talk in the hallway about what was accomplished.

If necessary, identify *how* to communicate with the target audience such as face-to-face, by email, and so on. For even more complex communication plans, further determine frequency or how often to set up regular communications.

COMMUNICATIONS PLAN

An actual *Communications Plan* involving multiple audiences, messages, vehicles, and timing should be taken one step at a time since there is a one-to-many relationship throughout. Each audience may require multiple messages, and each message may require multiple delivery methods and each delivery method may require scheduling or sequencing. So, identify one at a time . . .

- Audiences for communications

- Messages to be delivered (to each)

  - Sequence of the messages

- Vehicles for delivery (for each)

  - Sequencing of the vehicles

- Timing of communications (for each)

  - Layering who hears what and when

NOTE: It may be necessary to schedule the communications so that the superiors are informed before other stakeholders. Failing to plan, meeting participants will use varying methods and different rhetoric that may cause confusion among stakeholders and potentially problems as well. Amplify this confusion when there are additional language translation requirements.

11. Review and Wrap (Conclusion) Agenda Step

Follow the four-activity sequence for the *Review and Wrap* more fully explained in chapter 5. None of the four activities should ever be skipped entirely, so expand and contract based on your situation and constraints.

NOTE: Daniel Pink's research on timing (2018) indicates the *Review and Wrap* is more important than a smooth *Launch* because the recency effect of "what did we accomplish in that meeting" reverberates louder and stronger in the hallways than the primacy effect of a smooth beginning.

ACTIVITIES

1. *Review*: Do not relive the meeting; simply review the outputs, decisions, assignments, and so on. Focus on the results and deliverable of each *Agenda Step* and not on how you got there. Participants do not need a transcript of the meeting; they need to be reminded about the takeaways and to be offered the opportunity to ask for additional information or clarification before the meeting ends.

2. *Open issues and follow-up:* There are various methods and treatments of open items and formal assignments, such as roles and responsibilities. Once post-meeting assignments are clear, the meeting is almost over.

3. Skip *Guardian of Change* because a *Communications Plan* was completed in the prior *Agenda Step*. For *Meeting Approaches* that did not include the *Guardian of Change* as a separate *Agenda Step,* invest a few

minutes to get the group to agree on what they are going to tell others when asked, "What happened in that meeting?"

4. *Assessment:* Get feedback on how you did. Set up or mark a whiteboard by the exit door and create two columns, typically *Plus* and *Delta* (the Greek letter Δ, which stands for "change"). Have each participant write down on a small Post-it note at least one thing they liked about the meeting (+) and one thing they would change (Δ). Ask participants to mount each note in its respective column when departing the room.

QUALITY CONTROL

Effective leaders will not disband their meetings until participants have been offered a final opportunity to comment or question, actions have been assigned, messaging has been agreed to, and feedback for continuous improvement has been solicited.

Quick Summary on Planning

You now have both the tools and logic to facilitate any type of planning session, from the boardroom to the boiler room. Stay focused on the questions rather than terms like *Mission*. Structure your logic so that *why* comes before *what* comes before *how*.

I find it interesting that the input to planning is *why* and the output is *what*. If you conduct further analysis during project or product support, you will discover that the input is *what* and the output is *how*—the trichotomy, or transformation from the abstract to the concrete.

> NOTE: While executive teams go off-site for strategic planning, it's unlikely they will permit the accounts payable department to go to an island resort to conduct planning. However, the accounts payable department is entitled to answers to the same questions, such as these:
>
> – Why are we here?
>
> – Where are we going?
>
> – What are our success measures?
>
> – What are we doing to succeed?

Therefore, while we may not complete a discrete *Mission, Values,* and *Vision* for accounts payable, we still need to know why the department exists, what it is doing to help the organization reach its *Measures,* and so on. Therefore, in chapter 7, "Deciding about Anything," we will learn about the *Purpose Tool* (chapter 7), a powerful device that integrates *Mission* (chapter 6), *Values* (chapter 6), and *Vision* (chapter 6) into one cohesive expression.

7

Deciding about Anything Approach

AGREE ON THE *WHY* BEFORE THE *WHAT*

Frequently you discover that people have similar purposes, values, and criteria, and yet they cannot agree. Why? People cannot agree because they have different priorities. For example, when choosing a new car, everyone values appearance and clean air. Yet while some prefer an aesthetically attractive appearance more than power efficiency, others may be unwilling to sacrifice their concern for carbon displacement, preferring a hybrid, even if an affordable hybrid for them looks less fashionable.

Significant business decisions are much more complex than personal vehicle decisions. This chapter shows you how to forge consensual decisions by developing purpose, options, and decision criteria. This chapter also provides another dozen *Tools* to guide you through simple, complicated, and complex decision-making for any type of group, organization, or situation.

Decision-Making Options

While there are highly elaborate forms of voting and authoritarian decisions, three forms of decision-making dominate the business landscape:

1. Authoritarian—decision made by a sole source such as a person or group

2. Voting—formal or informal; used when the leader is incapable or lacking the time or knowledge required to build consensus

3. Consensus—an interactive method particularly helpful when the deliverable is complicated, or an elevated level of commitment and ownership is required of the participants to yield successful results

Voting Sucks

Eric Maskin and Amartya Sen considered Kenneth Arrow's *Impossibility Theorem*, which established a series of mathematical proofs based on Condorcet's work. Suppose a nine-person leadership team that wants to cut costs looks at three options: (a) closing plants, (b) moving from a direct sales force to distributors, and (c) reducing benefits and pay.[1]

> **—Kevin Dutton, "The Power to Persuade," *Scientific American Mind* (2010)**
>
> *Context is everything: a fancy label and a high price can fool people into thinking that wine tastes better than wine from seemingly cheaper bottles.*

While any executive can rank their preferences, it is mathematically possible for a majority to simultaneously support each alternative. Five members might prefer "closing plants" to "moving sales to distributors" (a > b), and a distinct set of five might prefer "moving sales" to "reducing benefits and pay" (b > c). Through the transitive property, "closing plants" should be preferred to "reducing benefits and pay" (a > c). The paradox is that five members could rank "reducing benefits and pay" over "closing plants" (c > a).

Maskin and Sen demonstrate that no voting method—neither allocation of points nor rank-ordering of choices—will generate a shared favorite. Although this concept is frequently understood in political science and economics, it is rarely acknowledged in organizational management. Understanding the paradox of the impossibility theorem improves the likelihood that you will build consensus, because the theorem proves that the best decision might not be anyone's favorite.

Three Requirements for Any Decision

Whether you are deciding which new software to use, which product to develop, or which corporate acquisition will be your most valuable target, three building blocks are required for all decisions, simple (personal) and complex (consensual).[2]

1. Purpose of the object (for example, vehicle, product, or corporate acquisition)

2. Options[3]

---

[1] Eric Maskin and Amartya Sen, *The Arrow Impossibility Theorem* (2014).

[2] I encourage a fourth activity, testing for decision quality, so that you can avoid another meeting.

[3] Some styles call these "alternatives," but strictly speaking, in the English language, an alternative is one of two. If there are more than two, they are called options.

3. Criteria

4. Testing (optional but encouraged)

PURPOSE OF THE OBJECT

Even if you purchase a new shirt or blouse, you first determine *why*. Your *purpose* has a significant impact on deselecting. If you need a T-shirt for exercising, you won't be looking at dress shirts with French cuffs. Conversely, if you plan to attend a formal wedding, T-shirts are not an appropriate style to consider.

OPTIONS

For a new blouse, brick-and-click retail establishments provide lots of *options*—in the store, racks and retail displays of products, and online, page after page of shirts and blouses. How do you decide? If you visit a store, you may even take less shopping time than you will online. Why? Because there are fewer options in a store to consider than when you shop online.

CRITERIA

At the same time you will consider your selection *criteria*. For a standard T-shirt, you may consider features such as availability, brand, color, country of origin, fabric, quantity, price, size, style, weave, and so on. The human mind integrates all your decision criteria into one sparkline representing the optimal profile you seek.[4]

If the shirt or blouse on the shelf or your screen has an identical sparkline, the deal is done. Since this rarely occurs, you evaluate the variances. When you are assessing, you also allocate value according to the relative importance or weighting of your criteria, thus complicating your decision further.

As implied by the sparklines in figure 7.1, availability for the dress shirt is much more important. There is a sense of urgency and timing for the wedding rather than the immediate need for another T-shirt. The brand of the dress shirt is also more important than the brand of the T-shirt, although brand is much less important than size for both shirts. There's more price sensitivity to the T-shirt, meaning that you are willing to pay more of a premium for the dress shirt than the T-shirt. And since the style of most dress shirts remains similar, the T-shirt style is more important since you may want to avoid a V-neck or tank top.

---

[4] A sparkline is a brief line including multivariable information. The term comes from Dr. Edward Tufte's remarkable work, much focused on the graphical and qualitative display of quantitative information. See *The Visual Display of Quantitative Information* (2001) and his other wonderful works.

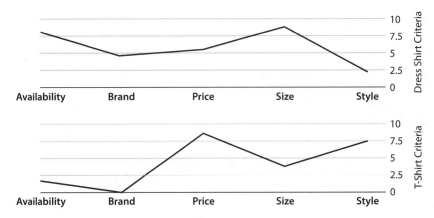

Figure 7.1. Large-Scale Sparklines of Shirt Profiles

NOTE: Personal plans and decisions (such as purchasing a new shirt or blouse) are both simpler and more concrete than business plans and decisions (such as launching a new product) that are more complex and abstract. However, both require the same three components to test for decision quality.

Two Scenarios

SCENARIO 1: NEW CLOTHING

Suppose you are making an individual decision, let's say some type of clothing, although it doesn't really matter because any decision-making requires all three components: purpose of the object, options, and criteria.

Deliverable

A decision about some object (for example, a shirt or blouse to buy).

Procedure

Although it happens so quickly as to be transparent to you, even for simple purchases, your mind will hastily consider purpose, options, and criteria. Therefore, to build consensual decisions around straightforward business decisions, use the seven *Agenda Steps* provided.

SCENARIO 2: RETIREMENT GIFT

Suppose you are asked by your leader to conduct a meeting and make a decision about what gift should be given to a valuable individual who is retiring. Since the example is both concrete (physical) and straightforward, the same *Basic Agenda* below works perfectly.

Deliverable

A decision about a retirement gift with budget of US$500 to be presented at a retirement party on October 1, 20__.

Procedure

Adapt, leverage, or modify the seven *Agenda Steps* below.

> NOTE: Adapt or modify this *Deciding Approach* whenever your group needs to prioritize or make a consensual decision. What changes will be the *Tool* you use to analyze your options against the criteria. This chapter provides nine new *Tools* to consider.

BASIC AGENDA

1. Launch (chapter 5)

2. Purpose of the object (for example, shirt or blouse, or retirement gift)[5]

3. Options (for the objects)

4. Criteria (about the objects)

5. Deselection and Decision (prioritization)

6. Testing (for decision quality)

7. Wrap (chapter 5)

NOTE: A quick comment on sequencing—indeed, you can invert the agenda sequence and build criteria before options. In fact, most un-trained groups usually begin with criteria; here's why.

They claim that starting with criteria is faster because you do not waste time on ideas that fall outside the parameters of the criteria. However, they also concede that the "answer" they develop is constrained and produces a result that is not innovative—a decision that remains "in the box" rather than outside of it.

My structured method suggests beginning with options when you seek innovation or breakthrough. Far-fetched ideas can lead to a practical alternative that no one thought of before. As a gift idea, a "trip to Tahiti" could lead to "digital binoculars for bird-watching" that no one considered until they deliberated about the question, "Why Tahiti?"

In addition, I am fastidious about the rules of *Brainstorming*, so while enforcing high energy, I do not permit *any* discussion during the

---

[5] Terms that are grayed out are for your eyes only and not to be shown on the *Basic Agenda* you provide meeting participants.

Listing activity.[6] If groups maintain high energy only for 6–8 minutes, then the most amount of time wasted is 6–8 minutes, yet I've increased the likelihood of an innovative result.

Visual Aids to Anticipate

- Meeting purpose, scope, and deliverables in writing. Use handouts or large-format paper for in-person meetings and optimally a handwritten and handheld artifact for online meetings.

- Basic and easily accessible agenda (included in the pre-read)—also a suitable candidate to use as an artifact for online meetings.

- Definitions for each of the key terms, especially *Options*, *Criteria*, and *Testing*.

- *Ground Rules* (chapter 4), readily available as a poster or as a handheld artifact.

- *PowerBalls* (chapter 7) and *Prioritization* legends (chapter 7).

- *Scorecard* or *Quantitative TO-WS Analysis* spreadsheets (chapter 6).

- *Parking Lot* and *Plus-Delta* (chapter 5).

1. Launch (Introduction) Agenda Step

Follow the seven-activity sequence for the *Launch*, which is fully explained in chapter 5. Keep in mind that the *Launch* is the "preachy" part for a meeting facilitator. My own *Annotated Agenda* for the *Launch* is always around three pages. If you want to rehearse anything, try explaining the white space behind your *Agenda Steps*—a terrific opportunity to develop confidence among your participants.

> NOTE: For multiple-day workshops, cover the same items at the start of subsequent days. Additionally, review content that was built during the preceding day or days and reinforce how that relates to the progress being made toward completing the deliverable.

Before you begin your meeting *Launch*, have your physical or virtual room set up to provide a visual display of the meeting purpose, scope, and deliverable. Let me repeat that if you do not know what the deliverable looks like, then you do not know what success looks like.

---

[6] The first person to normally violate this rule is the meeting facilitator making comments like "We already have that" or "What did you mean by that?" Look how often in a meeting the easel has two or three items after 20 minutes because the group is discussing each one. That is *not Brainstorming* and reflects an unstructured style not covered or encouraged by me or this book.

PROCEDURE

Follow these activities in this sequence for a robust start.

- Introduce yourself and stress the importance of meeting roles. Stipulate how much money or time is at risk if the session fails.

- Unveil your meeting purpose, scope, and deliverable. Seek audible assent from all. Ensure that all the participants can support them.

- Cover "administrivia" to clear participants' heads from thinking about themselves, especially their creature comfort. Explain where to locate lavatories, fire extinguishers, emergency exits, and other stuff they may be thinking about. Provide a check-in activity or icebreaker, especially for online meetings and workshops.

- Carefully explain the logic behind the sequence of your *Agenda Steps*. Explain how *Agenda Steps* relate to one another. Link *Agenda Steps* back to the deliverable so that participants see how completing each *Agenda Step* provides content that helps complete the deliverable.

- Share *Ground Rules* (chapter 4). Supplement your narrative *Ground Rules* with audiovisual support, including humorous clips, but keep them brief.

2. Purpose of the Object

The purpose of the object (gift, shirt, or business object) establishes the *why* before the *what*.

DELIVERABLE

A run-on sentence, 50 words or less, that describes the general purpose, reason, and rationale for the object. This may include some benefits and features but is not likely to include all of them.

RELATIONSHIPS

The purpose of the object establishes the foundation for the decision and enables trade-offs and prioritization. If the object is a gift and the purpose is to provide a gag gift, the decision will be entirely different, based on the purpose, not on the options or criteria. If the object is a shirt for a mud race, expect a decision different from a decision about a wedding shirt, based on the purpose.

PROCEDURE

Use the *Purpose Tool,* fully explained in the next section. Optionally, consider substituting *Breakout Teams* (chapter 6), *Creativity* (chapter 8), *Coat of Arms* (chapter 6), and *Categorizing* (chapter 6) to yield a 50-word (or shorter) expression that everyone supports.

In addition, I've included a wonderful transition *Tool* for *Agenda Steps* called the *Clarifying Tool* (chapter 7). In place of the overgeneralized question, "Can we move on?" substitute the *Clarifying Tool*, which confirms clarity, deletions, and additions by asking three discrete questions, before moving on to the next *Agenda Step.*

CLOSURE

Once the group is comfortable with the stated purpose of the object, apply your analogy, and move the agenda indicator for a smooth transition.

Purpose Tool

Understanding *why* is so critical to building consensus that it needs to be listed as a separate *Agenda Step,* even though it may take less than 10 minutes to accomplish. Use the *Purpose Tool* to construct a basic requirement[7] (I want X so that I can do Y) or to build consensual expressions that capture the benefits, intent, purpose, and reason for any scope of work.

This *Tool* is perhaps the best *Tool* in this book that you did not know about previously.

The *Purpose Tool* provides the group a consensually built foundation to reconcile arguments—and help galvanize consensus around the criteria, prioritization, and decision making that follow.

PROCEDURE

Either on one or two separate easels, or a split screen, build out the visual prompt in advance. Because the prompt itself is context and not content, use a nonprimary color: "The purpose of [insert object] is to . . . So that . . ."

- Prompt your participants: "The purpose of [insert object] is to . . ."

- Do not forget the word "to" because it forces a verb (an action).

- Maintain cadence. As you are scribing, if the room is silent, as you print the last word, prompt quickly with "so that . . . ," because you want to keep the energy high.

- I frequently say, "Why else do you want ____?" since this is the *why* before the *what.* You may also consider the "so that . . ." as the benefit or value-add.

- Use commas when you capture input as you are helping participants to build one long run-on sentence.

---

[7] The term "requirement" is abused and misunderstood. To me, it represents *who* does *what* by *when* for what purpose (*why*) and *how* they do it.

- Do not allow arguments whether something belongs in the "purpose is to . . ." section or the "So that . . ." section; in a run-on sentence, it does not matter where the clause is located.

- Likewise, do not allow arguments over whether something belongs at all. If one participant's purpose is X and another's purpose is Y, then the integrated purpose is X *and* Y, not X *or* Y. Be prepared to emphasize and defend this advice. If my purpose for the shirt is comfort and your purpose is style, than our integrated purpose is both comfort *and* style. We'll solve for how to accomplish both later.

- Do not wordsmith the results, but be certain to reread, review, and confirm that participants have created an expression that everyone can support. You have now created a strategic plan at the level of a business area or process or activity—*why* something is important.

- Refer to this statement during the meeting as an appeal to ensure that contributions support the purpose. If necessary, either take out-of-scope conversations and ask that they be placed in the *Parking Lot* (chapter 5) or go back and modify the purpose expression to include their concern.

> **The Purpose of _____ Is To . . .**
>
> **So That . . .**

Clarifying Tool

The *Clarifying Tool* makes it easy to clear up ambiguities that can impede progress.

WHY?

I have seen participants who were in violent agreement with each other but were using different definitions for terms or defined the same term differently. Additionally, and counterintuitively, we should slow down during transitions when most participants get confused. The *Clarifying Tool* helps in those situations.

PROCEDURE

"Scrubbing" means cleaning or clarifying input and any unedited lists or content:

1. What, if anything, remains unclear about _____ ? (clarity)

2. What, if anything, needs to be removed from _____ ? (deletions)

3. What, if anything substantive, needs to be added _____ ?
(additions)

NOTE: The last question does not ask for "anything." Rather, it speaks to something *substantive*—important or critical. Asking a group of smart people, "Is anything missing?" will usually result in something, typically with low-value yield.

3. Options (for the Object)

DELIVERABLE

A list of options, the myriad of objects from which to choose. Depending on the situation, these could range from a few (for example, half a dozen) to many (dozens). Use the *Definition Tool* (chapter 6) when a description of the option remains too vague to confirm that everyone shares the same understanding about specific attributes, characteristics, or features of an option.

PROCEDURE

Use any of the Listing activities suggested with *Brainstorming* (chapter 6). Facilitate a quick and thorough Listing with no discussion. Encourage all ideas because my procedures are self-correcting and will eliminate options that are inappropriate or unacceptable.

For example, when deciding on a retirement gift for someone, permit ideas that may be clearly beyond the budget. The subsequent Analysis activity might challenge the reasons for mentioning "ridiculous" options. Their rationale may provide insight into new and potentially powerful options not previously mentioned.

For example, the idea of a trip to Tahiti may reveal that our retiree loves bird-watching, and while we cannot afford to give a trip to Tahiti, further conversation unveils a new gift idea—a pair of digital binoculars with a built-in camera. An ideal gift option that did not "walk into the room"—rather, it was created in the room.

Use *Breakout Teams* (chapter 6), *Creativity* (chapter 8), and *Perspectives* (chapter 8) for generating additional options. The options for business decisions are rarely found on a shelf, so be prepared to inspire and stimulate your participants with *Warm-ups* (chapter 8). More ideas equate to higher-quality decisions, and when we apply *decision criteria* during the *Deciding Agenda Step*, suboptimal ideas will be eliminated.

CLOSURE

Once the group is comfortable with the list of options, apply your analogy and move the agenda indicator for a smooth transition. Remember, set this list aside and do not begin to talk about it or define items yet. We are still in a Listing mode, although next we will list the decision criteria.

4. Decision Criteria (for the Object)

DELIVERABLE

The result is a list of decision criteria, well defined and prioritized. Depending on the situation, these could range from a few (for example, half a dozen) to one or two dozen.

RELATIONSHIPS

Decision criteria capture the reasons for deselecting or getting rid of poor options. Whether you rely on narrative, graphic, or illustrative input, list decision criteria first and then *Clarify* (chapter 7) or use the *Definition Tool* (chapter 6) before you prioritize the decision criteria.

> NOTE: Please don't fall into the trap of prioritizing your options. First, you need to prioritize your decision criteria. Then, you will apply prioritized decision criteria to your *options*. When buying a shirt or a blouse, size is especially important and usually has a higher priority than material or weave—so size is a prioritized decision criterion. Begin the Analysis activity by prioritizing decision criteria.

PROCEDURE

While engaging in some Listing activity associated with *Brainstorming* (chapter 6), do not mandate or enforce that "all ideas will be allowed." Here we are restricting ourselves to appropriate reasons. Embrace the sense of "no discussion," but also confirm appropriateness if there is any doubt.

Some assumptions may be brought into the scenario that also function as decision criteria. Using the retirement gift example, budget and timing must be respected as high-priority decision criteria. The organization may also issue other mandates such as the need to include the company logo on the items selected.

> NOTE: A decision about the retirement gift might include more than one item. See the *SCAMPER Tool* (chapter 8) for additional questions to ask.

Use *Breakout Teams* (chapter 6), *Categorizing* (chapter 6), and *Perspectives* (chapter 8) for generating additional decision criteria. With *Breakout Teams*, when more than one team returns with the same or similar criteria, consensus becomes (almost) automatic. Use the *Definition Tool* (chapter 6) when there appears to be misunderstanding about any specific attributes, characteristics, or features of the decision criteria.

CLOSURE

Once the group is comfortable with the decision criteria, apply your analogy, and move the agenda indicator to *Deciding* for a smooth transition.

5. Deselecting and Decision

DELIVERABLE

The result is a consensually agreed-on decision, selection, or determination of the object (for example, a retirement gift).

RELATIONSHIPS

Deselecting and *Decision* smash together the options and decision criteria. One size does not fit all. Therefore, in the pages that follow, I will look at seven *Tools* to guide you from simple decisions through complicated ones and even complex decisions. Additionally, you can use the *PowerBalls Tool* (chapter 7) to make the other *Tools* more effective.

> NOTE: The word "decide" comes from "to cut off," from *de* ("off") and *caedere* ("to cut").

PROCEDURE

If an apparent consensual decision has not become evident or has not been promoted by someone immediately:

- Eliminate any options that do not satisfy mandatory requirements such as not exceeding budget.

- Eliminate any options participants personally object to after they give specific reasons for their objection and those reasons are considered valid by others. Once everyone has rejected their own personal "pet peeves," then technically you have consensus, although you don't yet have your decision or deliverable.

- By deselecting we are eliminating objectionable options and can optimize the decision even further by using a tool for applying prioritized decision criteria to the surviving options.

Numerous *Tools* are appropriate for prioritizing depending on the type of qualitative or quantitative *Criteria*. Let's look at prioritization *Tools*, beginning with simple situations, next more complicated situations, and finally complex situations (see figure 7.2).

Simple Criteria: Use PowerBalls or Estimation

The simplest and most frequently used *PowerBalls Tool* (chapter 7) provides quick support, especially for deselecting. Keep in mind that it is quicker to get a group to deselect, making it easier to focus on the best candidates.

> CAUTION: Do not use *PowerBalls* without using *Bookend Rhetoric* (chapter 7).

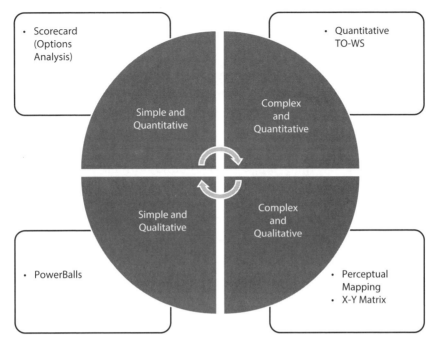

Figure 7.2. Prioritization Tools

Complicated Criteria: Use Decision Matrix or Weighted Scorecard

When the basic *PowerBalls Tool* is insufficient alone, particularly when there are dozens of *Decision Criteria* or many of the criteria can be assigned quantitative values, consider the *Decision Matrix* or *Scorecard Tool.*

Complicated Criteria: Use X-Y Decision Matrix

Whether we take the time to build a comprehensive *Decision Matrix* (chapter 7) or not, decisions could be arrayed on a single sheet or slide that compares each option with each criterion. We can use the *PowerBall Tool* to ascertain the degree of impact each *Option* provides against each criterion. When you have spent most of your time in a management meeting on one slide in your deck, the *Decision Matrix* is that slide.

Complicated Criteria: Use Weighted Scorecard

The *Scorecard Tool* (chapter 7) may be an entire meeting by itself. It may also fail to yield "the decision." However, it builds solid consensus around what *not* to select. By eliminating some of the options, your group can focus on the best options by appealing to some of the subjective criteria (for example, "strategic fit") or even taking a "test drive." Information technology groups isolate the best candidates to test, avoiding the time and expense of testing marginal options. As if you were purchasing a new vehicle, the *Scorecard Tool* helps generate the top three to five candidates that you might want to test drive further, without being required to drive dozens of vehicles (or middleware applications).

Complex Criteria: Use Perceptual Map

When your situation remains too complicated for the *PowerBalls Tool* and yet most of your criteria remain qualitative and abstract, array your options within *Perceptual Maps* (chapter 7). Yes, that's plural. No law prohibits you from building more than one *Perceptual Map*. Consider using the *PowerBalls Tool* to isolate the most critical decision criteria and then transpose them to numerous two-by-twos so that you can visually compare your options.

With *Perceptual Maps*, groups can leverage pattern analysis. You are not restricted to one *Perceptual Map*; when you build multiple maps, patterns appear that make it easier to secure consensus:

1. Weak candidates consistently show poorly and therefore are eliminated, frequently without any further conversation.

2. Strong candidates reappear, and when you get a group of smart people to focus on the same thing at the same time, magic happens. You can discover a cure or get to Mars faster than you ever thought possible.

Highly Complex Criteria: Use Quantitative TO-WS Analysis (Chapter 6)

An approach that helps analyze dozens of internally controllable Strengths and Weaknesses against dozens of externally uncontrollable Opportunities and Threats, empowering groups to prioritize hundreds of options.

Highly Complex Criteria: Use Real-Win-Worth

When your situation becomes extremely complex, understand the logic, and then adapt the questions recommended for a *Real-Win-Worth* (chapter 7) analysis. It includes three stages to minimize wasted time. In sequence, *Real-Win-Worth* analysis helps you understand . . .

1. Is the solution, decision, product, or project **Real**? (if not, go no further)

2. Given the solution, decision, product, or project, can we **Win**? (if not, go no further)

3. What is the solution, decision, product, or project **Worth**?

CLOSURE

Once the group is comfortable with its decision, apply your analogy, and move the agenda indicator to *Testing* to ensure decision quality and thus avoid the worst deliverable from any meeting: another meeting.

> NOTE: If all these *Tools* fail, take a break. Regather. Resuscitate. Rejuvenate. Gestate. During the entire history of humankind, it has never been recorded that a meeting participant was disappointed when the

leader said, "We're going to take a break." Alternatively, refer to the four activities for *Conflict Management* (chapter 4), based on appealing to your organizational objectives.

PowerBalls Tool

PowerBalls are truly powerful. They transport iconic, narrative, and numeric meaning and intent. They are simple to use and highly flexible. In fact, they are used within a variety of other tools such as *Alignment* and *Decision Matrix*.[8]

WHY?

PowerBalls help a group quickly and simply prioritize, using the Pareto principle (also known as the 80-20 rule) to help a group deselect and eliminate as many options as quickly possible. Deselection helps the group stay focused on the most important or commanding options.

> CAUTION: The most effective tactic suggests that you should first and always prioritize your *decision criteria*, before applying them to options. Untrained facilitators prioritize options and not *decision criteria*—oops!
>
> You can remedy this faux pas by reverse engineering. Why did each option receive its ranking? The answer yields *decision criteria*, the driving force behind decisions.

PROCEDURE

PowerBalls are flexible instruments for measuring anything. For simple decision-making, use the following activities:

- Establish the purpose of what the team is doing (for example, using the *Purpose Tool* in chapter 7).

- Build a list of options (for example, *Brainstorming*, chapter 6, and *Categorizing*, chapter 6). Set the options aside.

- Build a list of criteria (be prepared to further define specific criteria).

- Look at the criteria to see whether any options are in violation. For example, if Sally is allergic to flowers, then "buying her flowers" is an option we should eliminate (if we want to show appreciation).

- Ask the participants if they can support the remaining options. If someone objects, then eliminate that *Option* once the group understands and accepts their rationale. Once everyone can support the balance, you have consensus (but not a deliverable).

---

[8] These are also known as "Harvey Balls," but some of our students requested that we change the term. When asked for a name they would prefer, students offered up "PowerBalls."

- To improve the quality of the decision, unveil a legend for *PowerBalls* and the accompanying definitions.
  - ●—High means "pay any price."
  - ○—Low means "want it free, not willing to pay extra for it."
  - ◑—Moderate is the stuff in between, meaning we are "willing to pay a reasonable amount" (without being forced to define "reasonable").
  - ∅—Null means "will *not* have" (only if it comes up)
- The economic definitions listed here can be applied to all types of logic, for example:
  - Attraction versus repulsion (strong—weak—moderate)
  - Frequent versus seldom (frequent—rare—occasional)
  - Full versus empty (full—empty—half full)
  - Liberating versus restricting (free—constrained—compromised)—and so on
- Apply *Bookend Rhetoric* (next section) to isolate the one-third most and one-third least important criteria.
- Code or score the remaining one-third as moderate by default, without discussion (usually).
- Attempt to force-fit one-third of the candidates to each category—high, low, and moderate—but be flexible. When you take on more than one-third of either high, low, or moderate, reestablish balance by taking on slightly less than one-third elsewhere.
- Appeal exclusively to the high criteria and isolate the options that best support the *high* criteria.

IF THIS PROCEDURE FAILS

Using only the most important one-third ("pay any price"), indicate that some options now appear best because they strongly support the most important criteria. And yet disagreement might still result, so these are your next steps:

- For misunderstandings, further challenge, define, and discover the supporting rationale.
- You may need a tool more robust than *PowerBalls,* so begin another analysis activity with a *Tool* capable of managing more complicated situations.

- If the dynamic is highly political, use the four steps in *Conflict Management* (chapter 4).

SURROGATES OR SIMILARITIES

The Agile and Design Sprint communities (typically supporting product and project management) use similar logic with different legends.

MoSCoW

One mnemonic being used is *MoSCoW*; the letter *o* is irrelevant, but the consonants represent the following:

- **M**ust Have (●)
- **S**hould Have (◑)
- **C**ould Have (○)
- **W**on't Have (∅)

Traffic Lights

With similar logic, the traffic light style, frequently used in scorecards, uses colors instead of symbols whereby green signifies Go (good), red signifies Stop (not good), and yellow signifies Caution (needs modification or be wary).

Bookend Rhetoric Tool

Effective facilitators shy away from analyzing lists in a linear, top-down manner. *Bookend Rhetoric* imposes a natural habit of squeezing the gray areas toward the middle, rather than wasting time on the least important stuff.

The *Bookend Rhetoric Tool* **is perhaps my favorite *Tool* because it's powerful, effective, and will get you DONE fast.**

Groups tend to argue about gray areas ("*moderate* importance"; "pay a *reasonable* amount") and frequently the **moderate factors have little to no impact on decision quality.** For instance, with *PowerBalls* (chapter 7), you can envision some participants arguing about whether something is more than moderately important but less than highly important. I know from experience that the extreme criteria (high and low) drive decision quality, so *Bookend Rhetoric* helps me identify the most important criteria quickly.

When untrained facilitators start in a linear fashion with the first item and ask whether something should be categorized as of high, medium, or low importance, they end up with a list that is 80 percent high. The list becomes less valuable, not more. We should concede that items on the list *all* represent the most important considerations, but that a few items are slightly more or less important than the others. So we can turn to the *Bookend Rhetoric Tool* for help sorting them.

PROCEDURE

When your cleanly defined list of criteria needs prioritizing, compare and contrast different items with the *precise questions* detailed here, moving from one end to the other and back:

- Ask, "Which of these is the most important?" (Code the answer with the filled circle *PowerBall* icon.)

- Next ask, "Which of these is the least important?" (Code the answer with the empty circle *PowerBall* icon.)

- Then return to the *next most* important.

- And next return to the *next least* important.
  - Return and repeat until the list has been two-thirds scored. Code the remaining one-third as moderate by asking the group, "Will you lose any sleep over making the remaining moderate?"

NOTE: Always ask in the singular: "which is," not "which are." When two or more participants speak at once, be prepared to take them all. In advance, divide the list quantity (N) by three. You are seeking three evenly distributed buckets. However, you can be flexible and reestablish balance if forced to add an additional "high," for example. With 12 criteria, we are seeking three buckets with four per bucket. If forced to add a fifth bucket, we simply offset that with three in one of the other buckets.

If force-ranking, apply the highest available number followed by the lowest available number and repeat until each ranking number has been used.

- If comparing or contrasting illustrations, consider these questions:
  - Which is most similar?
  - Which is least similar?

- For general conversations, ask opposing questions:
  - What is your greatest strength?
  - What is your greatest weakness?

NOTE: I do not encourage the use of one-quarter or three-quarter PowerBalls, but remain flexible, if doing so will mitigate an argument and get us back on track. Likewise, I don't encourage "null," but you should know what to do if participants say they "will not have" some option.

If needed, here is a five-level list of *PowerBall* options, plus null:

- ● High importance
- ○ Low importance

- ◑ Moderate importance

- ◕ Moderately high importance

- ◔ Moderately low importance

- ⦰ Null or will not have

Decision Matrix Tool

WHY?

The *Decision Matrix* supports decision-making at every level in the holarchy, from the organization through project and product teams. The *Decision Matrix* can be viewed as the "logic" behind *all* decisions. It provides the reasons and explicit support behind selecting or deselecting the options. In a portrait format, when there are more options than criteria, the options are listed vertically (Y-axis), and the criteria arrayed horizontally (X-axis). In a landscape format, or if there are more criteria than options, the largest group is arrayed across the X-axis horizontally and the smallest group is located on the Y-axis vertically.

PROCEDURE

Once the *Purpose of the Object* (chapter 7) (or of the topic) has been agreed on, use *Creativity* (chapter 8) or narrative Listing to develop the options being considered and the criteria to evaluate the options. By applying *PowerBalls* and carefully wording your questions, you can now assess the impact of each criterion on each of the options with a straightforward, yet powerful matrix.

For example, if we want to know which sports to target in a marketing campaign, we might develop two lists and populate the matrix as shown in table 7.1. At the intersection of each criterion and option, precisely recite the following question: **"To what extent does X impact (or affect, support, and so on) Y?"** From the example in table 7.1 we might determine that from the perspective of a sports drink company, basketball captures a much more desirable marketing profile than curling, even if we know nothing about either sport.

> CAUTION: Avoid asking the close-ended question "Does X involve Y?" There is always a subject matter expert who can establish a correlation when you use a close-ended question. We are not seeking an answer to the question "Does it?" Rather, we are seeking the degree, intensity, level, or extent that it does.

BENEFITS

Provide your executive sponsor or steering team with a *Decision Matrix* that renders visual support for your decisions. This iconic *Tool* preempts the common question, "Why did you select X?" The *Decision Matrix* displays the rationale and trail of logic. If executives want to change the decision, the *Decision*

Table 7.1. *Decision Matrix*: **Which Sports to Target?**

Criteria/Sports Examples	Sweat (Dehydration)	Participant Growth	Online Audience	etc.
Curling	○	◔	○	
Basketball	●	◕	●	
Tennis	◕	◑	◑	
etc.				

> **—Albert Einstein**
> *Not everything that can be counted counts, and not everything that counts can be counted.*

Matrix forces them to share their logic, enabling your team to become more consistent with their subsequent decisions by basing them on the updated or refreshed rationale from the executives.

Scorecard Tool

COMPLICATED DECISIONS

Criteria are used to evaluate lists of ideas or options and may be used to prioritize lists or select one or two items from a list. Robust criteria are difficult to develop. The depth of criteria makes the difference between a high-quality decision and a questionable one.

WEIGHTED CRITERIA

A criterion provides a factor against which you can objectively assess options. For example, in buying an automobile, one would look at criteria such as air-conditioning, city gas mileage, heated seats, and styling. Each needs to be considered. A criterion is most effective when it is well defined and a clear, objective set of numeric values can be determined.

Criteria may be drafted ahead of time or developed in the meeting. If drafted ahead of time, list those criteria and check with the group to ensure that participants understand the criteria clearly.

There are three tests (scrubbing) for advancing consensus:

1. First, do participants understand the criteria? (validity)

2. Can participants support the criteria? (relevancy)

3. Which substantive criteria are missing? (omissions)

PROCEDURE

To develop criteria in the meeting:

- Start with a clear and finite set of options to apply the criteria; if you don't have this yet, use the Listing activity of *Brainstorming* (chapter 6) to create options the group will consider.

- Next list criteria that participants consider valid and real—criteria participants intend to use in supporting their decision. (Do not mandate SMART criteria when you are in the initial Listing mode.)

- When you list criteria, participants will frequently offer subjective criteria (such as comfort). Do not immediately reject these. Ask participants what they care about, what they need to measure. With enough time and money, you can always find an objective measurement buried within subjective criteria (think Lean Sigma or Six Sigma).

- Scrub each criterion with the three tests (scrubbing) listed earlier. Before going further, make sure each scrubbed criterion is understood and accepted by everyone. In scrubbing, you may need to consider defining or categorizing similar criteria and deleting criteria that may be contradictory. For example, it may not be possible to require both a convertible and a traditional glass sunroof. If the group is uncertain, return to a specific criterion later. Do not allow one criterion to bog down your meeting.

- When scrubbing, apply one of the following icons to each criterion. There are several types of criteria, so explain your legend by posting a visual icon alongside each of the criterion types:

    - Deal-breaker = ◆ (mandatory and binary, as in "yes" or "no")

    - Desired = ✚ (desired and binary)

    - Fuzzy = ☁ (desired and subjective)

    - Scalable = ☰ (mandatory and measurable—note that most scalable criteria are also mandatory, but you should always prefer scalable to binary criteria).

- Explain the difference between binary criteria, determined by whether something exists or not, on the one hand, and mandatory or simply desired criteria, on the other. For example, when buying a car, you might consider:

    - Air-conditioning (mandatory and binary requirement—the desired feature either exists [YES] or it does not [NO]) ◆

- City gas mileage (mandatory and scalable, where more is typically better) ≡

- Run-flat spare tire (desired and binary—the desired feature either exists [YES] or it does not [NO] but it is not mandatory) ✚

- Styling (desired and subjective or fuzzy) ☁

- Have the group confer and code each item as one of the four types. Carefully provide reflective feedback and confirmation to ensure that everyone understands the supporting rationale.

- Remember *Definitions* (chapter 6) and as appropriate, use separate flip charts to carefully define criteria that remain unclear or uncertain. As definitions are built, eliminate other criteria that can now be folded into the updated definition or more fully extract, define, and code new criteria that develop.

- Binary requirements are answered with yes or no. Validate each deal-breaker item [♦] and (one at a time) change binary criteria that are not mandatory to desired [✚]. In my vehicle example, a binary requirement may be "must have air-conditioning." Create a final list of mandatory (deal-breaker) criteria to document as a separate list of mandatory requirements.

- Do not mix binary requirements with scalable criteria. Either we are satisfied leaving a mandatory criterion as binary (yes or no), or we need to scale the criterion (what is the quantified capacity of the air-conditioning system?).

- For binary items that are optional or desired, but not mandatory, move them to a separate "desired" category that we will score later when combining them with the fuzzy or subjective criteria.

NOTE: Never merge binary requirements with scalable criteria. Binary criteria that are desirable but not mandatory need to be moved to the *desired* (not *mandatory*) category. The four types of criteria need to be separated (coded) to be effectively used. Please provide a visual legend to assist your participants with identifying which of the four types of criteria each item represents.

- Next apply the mandatory criteria list against the options (for example, a vehicle list) to see whether each option is available with the mandatory criterion. If not, *eliminate the option.*

- With the scalable items, stipulate the unit of measurement for each item. For example, with "gas mileage" the unit of measurement might be "miles per gallon—city."

- Write the numbers *0* and *10* underneath each scale with the number *0* on the left edge of the paper and the number *10* on the right edge. Remember, bigger numbers (more) are better, although there are some reverse scales (less carbon emissions are better).

City fuel performance measured in miles per gallon (MPG)

0	10

- Fully document scalable items, challenging participants with questions like these:
    - What is the unit of measurement?

    - What are you measuring?

    - What is the source of your data?

    - What calculation would you use so that you and your grandmother would arrive at the same answer? Have the group define the values that correspond to 0 and 10—do not use subjective terms such as "slow" or "fast." Ten is *outstanding*, and 0 is *lousy*. In the example, 0 may be "less than 10 MPG in city driving," and 10 may be "greater than 30 MPG." As 5 is midway between 0 and 10, so 5 would be equal to 20 MPG in my example.

- To build the scales, use the following questions **precisely**, and do not vary your rhetoric:
    - Measured in terms of _____, what is **outstanding** performance?

    - Measured in terms of _____, what is **lousy** performance?

City fuel performance measured in miles per gallon (MPG)

< 10 MPG	< 30 MPG
0	10

- After the scales have been built, gather actual values (above the line) for each remaining option.

- There are several ways to complete the scoring. You may use individuals, teams, and even overlap. Consider using *Breakout Teams* (chapter 6) based on business units, departments, discipline (such as technical versus business), or other meaningful categories. Complete the scoring and aggregate the scores. Select the best method to assign scoring instructions based on your resources, situation, and constraints.

- If individuals or teams score duplicates, you can make scoring comparisons to ensure that all the scores are identical. Then identify and analyze outliers that may be in error.

- Use examples (like those given here or your own analogy) to help illustrate. Within a business community, "importance to business" may be listed. However, counting how many people scream for something may be a poor unit of measurement. Counting how many corporate objectives are supported by an option may provide a better measurement of importance.

Weighting

We know that not all criteria are weighted equally. Weighting supports the rationale behind prioritization and helps to document assumptions.

PROCEDURE

- Start with the scalable criteria and the scores developed in the *Decision Criteria Agenda Step*. Remember, a score of 1 is lousy performance and 10 is outstanding performance. The scale is linear, and the midpoint can be easily calculated without violating neutrality.

- Bring the individuals or teams and scores together and collect the worksheets.

- Off-line or with the help of a documenter, calculate the scores, per criterion, for each option being prioritized and record on a group worksheet. Speed up the group activity by using an electronic spreadsheet.

- Next, without displaying the results, use the *Bookend Rhetoric Tool* (chapter 7). Have the group assign a weighting factor for each criterion. The weighting factor is based on a scale of 1 to 5. Again, bigger numbers are better. The most important criterion rates a 5, where more is better. Strive for balance so that you have an equal or approximate number of low, medium, and high priorities. Participants should be able to justify their weightings by appealing back to organizational, departmental, or product or project goals and objectives.

- Apply each criterion weight to the worksheet (see figure 7.3 for a blank scoring sheet). The spreadsheet will multiply the weight by the score and calculate a total for each criterion for each option (multiply the score for each criterion times the weight of the criterion).

Solution:					
Criterion:					
Performance:			Weight:		Score:
1 2 3 4 5 6 7 8 9 10	Times	1 2 3 4 5			
Criterion:					
Performance:			Weight:		Score:
1 2 3 4 5 6 7 8 9 10	Times	1 2 3 4 5			
Criterion:					
Performance:			Weight:		Score:
1 2 3 4 5 6 7 8 9 10	Times	1 2 3 4 5			
Criterion:					
Performance:			Weight:		Score:
1 2 3 4 5 6 7 8 9 10	Times	1 2 3 4 5			
TOTAL SCORE:					
COMMENTS:					

Figure 7.3. Blank Scoring Sheet

- Sum all the criterion scores for each option. Display the results with the options force-ranked from highest to lowest scores, on a flip chart, handout, or screen.

- Ask the group to review the list. If participants feel compelled to alter or modify the results, have them justify the changes and document their reasons.

- Look for a natural separation (such as a line break) between the highest and lowest scoring groups. The lowest-scoring options should no longer be mentioned; they should be eliminated. Keep the conversation focused on the group with the highest scores, such as the top three to five options.

- I frequently stop here because we have painstakingly determined the absolute best options and can now conduct a test drive or go off-line to conduct further research on the limited few remaining options.

- If needed (no decision has been made yet) use the remaining desired and fuzzy criteria by taking the remaining options (the top three to five) and appealing to the most important desired and fuzzy criteria to guide a final decision (such as picking a stylish vehicle).

- Prioritize these criteria as high, medium, or low using *PowerBalls* (chapter 7), and compare the remaining options to the most important priorities. However, use the desired and fuzzy criteria only if absolutely needed—to help optimize a decision or solve for an impasse.

NOTE: This *Agenda Step* takes from 60 minutes up to four hours or longer. Defining clear, measurable criteria in advance will accelerate your conclusion.

Perceptual Mapping Tool

WHY?

To help a team compare and prioritize its options using graphical indication of prioritization, *Perceptual Mapping* helps convert qualitative factors into quantitative assessments. Use this *Tool* to solicit supporting arguments about how options should be ranked against criteria and which options may demand urgent attention or priority.

PROCEDURE 1

After you have helped the team build their options (actions to take), consider arraying them along the *Payoff Matrix,* criteria dimensions including the ease of implementation and the impact of the solution.

- If you have dozens of options, consider using a whiteboard or large wall display. You may want to use Post-its because participant input will change and cause you to move them around, making frequent adjustments to the relative position of some options (the Post-it notes).

- Be careful to fully explain and define the "high" and "low" of each criterion, and to the extent possible draw from your personal analogy.

- Start in the middle, one axis at a time (holding a small Post-it note), and ask, "On this dimension, is the option more, less, or somewhere in the middle?" Use the same question on the second dimension, but do not ask about two dimensions at once.

- As you move in the direction of an existing Post-it note, add the following question: "Is it more or less than _____?" Here the team provides you with their "perceptional" or "relational" logic for placing the note.

- Use active listening and frequently challenge to find out what type of evidence can be used to support participants' beliefs and claims.

- The illustration in figure 7.4 is called a "Two-by-Two" although it can be modified by adding a third, moderate range, making it a "Nine-Block Diagram" (figure 7.5).

- When you have lots of options (Post-it notes) crammed in one area, put a large "dot" on the Post-it to indicate precisely the point being mapped.

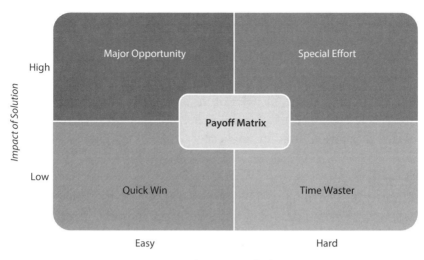

Figure 7.4. Payoff Matrix

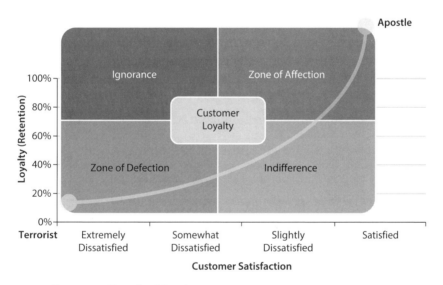

Figure 7.5. Customer Loyalty Matrix

NOTE: For the matrix in figure 7.5, consider substituting "probability of success" for "implementation," resulting in four new categories: "Quick Wins," "Tried and True," "Wild and Crazy," and "Hail Mary Passes" (clockwise).

PROCEDURE 2

You can facilitate any custom *Perceptual Map* by doing the following:

- Identify the primary criteria that affect the decision or situation.

- Typically, you would arrange from low to high, but be prepared to define what is meant by "low" or "high." See *PowerBalls* (chapter 7) for economic definitions (for example, "pay any price").

- If you need to use a third dimension, such as quantity, then consider varying the size, shape, or color of the symbol by modifying your Post-it notes. Allow the notes' color, height, shape, or width to equate to a third criterion or additional criteria.

PROCEDURE 3

The illustrative example in figure 7.6 requires ranking each stakeholder's *power* to influence other stakeholders or control resources (horizontal) with their *interest* (vertical) or how much they care, to determine the most and least important stakeholders.

Real-Win-Worth Tool

WHY?

Real-Win-Worth (R-W-W) isolates the absolute best candidate (for example, process or product) using a three-stage screening process:

1. How *real* is the opportunity?

2. To what extent can we *win* compared with competitive options?

3. To what extent is the opportunity *worth* doing?

I have long been an advocate of decision matrices; this *Tool* benefits from an assist from George Day.[9]

> "The R-W-W screen is a straightforward but powerful technique built on a series of questions about the innovation concept or product, its potential market, and the company's capabilities and competition."—George Day

The *R-W-W Tool* provides objective scores but also requires expert reviews at each stage. If the idea is "great," for example, but we cannot win—then there is no need to go further. Even if we have the capacity to win, if the concept is not worth much—there is no need to go further. As a consensus-building *Tool*, *Real-Win-Worth* provides a disciplined method for exposing assumptions while also identifying knowledge gaps (or areas of superiority).

Successful screening depends upon the quality of the questions you use. To arrive at consensual understanding using *R-W-W*, develop a robust set of detailed

---

[9] See George Day, "Is It Real? Can We Win? Is It Worth Doing?" (2007).

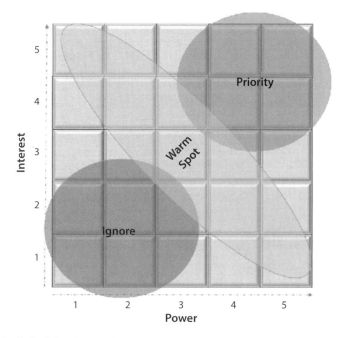

Figure 7.6. Stakeholder Power-Interest Matrix

questions. Neither I nor George Day can tell you how to modify the basic questions listed here, so first understand their intent and then determine what modifications you need to make an informed decision during each of the three phases.

PHASE 1: TO WHAT EXTENT IS THE OPPORTUNITY *REAL*?

Consider two critical vectors.[10] Assess the *feasibility* of the product, service, or solution and the extent to which it is *attractive* (for example, to internal or external customers). Assess these vectors by exploring the dimensions they represent. Eight representative questions (dimensions) are provided in the illustration in figure 7.7. Rarely should the questions be posed as close-ended. Rather, by exploring the *extent* to which they apply, you will assess actual values across each dimension. Your most attractive options score higher relative to others.

TO WHAT EXTENT CAN WE *WIN* COMPARED WITH COMPETITIVE OPTIONS?

After determining the extent to which your customer demand and solution are both *real*, next assess your ability to succeed against competitive options. According to Day,

---

[10] A "vector" is the aggregate of multiple dimensions, with each dimension representing a range of potential values.

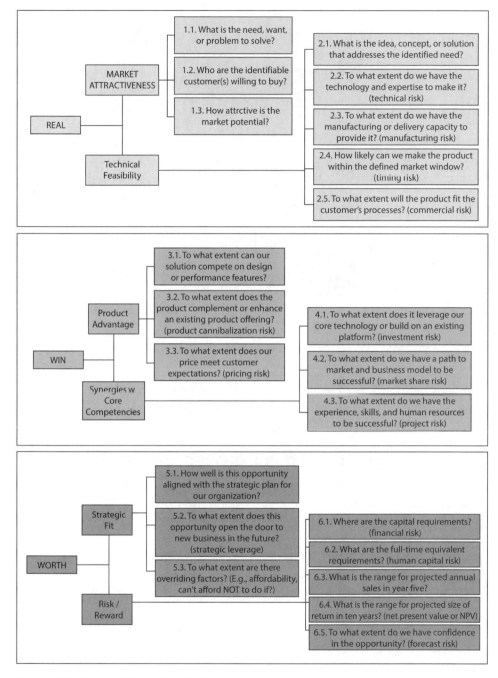

Figure 7.7. Real > Win > Worth Questions

Two of the top three reasons for new-product failures, as revealed by audits, would have been exposed by "Can we win?" Analysis: Either the new product didn't achieve its market-share goals, or prices dropped much faster than expected. (The third reason is that the market was smaller, or grew more slowly, than expected.)[11]

Begin by reviewing a set of six new questions that explain the two vectors called *synergies* and *advantages*. Consider pulling in the results from any research efforts to help answer the questions. Focus on the open-ended nature of answers or projections.

TO WHAT EXTENT IS THE OPPORTUNITY *WORTH* DOING?

The final phase addresses predictive vectors including *financial risk and reward* and *strategic fit*. Financial projections can be general or refined, but apply a consistent level of rigor to all dimensions you assess. Keep in mind that the forecasts of financial returns from innovative solutions are notoriously unreliable. Day notes from his research:

> "Given the susceptibility of financial forecasts to manipulation, overconfidence, and bias (heuristics), executives should depend on rigorous answers to the prior questions in the screen for their conclusions about profitability."[12]

Build ranges and adapt them to your scale. Keep in mind that risk and reward factors, while specific, are nevertheless projections. There is no better time to use a large group for assessment since *The Wisdom of Crowds* suggests that nobody is smarter than everybody.[13]

MEETING FACILITATOR CONSIDERATIONS

Facilitate a session or sessions to build your questions (dimensions) as well as your assessment continuums. You may discover that by having individuals score the candidates privately and then aggregating results, you have a solid foundation to launch another decision-making session that will anchor the final assessment or decision. Keep in mind that the highest-scoring idea does not necessarily claim victory, but you will not waste time discussing suboptimal ideas, allowing the group to focus on the best candidates, those appealing to their most compelling reasons.

---

[11] George Day, "Is It Real? Can We Win? Is It Worth Doing?" (2007), 12.

[12] Day, "Is It Real? Can We Win? Is It Worth Doing?" (2007), 16.

[13] See *The Wisdom of Crowds: Why the Many Are Smarter than the Few and How Collective Wisdom Shapes Business, Economies, Societies, and Nations* by James Surowiecki (2005), who also states: "With collective intelligence . . . you could say it's as if we've been programmed to be collectively smart. . . . Any major decision should be taken by as large a group of managers as is logistically feasible."

Real > Win > Worth Potential Questions and Scoring Continuums

		Criterion/Weight	0 (Uncertain?)	1	3	9
Real	**Market Attractiveness** / Is the Market Real?	1.1. What is the need, want, or problem to solve?	Unknown or no apparent need.	Not clear or not well defined need/want/problem to solve or market development required.	Clearly defined and identifiable need/want/problem to solve.	Need/want/problem is clear and is a validated by a customer or market.
		1.2. Who are the identifiable customer(s) willing to buy?	No interest or no known fit with a customer or a market segment.	Anecdotal customer(s) interest in buying the product/solution	Well-defined customer(s) interest in buying the product/solution	Well-defined interest and urgency in buying the product/solution
		1.3. How attractive is the market potential?	Market Potential <$4MM	Market Potential <$8MM	Market Potential <$20MM	Market Potential >$20MM
	Technical Feasibility / Is the Product Real?	2.1. What is the idea, concept, or solution that addresses the identified need?	Solution is not evident or no idea or concept currently exists that addresses the need.	Early ideas or concepts exist that address the need.	Several potential alternatives have been identified to solve the need.	At least one clear solution to the need has been identified.
		2.2. To what extent do we have the technology and expertise to make it? (technical risk)	New Technology or Invention is required.	Major development is required (reformulation, etc.).	Minor development is required (liner, thickness, color).	No development required.
		2.3. To what extent do we have the manufacturing or delivery capacity to provide it? (manufacturing risk)	New Manufacturing Process or Capability needed.	Major modification needed (equipment upgrades).	Minor modification needed (process settings, etc.).	Need can be filled with existing capability.
		2.4. How likely can we make the product within the defined market window? (timing risk)	Not possible to meet market window.	Low probability in meeting market window.	Moderate probability of meeting market window.	High probability of meeting market window.
		2.5. To what extent will the product fit the customer's processes? (commercial risk)	New customer manufacturing process(es) required.	Major manufacturing process modification(s) required.	Minor manufacturing process modification(s) required.	No changes required in customer manufacturing process(es).

Win							
Product Advantage		Is Product Competitive?	3.1. To what extent can our solution compete on design or performance features?	Has many attributes inferior to competition with key customer requirements.	Is equal to but is sometimes inferior to competition with key customer requirements.	Is equal to and sometimes exceeds competition with key customer requirements.	Clearly exceeds competition with key customer requirements.
			3.2. To what extent does the product complement or enhance an existing product offering? (product cannibalization risk)	No expected enhancement to product, customer, or market position.	Enhances product position at a specific customer only.	Enhances specific market position and product position only.	Enhances specific market position and overall product portfolio.
			3.3. To what extent does our price meet customer expectations? (pricing risk)	Price has not been validated.	Price has been validated by internal sources only (e.g., sales rep).	Price has been validated by at least one customer.	Price has been validated by customers representative of market segment.
	Synergies w. Core Competencies	Is the Company Competitive?	4.1. To what extent does it leverage our core technology or build on an existing platform? (investment risk)	Leverages none of core technology platforms and technical strengths.	Leverages an insignificant level of core technology platforms and technical strengths.	Leverages some level of core technology platforms and technical strengths.	Leverages a significant level of core technology platforms and technical strengths.
			4.2. To what extent do we have a path to market and business model to be successful? (market share risk)	No path to market/new market/no business model	Elements missing from path to market/business model/new customer(s) within existing market	Existing path to market, existing business model, expanded offering to current customer(s)	Existing path to market, existing business model, replacement product for current customer(s)
			4.3. To what extent do we have the experience, skills, and human resources to be successful? (project risk)	No existing FTE resources available for project.	Major FTE resource additions or skill set improvements are required.	Minor FTE resource additions or skill set improvements are required.	Current FTE resources and skill sets meet requirements.

(continued)

Real > Win > Worth Potential Questions and Scoring Continuums

	Criterion/Weight	0 (Uncertain?)	1	3	9
Worth — Strategic Fit — Is It Strategic?	5.1. How well is this opportunity aligned with the strategic plan for our organization?	Business opportunity does not align with existing strategic objectives.	Business opportunity is partially aligned with strategic objectives.	Business opportunity is closely aligned with strategic objectives.	Business opportunity is well aligned and is a "must do" to meet strategic objectives.
	5.2. To what extent does this opportunity open the door to new business in the future? (strategic leverage)	No other business opportunities expected outside of this specific offering.	Opportunity may be leveraged in more than one customer application.	Opportunity may be leveraged in several customer applications.	Significant opportunity to become a leveraged platform within organization.
	5.3. To what extent are there overriding factors? (e.g., affordability, can't afford NOT to do it?)	No overriding factors.	Small overriding factors.	Strong overriding factors.	Strategic overriding factor.
Risk/Reward — Is It Profitable?	6.1. What are the capital requirements? (financial risk)	Very Large (>$370K)	Large ($37K–$370K)	Moderate ($1.5K–37K)	Minor (<$1.5K)
	6.2. What are the full-time equivalent requirements? (human capital risk) (financial risk)	Very Large (> $390K per year)	Large ($260K–$390K per year)	Moderate ($65K–260K per year)	Minor (<$65K per year)
	6.3. What is the range for projected annual sales in year five?	<$1MM	$1MM–2MM	$2MM–4MM	<$4MM
	6.4. What is the projected range for rate of return on capital invested?	(First Full Year) GM < 40%	(First Full Year) GM = 40%–55%	(First Full Year) GM = 55%–70%	(First Full Year) GM >70%
	6.5. What is the range for projected size of return in ten years? (net present value or NPV)	(Ten Year) NPV < $0	(Ten Year) NPV $1K to $800M	(Ten Year) NPV $801K to $3,900K	(Ten Year) NPV >$3,900K
	6.6. To what extent do we have confidence in the opportunity? (forecast risk)	Largely not validated (Confidence <30%)	Validated (Confidence >30%)	Validated (Confidence >60%)	Validated (Confidence >90%)

Figure 7.8. Real > Win > Worth Detailed

NOTE: Remember, the questions and illustrative answers and ranges presented in figure 7.8 are illustrative, directional, and should be liberally adapted to your situation.

6. Testing (Decision Quality)

What is the worst deliverable from any meeting? Inferior quality you say? Wrong deliverable perhaps? There is something worse. From the perspective of all participants, *the worst deliverable from any meeting is **another** meeting.*

DELIVERABLE

Therefore, my method encourages a procedure to test the deliverable for decision quality so that we can avoid needing to meet again. With material you have already built during this meeting, testing will be quick and comprehensive.

PROCEDURE

Take your decision and return to the original *Purpose* (chapter 7) expression created in the second *Agenda Step*. Parse the expression because it's not possible to facilitate a group by asking participants to analyze "many to many." Rather, take the entire solution, one that may include many parts or characteristics, and ensure that they all harmonize and support each discrete phrase or clause in your *Purpose* expression, one at a time.

If you experience further challenges or prefer leaving an exhaustive documentation trail for your decision, then consider using the more complex *Decision Quality Spider Chart* explained in the next section.

CLOSURE

To the extent that your final decision resonates solidly with the *Purpose*, the deliverable appears valid, and the meeting is complete. If there are gaps or uncertainties, focus group participants on either modifying their decision, better defining the *Purpose*, or discounting any "disconnects" as being too minor to consider any further.

Either way, you have helped your group build something glacial (very cool). You have structured an activity that ensures decision quality. Your participants have performed quality control on their deliverable. This is especially cool (super glacial) since decision-quality testing is missing from most meetings; most people are simply happy to get out. Arguably, most meetings never end—they simply stop.

Decision Quality Tool

WHY?

When making decisions, always test for decision quality (DQ) so that you can avoid having another meeting. Therefore, as explained in the previous section, a quick method involves testing your decision against the *Purpose* statement to gauge an amount of alignment and support. The *DQ Spider Chart* offers an even more robust method.[14]

Remember that my method defines consensus as a decision good enough that it "will be supported" (not thwarted in the hallway or uprooted in the boardroom) and not cause anyone to lose any sleep rather than being anyone's favorite option or making anyone happy. Consensus does *not* mean that participants will all leave the meeting singing "Kumbaya." Rather, consensus relies on the prowess of structured facilitation and detailed questions.

PROCEDURE

When testing for decision quality, score these six vectors, which have the greatest impact:

1. Appropriate Context (Frame)
- How clear is the background, context, and impact of the decision?
- How well do stakeholders understand the problem?
- To what extent do stakeholders prioritize the problem?
- To what extent has the decision been quantified for its impact, typically in dollars or FTP?
- To what extent do you have an articulate problem to address?

2. Options Development
- Are any potentially critical options missing?
- Should any inconsequential options be eliminated?
- What are the viable solutions (decisions)?
- With remaining options:
  - To what extent are they realistic (doable)?
  - If the option is selected, to what extent will we win?

3. Meaningful and Reliable Information
- To what extent do we know what we need to know?
- To what extent do we *not* know what we need to know?
- How trustworthy are our sources of information?
- To what extent will this be a fact- or evidence-based decision?

---

[14] Microsoft Excel refers to this chart as a "radar" chart.

4. Clear Decision Criteria

- To what extent have we identified and clarified the most critical criteria?

- How well have the criteria been prioritized to reflect our internal value drivers?

- How comprehensive are the criteria to help measure success against the project or organizational goals and objectives?

5. Logic and Reasoning

- How solid and thorough are our research, logic, and findings?

- How well can we explain our choice for and choices against our options?

- To what extent have we applied appropriate tools and rigors to evaluate our proposed solution?

6. Action and Commitment

- How confident are we in projecting the outputs or outcome of this option?

- How ready are we to commit ownership and resources to this option?

- To what extent have we missed anything substantive that could impact the quality of this decision and its results?

HOW TO COMPLETE THE DECISION QUALITY SPIDER CHART

Consider this quick method for scoring by using a low score of 1 and a high score of 5.

Instruct each team member or stakeholder to generate an individual score for each of the six vectors just listed for any option or decision. Using a spread-sheet application, or simply drawing on a large-format Post-it paper or white-board, put a dot on the average value. Also place a dot on each outlier, the lowest and highest score, along each of the six vectors.

Analyze the outliers so that everyone can support the original average or move the average value either lower or higher based on the arguments and consensual understanding.

Facilitate understanding around the results, and consider the following questions:

- Do the values look defensible?

- To what extent do the differences represent real risk or simply differences of opinion?

- Which scores appear too high or low relative to the project or initiative they are supporting? (Adjust the score if needed)

You may want to force-rank the six vectors, if some are more important than others. Tell the group to consider the ranking during the assessment, and if necessary, change the values based on a calculation of the reduced or increased weight of each vector.

In my illustration in figure 7.9, stakeholders would favor Option 3 if ownership and commitment are more important than logic or reliable information.

Likewise, stakeholders would favor Option 1 if context and logic become more important than criteria and information.

7. Review and Wrap (Conclusion) Agenda Step

Follow the four-activity sequence for your *Review and Wrap* explained in chapter 5. None of the four activities should ever be skipped entirely, so expand and contract based on your situation and constraints.

ACTIVITIES

1   *Review:* Do not relive the meeting; simply review the outputs, decisions, assignments, and so on. Focus on the results and deliverable of each *Agenda Step* and not on how you got there. Participants do not need a transcript of the meeting; they need to be reminded about the takeaways and to be offered the opportunity to ask for additional information or clarification before the meeting ends.

2   *Open issues and follow-up:* There are various methods for dealing with open items and formal assignments, such as roles and responsibilities. Once post-meeting assignments are clear, the meeting is nearly complete.

3   *Guardian of Change:* Invest a few minutes to get the group to agree on what they are going to tell others when asked, "What happened in that meeting?" Use a T-Chart and build separate messages for superiors and peers (or other stakeholders).

4   *Assessment:* Get feedback on how you did. Set up or mark a whiteboard by the exit door and create two columns, typically *Plus* and *Delta* (the Greek letter Δ, which stands for "change"). Have participants write down, on a small Post-it note, at least one thing they liked about the meeting [+] and one thing they would change [Δ]. Ask participants to mount each note in its respective column when departing the room.

QUALITY CONTROL

Effective leaders will not disband their meetings until participants have been offered a final opportunity to comment or question, actions have been assigned, messaging has been agreed to, and feedback for continuous improvement has been solicited.

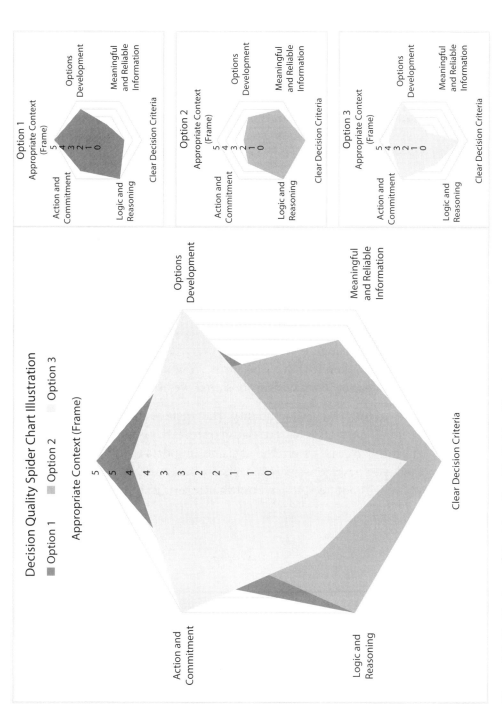

Figure 7.9. Six Vectors of Decision Quality Spider Chart

Quick Summary on Decision-Making

In practice, decision-making and prioritization are anything but linear. You will find yourself frequently going back and forth to fortify the purpose and add new ideas, new criteria, different criteria weights, and so on. When you know *where* you are going, it's quite easy to jump around and yet maintain control.

Here are some practical reminders on decision-making:

- Do not allow arguments about the *Purpose* (chapter 7) statement. If my purpose is different from your purpose, the statement needs to reflect *both* purposes, as an aggregate. We'll solve for it later.

- The statement itself is *not* technically part of the deliverable. It exists to support building consensus and quality control—to make sure that we don't forget or miss something, such as some type of intended purpose without a corresponding feature in the selection.

- Be prepared to upgrade your *Tool*. If the *PowerBalls Tool* (chapter 7) proves insufficient, step it up to a *Decision Matrix* (chapter 7) or *Perceptual Map* (chapter 7) *Tool*. More is better with decision-making.

- The best use of *Tools* comes from deselecting, getting groups to agree on what *not* to consider. If we eliminate everything that causes personal objections, then we have consensus. We may not have a decision, but it is much easier to make decisions *after* we have consensus.

- Remember to test for decision quality. The *Purpose* statement is invaluable when you parse it. Take one clause or feature or benefit at a time and determine to what extent the decision supports each. When amply supported, you have consensus, a decision, and a successful test that suggests we will not need to have another meeting about this decision.

8

Creative Problem-Solving Approach

MANAGING MORE THAN ONE RIGHT ANSWER

Leading a group from "here" to "there" presupposes more than one right answer. Facilitation strives to articulate the best answer for each group of participants, eschewing the thought that some universal "best answer" exists.

When preparing for problem solving or gap analysis, the meeting designer alone bears a tremendous burden to design optimal meeting activities that will kindle consensus. No one can prove certainty about the future, so I'll also recommend building different scenarios and ranges of possibilities. Therefore, creative thinking remains paramount for exceptional problem solving or gap analysis. Facilitators may be more challenged than ever, but this chapter will make it easier for you, especially once you learn how to manage "many-to-many."

This *Problem-Solving Approach* solves problems by creating focus when there are many symptoms, many causes, many preventions, and many cures that ought to be considered. This *Problem-Solving Approach* also keeps participants, especially those who jump around, on track.

Many meetings waste time because they lack structure, not because they fail to generate some promising ideas. Meetings are challenged by people who never know when they are done, how they can measure their progress, and how much work remains to be done. They don't know what they missed. They don't know what they don't know. This disciplined *Problem-Solving Approach* helps you to structure activities and ask precise questions that will unveil practical and obscure solutions.

Problem Definition

Early emphasis should not be on trying to solve the problem but instead on finding unusual ways of looking at and describing the problem situation. The more general the expression of a problem, the less likely it is to suggest answers. As the problem definition becomes more specific, it sharpens potential solutions.

> —Jeffrey Dyer, Hal Gregersen, and Clayton Christensen, *The Innovator's DNA: Mastering the Five Skills of Disruptive Innovators*
>
> *Innovative people systematically engage in questioning, observing, networking, and experimenting behaviors to spark new ideas. Similarly, innovative organizations systematically develop processes that encourage questioning, observing, networking, and experimenting by employees.*

NOTE: Problem definition is far more critical than most people understand. For example, while traveling on a deserted road, an automobile gets a flat tire. The occupants discover that there is no jack in the trunk. They define the problem as "finding a jack" and decide to walk to a station for a jack. Another automobile on the same road also blows a tire. The occupants of the second car also discover that there is no jack. They define the problem as "raising the automobile." They see an old barn, push the auto there, raise it on a pulley, change the tire, and drive off while the occupants of the first car are still trudging toward the service station.[1]

While J. W. Getzels, who came up with this example, does not mention a third option, another group might push the vehicle to the side of the road and, using their hands, rocks, sticks, or different implements, dig a hole around the bad tire. The problem statement might more accurately reflect the need for "clear access to the axle and surrounding area," rather than lifting the vehicle. Depending on the cause of the flat, there may be more problem definitions as well.

---

[1] J. W. Getzels, "Problem Finding and the Inventiveness of Solutions" (1975).

To create divergent solutions, vary the descriptions of the problem. When focused on describing the problem, using mountaineering as an analogy, you might consider the following:

First, consider rewriting or versioning problem statements:[2]

- ***Broaden focus, restate the problem with larger context:***

  - Initial: Should I keep a diary?

  - *Paraphrase: How do I create a permanent memory of our ascent?*

- ***Paraphrase, restate the problem using different words without losing original meaning:***

  - Initial: How can we limit congestion around the base camps?

  - *Paraphrase: What can we consolidate to keep the congestion from growing?*

- ***Redirect focus, consciously change the scope:***

  - Initial: How do we get all our supplies to 16,000 feet?

  - *Paraphrase: How do we reduce our consumption and need for supplies?*

- ***Reversal, turn the problem around:***

  - Initial: How can we discourage people from climbing this mountain?

  - *Paraphrase: How can we get people to go to a different mountain?*

Second, consider changing *Perspectives* (chapter 8), which stimulates other worthwhile aspects that further help detail and describe the problem. Mountaineers might embrace perspectives from their climbers, Sherpas, legal authority, nearby residents, other climbers, and so on.

PROCEDURE

Adapt the *Problem-Solving Approach* for your situation. This chapter explains the prototype for solving problems and analyzing gaps that gets us from where we are now to where we want to be in the future. I'll use an example suggesting that an organization has determined that a problem of "burnout" permeates the Cybersecurity Department. We will use the *Problem-Solving Approach* to draft creative and practical solutions.

---

[2] For other ideas and more detail, see *The Thinker's Toolkit: 14 Powerful Techniques for Problem Solving* (1998) by former CIA agent Morgan D. Jones.

ILLUSTRATIVE DELIVERABLE

A solution of proposed actions to prevent, mitigate, and cure the causes of "burnout" within the Cybersecurity Department.

BASIC AGENDA

1. Launch (Introduction) (chapter 5)

2. Purpose of the Cybersecurity Department *(description of ideal future state)* (chapter 7)[3]

3. "Burnout" *(definition of problem and current state)*

4. Symptoms *(externally observable factors)*

5. Causes

6. Actions[4]

   – Preventions *(x-axis, Timeline 1)*

   – Cures *(x-axis, Timeline 2)*

   – Cybersecurity Department Personnel *(y-axis, Persona A)*

   – Management *(y-axis, Persona B)*

7. Testing[5]

8. Review and Wrap (Conclusion) (chapter 5)

1. Launch (Introduction) Agenda Step

Follow the seven-activity sequence fully explained in chapter 5.

Here is a brief exercise that illustrates the difficulty of managing information in our heads (that is, without external aids or other people).

Picture an apple in your "mind's eye." Can you do that? Can you picture 2 apples in your mind? Three? Clearly picture 3 apples in your mind. How about 4 . . . 5 . . . 6 . . . 10? Few people will claim they can hold the images of 10 or more apples at once.

Humans have cognitive limitations and limited information-processing capacity. Apples are basic objects. We can "hold" several of them in our mind at

---

[3] Terms that are grayed out are for your eyes only and not to be shown on your *Basic Agenda*.

[4] While this *Problem-Solving Approach* appeals to the *Purpose* expression to ascertain the value of proposed actions, you may add an additional *Agenda Step* to develop a set of criteria (or constraints) that optimal actions should support.

[5] On a practical note, when the topic is "politically sensitive," *Change Management* might be an additional *Agenda Step*—to develop a plan to reduce resistance to the proposed actions (solution).

once. But increase the number, or increase their complexity (make that 1 large, red Macintosh apple; 3 smallish green Granny Smiths; 4 average-sized Fijis; and so on) and it becomes more difficult to hold a picture. In a group setting, each person might be picturing a different variety or size of apple and not be aware that his or her vision is entirely different from others'. When individuals and groups confront a complex decision, they may talk in circles without keeping track of all the details and relevant information, beyond what they can see in their mind's eye.

Therefore, my *Problem-Solving Approach* respects the fact that all of us can recall, remember, and visualize more possibilities as a team than as individuals. Participants with specialized expertise also increase the likelihood that more accurate cause-effect relationships may be identified. Collaboratively, we are much more powerful, and that's why nobody is smarter than everybody.

2. Purpose of the Cybersecurity Department (Future State)

PROCEDURE

Use *Breakout Teams* (chapter 6) and the *Creativity Tool* (next section) to illustrate the ideal state for the Cybersecurity Department, devoid of any "burnout." It might be faster and potentially more effective to build a narrative expression using the *Purpose Tool* (chapter 7).

If you use any illustrative tool, you develop some good "eye candy" for posting throughout the session. Plan to use the logic of *Categorizing* (chapter 6) and *Bookend Rhetoric* (chapter 7) when you convert any illustrations into narrative expressions. Either way, narrative or illustrative, be prepared to use the *Definition Tool* (chapter 6) to socialize understanding about terms or phrases used by the participants.

> NOTE: By confirming the purpose of the future state or the ideal condition, we are describing the way things ought to be when there is no problem, when everything is working according to design.

Creativity Tool

WHY?

Use the *Creativity Tool* during the ideation or Listing activity of *Brainstorming* (chapter 6). Requiring participants to illustrate their answers enables them to express complex ideas more easily, even when they prefer to do it narratively. The *Creativity Tool* is especially beneficial for developing visions of the business or organization; use when defining terms or solutions, especially intangible products and services.

Figure 8.1. Creativity Tool Example

PROCEDURE

Creativity allows each team to draw many illustrative answers to one specific question or provide many solutions for one specific scenario (figure 8.1). For complex topics, *Creativity* frequently takes less time than getting participants to write down narrative descriptions.

- Use *Breakout Teams* (chapter 6). Plan how you want to blend them.

- Provide a time limit, flip chart paper (or Mural or Miro), and colored markers.

- When finished, have each team present their drawings. Use *Bookend Rhetoric* (chapter 7) for quickly identifying commonalities or items that may be extremely unique. Keep drawings mounted. Do *not* mark on them.

- Separately, document participants' narrative explanations. Get feedback and confirm that your narrative reflections are accurate and complete.

When you use *Creativity* early during your session, mount participants' output as wallpaper and they will refer to it during the session. Since teams, not individuals, create the output, you provide timid participants with permission to speak freely by enabling them to speak about what their team created.

VISION EXPRESSIONS

- Draw a picture of how the organization looks today.

- Draw a picture of how you would like the organization to look.

- Draw your vision of where you are going with the business.

NOTE: You can use one or more of the prompts listed here or use your own. If you have the teams draw pictures of *both* today and the future, you empower them with the ability to compare and contrast.

3. Problem State ("Burnout")

PROCEDURE

I would use the *Definition Tool* (chapter 6). There are other right answers. However, make sure you know what your deliverable looks like. To me, it looks like five responses for prompts from the *Definition Tool*:

1. Is not? (list)

2. Description (sentence)

3. Characteristics? (list)

4. Illustration (drawing)

5. Examples (narrative descriptions, paragraph each for two examples)

NOTE: Fully define the problem state or condition, building consensus around the way things are at present. This *Agenda Step* could be inserted ahead of the "ideal state." Do what feels natural to you.

I prefer to describe a "solution," then agree on the problem, and use the remaining time to get us from here (problem) to there (solution). Some argue that cybersecurity personnel might be bitching and moaning when the session begins, so let them get it off their chests by covering the problem first.

ALTERNATIVE PROCEDURE

You may want to use the *Force Field Analysis Tool* (next section). If the goals, objectives, and measures of the department are clear, *Force Field Analysis* helps build mutual understanding around forces, both controllable and uncontrollable, that are hindering or impeding participants' efforts to reach their target goals.

Force Field Analysis Tool

WHY?

Force Field Analysis improves upon a similar tool called "pros and cons." *Force Field Analysis* identifies and prioritizes actions based on opportunities for improvement. The creator, Kurt Lewin, viewed *Force Field Analysis* as a change management remediation, when change is not occurring quickly enough or the change occurring seems to lack clear direction.

Force Field Analysis makes it easier for groups to organize their thinking while encouraging thoughtful exploration. Once supportive and hindering forces are identified, the group analyzes impact, leading to actions that reinforce the positive and mitigate the negative forces.

PROCEDURES

Force Field Analysis begins by identifying the objectives, CTQs (Critical to Quality), or the targets of change. So, facilitate clear understanding about the objectives of the change. Next, for each discrete objective (typically built in advance of a meeting and provided in a pre-read as a slide or handout), ask the following questions, *one at a time*:

- What is hindering us from reaching this (specific target) (negative, or forces preventing change)?

  - Environmental forces (for example, ask "What environmental forces are hindering changes that will deter us from reaching our objectives?")

  - Structural or organizational forces

  - Technological forces

  - Individual forces

- What is helping us move toward this target (positive forces supporting change)?

  - Repeat using each of the four forces from above.

- Use additional forces related to *Perspectives* (chapter 8).

NOTE: Use the *Perspectives Tool* by selecting from the more than 30 points of view that will prompt for additional forces participants might consider.

ALTERNATIVE 1

Participants' responses generate two lists (positive, supporting forces and negative, hindering forces). Adapt the philosophy that it is easier to remove obstacles (hindrances) than to push harder (supports). Focus conversation on what we can do differently to overcome each hindrance, one at a time.

Once actions have been clarified, you may need to prioritize them. When you have more than a dozen actions, consider the Pareto principle (the 80-20 rule). If so, use *PowerBalls* (chapter 7), *Perceptual Maps* (chapter 7), or the *Decision Matrix Tool* (chapter 7) to prioritize. Note that your objectives are criteria, and actions are your options.

ALTERNATIVE 2

Associate each support or hindrance with an impact weight. A scale of 1 through 5 is commonly used, where 5 has greater influence. You could also force-rank based on how many items are in each column. Either way, assign the hindrances negative numbers, with –5 more harmful than –2. Compare

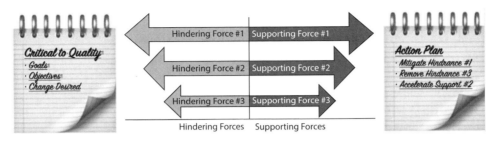

Figure 8.2. Force Field Analysis

the totals for an overall look, to the extent that the total for support factors may or may not exceed the total for hindrances being faced.

When building responses, begin with actions to oppose the hindrances. Time permitting, look at additional actions that improve leverage for the support factors.

> NOTE: My experience has shown that some hindrances require further *Definition* (chapter 6), some may be combined, and some forces may be so complex as to require *Root Cause Analysis* (chapter 8).

RIFFS AND VARIATIONS

By scoring the power or impact of the forces, with scaling from 1 through 5, you can graphically allow for the length or width of the arrows to indicate the relative weight of the supporting and hindering forces, as in figure 8.2.

4. Symptoms

PROCEDURE

What does your deliverable from this *Agenda Step* look like? To us, it looks like a list—and I am not a fan of lists. More important, what are you going to do with this list, and what questions need to be asked to convert this list of symptoms into an understanding of potential causes?

FORTIFICATION

Change the way participants look at the problem by changing *Perspectives* (next section) to identify symptoms they may have missed. The *Thinking Hats Tool* (chapter 8) provides additional perspectives on the situation.

> NOTE: Identify the potential symptoms that make it easy to characterize or confirm the problem or issue. Consider symptoms to be "externally identifiable factors" that can be seen and observed objectively, such as "tardiness." Some symptoms were captured during a description of the problem, but certainly not all of them.

Perspectives Tool

This tool is remarkably powerful and underused. Change participants' *Perspectives* to resolve an impasse or to capture innovative ideas previously not considered.

DETAILED PROCEDURES

When you ask your participants to "walk in someone else's shoes" by embracing a new perspective, you stimulate participants to change their point of view. More perspectives create more ideas, and more ideas drive decision quality. You may ask individuals or *Breakout Teams* (chapter 6) to each take on new perspectives. I've personally witnessed remarkable success using two specific *Breakout Teams*: monasteries and organized crime (it can be like night and day). I'm aware of alumni who love contrasting the Apple, Linux, and Microsoft perspectives.

The inputs provided by shifting perspectives are not necessarily definitive. By challenging and exploring them, we can surface problems and solutions that were not previously considered.

TEAM PERSPECTIVES AND PROCEDURE

WW_D: What Would _____ Do? Insert analogs of famous people, organizations, or teams. Ask, "What should we add from the perspective of _____?" (fill in the blank using one of the items in this section).

- Use *Breakout Teams* to develop responses contrasted with other specific points of view, such as the following:

  - A college or university compared with the military-industrial complex

  - A monastery compared with the Mafia or organized crime

  - Bill Gates (or Microsoft) compared with Steve Jobs (or Apple)

  - Jeff Bezos (Amazon), Sergey Brin (Google), or Mark Zuckerberg (Facebook)

  - Genghis Khan (warlike) compared with Mohandas Gandhi (peaceful)

  - Or create your own based on driving forces in your situation, such as antifragile technology (gets stronger), ants (collaborative), Drake or Lizzo (unrepresented voices), or weather (unpredictable yet returns to homeostasis)

- Then compare output from each team focusing on similarities that become symptoms or factors previously unrecognized and differences that should be explored and reconciled as valid possibilities.

NOTE: Use any of the perspectives suggested or make up your own perspectives to help participants focus their input from a specific point of view.

INDIVIDUAL OR TEAM PERSPECTIVES

The 6-M's, 7-P's, or 5-S's are frequently used as the main "bones" in an Ishikawa diagram. Take and choose from among the following 30 perspectives that are most germane and compelling to your situation. Also combine perspectives, including the classic views from de Bono's *Thinking Hats*.

The 6-M's perspectives:

- Machines

- Manpower

- Materials

- Measurements

- Methods

- Mother Nature

The 7-P's perspectives:

- Packaging

- Place

- Policies

- Positioning

- Price

- Procedure

- Promotion

The 5-S's perspectives:

- Safety

- Skills

- Suppliers

- Surroundings

- Systems

Perspectives (trends) from the World Future Society

- *Demographic perspectives:*
  - Family composition

- Public health issues

- Specific population groups (and so on)

- *Economic perspectives:*
    - Business

    - Careers

    - Finance

    - Management

    - Work (and so on)

- *Environmental perspectives:*
    - Ecosystems

    - Habitats

    - Resources

    - Species (and so on)

- *Governmental perspectives:*
    - Laws

    - Politics

    - Public policy

    - World affairs (and so on)

- *Societal perspectives:*
    - Culture

    - Education

    - Leisure

    - Lifestyle

    - Religion

    - Values (and so on)

- *Technological perspectives:*
    - Discoveries and effects

    - Innovation and effects

    - Science and effects (and so on)

Six value or utility levers perspectives:

- Convenience

- Customer productivity

- Environmental friendliness

- Fun and image

- Risk

- Simplicity

Seven Thinking Hats: see *Thinking Hats* perspectives in the next section.

NOTE: *Perspectives* can be used so many ways. For examples, use four perspectives to create a highly robust problem-solving panel. The intersection of common factors they may identify provides the basis for a MVP (minimum viable process or minimum viable product).

For example, if mountaineers, Sherpas, and legal authorities are all concerned with garbage and trash left behind by previous climbing parties, consensus about the importance of trash control is instantly apparent.

Thinking Hats Tool

WHY?

Use a structured *Tool*, inspired by Dr. Edward de Bono, that leverages existing ideas into new, better, different, or more substantial ideas.[6] Refine and bolster your ideas by asking questions from the following perspectives—for example, "Let's focus on the White Hat perspective. What are the facts and evidence?"

PROCEDURE

Thinking Hats forces perspective to capture additional, and frequently innovative, ideas and suggestions. Study the perspectives shown in figure 8.3, which are defined here:

- **Black Hat (risk averse)**

  - The logical negative, careful, cautious, and judgmental; contrary to the Yellow and Green Hats

- **Blue Hat (process control):**

  - The organizing hat (from start to finish) that controls the use of the other hats; contrary to the Green and Red Hats

---

[6] Edward de Bono, "Six Thinking Hats," n.d., https://www.debonogroup.com/services /core-programs/six-thinking-hats/.

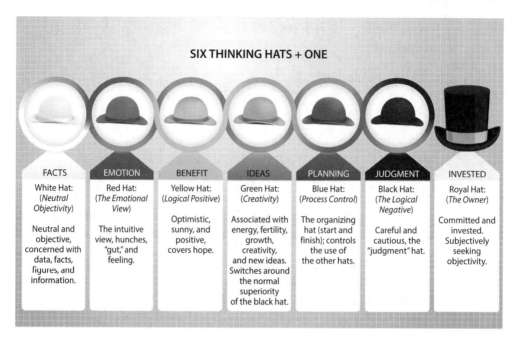

Figure 8.3. Six Thinking Hats + One

- **Green Hat (creativity):**
  - Associated with creativity, energy, fertility, growth, and innovative ideas; contrary to the Black and Blue Hats

- **Red Hat (emotional):**
  - The intuitive view, feeling, "gut," and hunches; contrary to the White and Blue Hats

- **Royal Hat (ownership):**
  - Committed and invested, subjectively seeking objectivity

- **Yellow Hat (risk begone)**
  - The logical positive, hopeful, optimistic, sunny, and positive; contrary to the Black Hat

- **White Hat (neutral objectivity):**
  - Neutral and objective, concerned with data, facts, figures, and information (evidence-based); contrary to the Green and Red Hats

Assign a hat (perspective) to *Breakout Teams* (chapter 6), the entire group, or each person, and then rotate the hats to encourage more ideas. Some claim better results from insisting that everyone wear the same color hat at the same time because it ensures everyone is looking from the same direction at the same time.

Use every hat as often as you like. Nothing prohibits you from returning to hats you have already used once.

There is no need to use every hat. Provide varying sequences of two, three, or more hats at once.

As meeting leader, permit either a pre-set order or one that is evolving. Do not, however, ask participants for the sequence (no facilitating context).

You may also use Post-it notes to have participants individually provide a bunch of ideas. If so, transcribe them so that they are legible by all participants, during a quick break.

Modify the definitions based on your own situation. However, be sure to post some type of visual legend or graphic prompt to explain the perspectives that you are seeking. See Dr. Edward de Bono's work for other riffs and variations.

5. Causes

What question or questions are you going to ask that will convert your list of symptoms into potential causes?

Technically, at this point, you might conduct *Root Cause Analysis* (next section). Another popular technique is called an *After-Action Review* (chapter 8) because it focuses on issues and not people. On a practical note, you might launch a Six Sigma project to identify leading indicators and other objective measurements. During most meetings, however, we could simply take each symptom, *one at a time*, and ask:

What are all the likely causes of [insert symptom; for example, "redeye"]?

Most important, you *cannot* ask, "What are all the probable causes for all of these symptoms?" That unstructured question would have people jumping around with replies such as "insufficient training," "wrong tools," "fatigue" (and so on). While valid ideas can be suggested this way, if you use an unstructured style, you simply don't know what you don't know. An unstructured style asks for all the plausible causes for all the possible symptoms (many to many). Structure recommends focusing on one symptom at a time, asking for all the probable causes of each symptom, one at a time.

Question: "What are all the probable causes of *redeye*?"

Replies:

1. "Air quality. When I'm working overtime, they shut down the air-conditioning and this building gets stale really quick."

2. "Allergies. Can't help it but I get sneezy and ugly during the spring when all the pollen starts flying around."

3. "Fatigue. They are working us 70 hours a week and my eyes always look like this when I get four hours of sleep."

What does your deliverable look like when you are finished identifying causes? It looks like another list—since each symptom may have more than one probable cause, an even longer list. While there could be some overlap (for example, fatigue), after *Clarifying* (chapter 7) your list, what are you going to do with this clean list of causes? You could prioritize, of course, but what questions will you ask to convert the most important causes into an actionable plan?

To draft a detailed and actionable plan, the secret is in the specificity of the questions you ask. You *cannot* ask an unstructured, global-hunger question, such as "So, what's the plan?" or "What should we do about it?"

Root Cause Analysis Tool

WHY?

The Ishikawa diagram (also known as a *fishbone diagram*; see figure 8.4) provides a systematic way of looking at potential causes or contributing factors of undesirable effects and is frequently referred to as a "cause and effect diagram." When you facilitate *Root Cause Analysis*, the starting illustration resembles the skeleton of a fish with large bones (categories—remember my explanation of the big *X*'s) and small bones (specific potential causes within each category—remember my explanation of the little *x*'s).

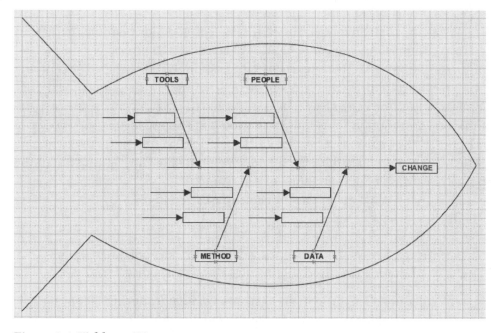

Figure 8.4. Fishbone Diagram

The *Fishbone Diagram* helps the team focus on the most important causes. It would be helpful to work with a Six Sigma Green Belt, Black Belt, or Master Black Belt (MBB) who can help with this *Tool* and provide statistical confidence about factors and measures.

PROCEDURE

- Draw the primary fishbone diagram.

- Agree on the purpose of the item or issue to change, if fine-tuned and fully working.

- List the problem or issue to be studied in the "head of the fish"—for example, "noisy mufflers."

- Label each major bone of the fish by selecting the most appropriate *Perspectives* (chapter 8) or primary bones, such as Tools, People, Method, and Data shown illustratively above (taken from among 30 categories explained with the *Perspectives Tool*).

- Use an idea-generating *Tool* to identify contributing factors within each category that could cause the problem, issue, or effect being studied.

  - For example, the facilitator could ask, "What are the possible *tools* issues affecting or causing the effect?" (for example, for noisy mufflers: "over-torqueing the bolts causing metal fatigue")

  - For example, the facilitator could ask, "What are the possible *people* issues affecting or causing the effect?" (for example, "drivers going too fast over speed bumps")

  - Or the facilitator could ask, "What are the possible *method* issues affecting or causing the effect?" (for example, "stacking mufflers outside before installation and they begin to oxidize or rust before installation")

  - Or the facilitator could ask, "What are the *data* issues affecting or causing the effect?" (for example, "the metallurgical reports from our supplier are not accurate or consistent")

  - Complete each category until you no longer get useful information when you ask, "What other issues could be causing the effect?"

- Repeat this procedure with any additional categories that are identified until you develop and create a final list of potential causes.

- Consider prioritizing the potential causes. If so, know in advance which *Tool* you want to use to prioritize, typically *PowerBalls* (chapter 7). Consider ranking the causes from high to low priority with the first item being the "most probable" or "most impactful" cause.

- Repetitive and more frequent causes may require more extensive analysis and should carry a higher weight.

- Separately confirm the decision criteria available from a prior initiative (such as cost and customer satisfaction). If not available, build the criteria for evaluation.

- Separate the SMART from the fuzzy criteria.

- Prioritize the criteria using *PowerBalls* with *Bookend Rhetoric* (chapter 7) or use a more robust *Tool* such as *Perceptual Mapping* (chapter 7), if required.

- After prioritizing, have the group agree on the most impactful and "most likely" causes. Frequently at this point, leaders instruct the group about the Pareto principle, seeking the 20 percent of causes that generate 80 percent of incidences.[7]

- Where the group remains uncertain, appeal to the fuzzy criteria to guide participants, but only let them use the fuzzy criteria when referring to the most important causes. Do not let participants waste time with the least important causes (except in the rare case that 100 percent diligence is required across every cause because of risks to life, health, or another critical value).

NOTE: Also consider applying the Pareto principle (80-20 rule) after you have prioritized solutions, so that you build consensus around the most important actions that should be endorsed.

After-Action Review Tool

WHY?

Use an *After-Action Review* (*AAR*) for debriefing what went wrong with a project, program, or initiative. An *After-Action Review* may also be called an after-action debriefing, a look back, a postmortem, or a hot wash, among other names. In the Agile community, a similar event is called a retrospective. The logic of an *AAR* supports building a reflection of what caused fixable problems so that we can improve future performance.

An *After-Action Review* is *not* intended to critique or grade success or failure. Rather, it identifies weaknesses that need improvement and strengths that might be leveraged and sustained.

---

[7] The Pareto principle (also known as the 80-20 rule) suggests that in most situations, 80% of outputs or effects are derived from 20% of inputs or causes.

PROCEDURE

After-Action Review answers four "learning culture" questions:

1. Purpose: What was supposed to happen?

2. Results: What did happen?

3. Causes: What caused the difference?

4. Implications: What can we learn from this?

The *After-Action Review* provides a candid conversation of actual performance results compared to purpose and objectives. Hence, participants contribute their subject matter expertise, input, and perspective. They provide their insight, observation, and questions that help reinforce strengths and identify and correct the deficiencies of the action being reviewed.

Learning cultures highly value collaborative inquiry and reflection. The US Armed Forces use *AARs* extensively, using a variety of means to collect hard, verifiable data to assess performance. The US Army refers to its evidence-based learnings as "ground truths."

AARs value openness, candor, and frankness. Participants identify mistakes they made as well as observations of others, without attributing the mistakes to any one or group of people. Few groups open up and provide complete candor, but facilitators should encourage full disclosure. Prohibit any other use of these candid conversations, especially performance reviews and personal evaluations.

Focus on *what* can be learned, not *who* can be blamed.

The US Army's technique uses five basic guidelines that govern its *AARs*, namely:

1. Call it like you see it.

2. Discover the "ground truth."

3. No sugarcoating.

4. No thin or thick skins.

5. Take thorough notes.

An *AAR* meeting takes from a partial day to an entire week. The *AAR* meeting may include 20 to 30 people or more, but not necessarily everyone at once. Hence, participation varies over the course of the meeting.

AFTER-ACTION REVIEW EVENT, MEETING, OR WORKSHOP AGENDA

- **Launch**

  - Use the seven-activity *Launch* (chapter 5). Emphasize the project objectives and expected impact of the project on the organizational holarchy. Carefully articulate key assumptions or constraints.

- **Success Objectives**

  - Results are compared to the SMART objectives. Items that worked or hampered provide input for conversation later. Be immediately cautious about scope creep. Questions that may be out of bounds at this time include why certain actions were taken, how stakeholders reacted, why adjustments were made (or not), what assumptions developed, and other questions that need to be managed later.

- **Goals and Considerations**

  - Compare the project results to the fuzzy goals and other considerations. Again, be careful with scope creep. Manage other questions later such as why certain actions were taken, how stakeholders reacted, why adjustments occurred (or not), and what assumptions developed.

- **What Worked and What Hampered Work**

  - Initially focus on the hard and inescapable facts of what did happen. Results-focused conversation stimulates talk about assumptions, conditions, evidence, examples, and options that impact future actions.

    - How stakeholders reacted

    - What assumptions developed

    - What worked and what hampered

    - Why certain actions took priority

    - What adjustments worked (or not)

    - Other questions as appropriate

- **Issues and Risks**

  - Assess or build a risk management plan and other follow-up actions (such as *Guardian of Change*) based on actual results.

- **Review and Wrap**

  - Use the four-activity conclusion

SPECIAL RULES

With more than 20 people, frequently use *Breakout Teams* (chapter 6). Do not hesitate to partition the meeting so that participants may come and go as required. You may need to loop back, cover material built earlier, and clarify or add to it. The *After-Action Review* shifts the culture from one in which blame is ascribed to one in which learning is prized yet team members willingly remain accountable.

Conduct *AARs* consistently after each significant project, program, or initiative. Therefore, do *not* isolate "failed" or "stressed" projects only. Special rules and guidelines that have proved successful in the past include these:

- Focus on the objectives first.

- Encourage participants to raise any potentially critical issues or lessons.

- Do *not* judge success or failure of individuals (judge performance, not the person).

For learning organizations, the following points support cultural growth:

- Some of the most valuable learning derives from the most stressful situations.

- Train the team to inspect and adapt itself.

- Transform subjective comments and observations into objective learning by converting adjectives such as "quick" into SMART criteria such as "less than 30 seconds."

- Use facilitators who understand the importance of neutrality and do not lecture or preach.

Effective use of *AARs* supports a mindset in organizations that are never satisfied with the status quo—where candid, honest, and open conversation evidences learning as part of the organizational culture. Learning cultures stress everyone's roles and responsibility, and such a culture begins with using hard data to analyze actual results.

6. Actions (Solutions)

If you use an unstructured question like "What should we do about this problem?," the cybersecurity technicians start talking about all sorts of things:

- "Management needs to hire more people."

- "Technicians should be required to use their PTO (paid time off)."

- "I need additional training on _____" (and so on).

They spend most of their meeting in scope (they are not talking about fútball the entire meeting). But when does the meeting end? Not when the list is exhausted. Rather, the meeting ends when the time runs out. Why? People have another meeting to attend; someone else reserved the meeting room; and so on.

If you can't measure it, you can't manage it. With the unstructured style, even though we captured good stuff, there is no way to know what we missed. The nature of "poor requirements" is that omissions can be more expensive than errors.

> NOTE: Although a separate activity, it will not take much time to identify the people, agents, or actors (personas) who will participate in the solution or plan (for example, participants, management, contractors).

PROCEDURE

If you embrace the structured tactic, you know exactly what to do and what four questions you are going to ask for each *and every* cause (for example, fatigue):

1. What can cybersecurity personnel do to prevent fatigue? (for example, improve their diets)

2. What can management do to prevent fatigue? (for example, provide ergonomic furniture)

3. What can cybersecurity personnel do to cure for fatigue? (for example, get to bed earlier)

4. What can management do to cure for fatigue? (for example, hire more people)

NOTE: Here you populate a matrix with the personas and timeline. The quickest way to proceed with the "x" dimension (horizontal or longitudinal—usually time runs from left to right) separately covers the before and after phases (such as what can be done to prevent each cause and then separately, what can be done to cure for each cause, repeating for each identified persona).

Which one of these four questions can you afford to skip? None of them, of course. But business is not always this elementary. Many times, there is a third type of persona: contractors. Sometimes there is a third point in time: during. Look at the matrix in table 8.1 and note that you might need to ask nine questions about each cause because you do not know which ones, if any, you can afford to skip.

I know table 8.1 gives a lot of people headaches. Knowing that to be thorough, participants must answer nine questions about each cause, the general reaction is, "Screw it—let's just have a meeting and discuss it."

How's that unstructured style working out for you? Don't forget that the terms "discussion," "percussion," and "concussion" are all related. If you have a headache when you depart a meeting, the reason is that the meeting was not structured and you are not sure what, if anything, was accomplished.

Table 8.1. Solution Stack (also known as Headache)

Timing / *Persona*	Before Burnout (preventative solutions)	During Burnout (mitigating solutions)	After Burnout (curative solutions)
Management	• List of causes A, B, C, and so on	• List of causes A, B, C, and so on	• List of causes A, B, C, and so on
	• Ideate preventions (1, 2, and so on)	• Ideate mitigations (11, 12, and so on)	• Ideate cures (21, 22, and so on)
Cybersecurity employee	• List of causes A, B, C, and so on	• List of causes A, B, C, and so on	• List of causes A, B, C, and so on
	• Ideate preventions (5, 6, and so on)	• Ideate mitigations (15, 16, and so on)	• Ideate cures (25, 26, and so on)
Contractors	• List of causes A, B, C, and so on	• List of causes A, B, C, and so on	• List of causes A, B, C, and so on
	• Ideate preventions (7, 8, and so on)	• Ideate mitigations (17 18, and so on)	• Ideate mitigations (27 28, and so on)

Innovation Warm-Ups Tool

WHY?

Warm-Ups may be used to set the tone for *Brainstorming* (chapter 6) or general problem-solving meetings. The *Warm-Ups Tool* helps groups to stimulate mind-expanding ideas and conversation, make unusual connections, and analyze relationships.

Warm-Ups can be conducted individually or with *Breakout Teams* (chapter 6); the *Tool* is very friendly to online meeting settings. Be creative and make up your own *Warm-Ups*, striving to select themes related to your meeting deliverables or product or project endeavors.

WARM-UPS

Simply give your group some basic commands. Most important, add your own objects ("things") to modify these questions:

- *Build a process flow diagram for . . .*

  – Washing a dog, mowing the lawn, cutting someone's hair, and so on

- *Coin a novel word for a . . .*

  – New soft drink, computer wizard, hyperactive customer, and so on

- *Describe a . . .*

  – New home on the moon, dessert with unusual ingredients, and so on

- *Design a new . . .*
  - Exercise machine, toy, breakfast food, food supplement, and so on
- *Draw a map of . . .*
  - Ideal playground, new type of amusement park, and so on
- *Give directions for . . .*
  - Making a peanut butter sandwich, tying a tie, and so on
- *Give new uses for a . . .*
  - Coat hanger, dental floss, carrot, whiteboard eraser, and so on
- *Make up a story that includes a . . .*
  - Space alien, garbage disposal, and watermelon
  - Sunflower seed, swimming pool, and 10-gallon hat
- *Name as many things as you can that . . .*
  - Come in pairs, include the word "ship," contain a color in the term (such as "red tape" or "yellow brick road"), and so on
- *Name as many things as you can that are . . .*
  - Soft and white, hard and can float, blue and edible, and so on
- *Name the ways you can . . .*
  - Make a friend, open a jar, thank someone, and so on
- *What would you do to improve . . .*
  - A drinking fountain, eyeglasses, fast food service, traffic congestion, high-rise buildings, and so on

SCAMPER Tool

WHY?

SCAMPER gives you a "hip-pocket" *Tool*—an unplanned way of developing appropriate questions on an impromptu basis. You may also use *SCAMPER* to take raw input (unedited lists) and challenge participants to clarify their input further, thus improving input.

PROCEDURE

Select appropriate questions using the mnemonic "SCAMPER" and challenge some of the initial input. Challenges help the group understand the objective nature of what is being described and encourage developing new options.

SCAMPER Checklist:

- **S** = **S**UBSTITUTE: Have a thing or person act or serve in another's place. Change a component or ingredient within an idea.

- **C** = **C**OMBINE: Bring together or unite. Combine components, ideas, or purposes.

- **A** = **A**DAPT: Adjust or suit to a condition or purpose. Look for surrogates or analogies. Look to the past or the future for parallels, riffs, and variations.

- **M** = **M**ODIFY: Alter or change in form or quality. Modify frequency, intensity, timing, size, and so on.

  - **M**AGNIFY: Enlarge or make greater in quality or form. Consider all appropriate dimensions such as frequency, intensity, timing, size, and so on.

  - **M**INIMIZE: Make smaller, lighter, slower, less frequent. Consider all appropriate dimensions such as frequency, intensity, timing, size, and so on.

- **P** = **P**UT to other uses: Use for purposes other than the one intended. See *Solving Creatively* for creative sparks and new thinking.

- **E** = **E**LIMINATE: Remove, omit, or get rid of a quality, part, or whole. Costs? Effort? Time? Waste?

- **R** = **R**EARRANGE: Change order or create new layout or scheme. See chapter 7 for separate *Tools* on purpose, options, and criteria.

7. Testing (Solution Quality)

Once we have a set of candidate solutions (*what* or *Actions*), we should test them for efficacy. To what extent do proposed solutions support the intended purpose (built in *Agenda Step* 2)? If clear objectives were built or are available, conduct *Alignment* (chapter 6). More important, will performing all these solutions get us from where we are to where we need to be?

If not, or if uncertain, we need to facilitate identification of the reason, immediately followed by identifying what other solutions should be considered. If thorough and acceptable, we can take the solutions and make assignments of *Roles and Responsibilities* (chapter 6) or, for now, simply wrap up.

Because no one can assuredly predict future states, prudent organizations rely on *Scenario Planning* to allow the possibility of sunny skies, stormy skies, or cloudy skies. Building scenarios and ranges begins in the next section.

Scenarios and Ranges Tool

WHY?

Probabilities consist of shared assumptions, beliefs, and outlooks about some future state or condition. Forward-looking deliverables such as five-year plans and shaping curves rely exclusively on the concept of probabilities, since no future state is certain.

How can a meeting facilitator help resolve arguments around conflicting probabilities, particularly when evidence supports multiple outcomes? The answer is by creating ranges and not relying on fixed numbers.

SCENARIO PLANNING RANGES

Strive to avoid building one set of "answers." Rather, build multiple answers—such as five answers. Facilitate mutual understanding around the following five scenario types.

Sunny Skies

Dare your participants to think positive. Ask them to relieve themselves from concerns about risks and other exogenous factors. Strive to build and agree on a "best likely" scenario, akin to sunny skies and clear sailing. Don't allow impediments or other negative throttles. While unlikely, the sunny skies scenario provides one *Bookend Rhetoric* (chapter 7) number or set of projections that would be unlikely to be exceeded within the period specified.

Stormy Skies

Take your participants in the opposite direction. Allow for every conceivable catastrophe or injurious situation. Try to fall short of "bankruptcy" or "going out of business," but relent if your participants make an urgent claim that complete "death" is one outcome.

Partly Sunny Skies

Having built the two prior scenarios, take a closer look at the sunny skies scenario and predict some of the most likely occurrences. Strive to make this view and set of projections positive, but not extreme. If necessary, use *PowerBalls* (chapter 7) to rank the importance of assumptions, and toggle or adjust only the most important outcomes, leaving the others untouched.

Partly Cloudy Skies

With *Bookend Rhetoric*, move again in the opposite direction by taking a closer look at the stormy skies scenario and toggle some of the least likely occurrences. Here you want to facilitate their development of a set of negative but not extreme projections. Have participants study past performance and downturns for reliable percentages. Again, if necessary, use *PowerBalls* to rank the impact of assumptions, and toggle only the most impactful outcomes, leaving the others untouched.

Probable Forecast

Take the four scenarios and projections to drive consensus around the most likely range. Force participants to defend their arguments with evidence, facts, and real-life examples. Have participants agree or disagree with the prioritized lists of assumptions, and revisit the prioritization if necessary. Along the way, begin to listen and note any projections being suggested as "most likely" because they can help establish an agreeable midpoint for final projections and ranges.

GOING FURTHER

Further analysis can take the range and establish targets and thresholds for on-target performance (green lights), cautionary performance (yellow lights), and intervention performance (red lights). Avoid an unstructured discussion. Carefully and extensively document and define assumptions. Remember to use *Definitions* (chapter 6), since you may discover participants in violent agreement with one another!

> NOTE: The value of a meeting facilitator is rarely greater than when serving as a referee for future conditions that cannot be proven, even using evidence-based support.

8. Review and Wrap (Conclusion) Agenda Step

Follow the four-activity sequence for the *Review and Wrap* explained in chapter 5. None of the four activities should ever be skipped entirely, so expand and contract based on your situation and constraints.

ACTIVITIES

1. *Review:* Do not relive the meeting; simply review the outputs, decisions, assignments, and so on. Focus on the results and deliverable of each *Agenda Step* and not on how you got there. Participants do not need a transcript of the meeting; they need to be reminded about the takeaways and to be offered the opportunity to ask for additional information or clarification before the meeting ends.

2. *Open issues and follow-up:* There are various methods and treatments of open items and formal assignments, such as roles and responsibilities. Once post-meeting assignments are clear, the meeting is nearly complete.

3. *Guardian of Change:* Invest a few minutes to get the group to agree on what they are going to tell others when asked about "What happened in that meeting?" Use a T-Chart and build separate messages for superiors and peers (or other stakeholders).

4. *Assessment:* Get feedback on how you did. Set up or mark a whiteboard by the exit door and create two columns, typically *Plus* and

Delta (the Greek letter Δ, which stands for "change"). Have participants write down, on a small Post-it note, at least one thing they liked about the meeting [+] and one thing they would change [Δ]. Ask participants to mount each note in its respective column when departing the room.

QUALITY CONTROL

Effective leaders will not disband their meetings until participants have been offered a final opportunity to comment or question, actions have been assigned, messaging has been agreed to, and feedback for continuous improvement has been solicited.

Quick Summary on Problem Solving

Problem-solving meetings are a hybrid of planning meetings and decision-making meetings; we typically combine parts of each to build a robust solution. Taking the time to be creative or to turn creative ideas into something innovative, something measurable, distinguishes problem-solving sessions.

To that end:

- Always embrace *Perspectives* (chapter 8), from every stakeholder's point of view.

- Explore unusual options because the best solutions often do not walk into the session, they are created during the meeting. Alex Osborn's keen appreciation for *Brainstorming* (chapter 6) was elevated because his participants leveraged one another's ideas to create solutions that were not apparent at the start of the meeting.

- Once you have a prioritized list of *Causes*, there are numerous paths you may take to develop *Solutions*, ranging from quick *Breakout Team* (chapter 6) sessions to extensive *Root Cause Analysis* (chapter 8). Have both a plan and a back-up plan depending on how well or quickly your meeting progresses.

- Remember that "poor requirements" usually indicate that something was missed or overlooked, not that the requirements gathered were incorrect. Therefore, be painstaking with detailed questions.

- You will find yourself in a position (eventually) where you don't have all the stakeholders in the meeting who need to be part of the solution. Anticipate that likelihood before your meeting and determine in advance how you are going to deal with that situation. Postpone? Call the stakeholders in? Or do something else?

- When building *Solutions*, remember the logic of *Scenario Planning* (chapter 8) and build ranges of numbers when projecting into the future, not one fixed number. Then prepare to review the work and toggle the ranges so that in some scenarios you hit the "most likely" end of the range, in others you hit the "least likely" end of the range, and so on.

- Allow time for rigorous *Testing*: to what extent will these *Solutions* (or this plan) get us from where we are to where we need to be?

9

Controlling

ONLINE CHALLENGES AND SPECIAL SITUATION TOOLS

This chapter provides additional devices (*Tools*) and highlights a few significant differences between facilitating in-person meetings and facilitating online meetings (without exploring or favoring specific application programs, brands, or technologies). While many facilitation experts recommend twice as much preparation time to get ready for online meetings (along with having two facilitators), I take a more practical approach, providing tips that will help you, the solo practitioner, prepare faster and complete on time while facilitating alone.

Finally, I did not want to close this book without also sharing a few special *Tools* and *Meeting Approaches* that I've learned to love. And for those of you also subjected to staff or board meetings, there are some special controls to help you get done faster, as leader *or* participant.

Online Challenges: Benefits and Concerns

Material covered thus far supports online meetings. Effective online facilitation requires line of site, listening skills, conflict management acumen, and meeting design. In fact, learning *what* to do remains most critical, because *how* you complete facilitated meetings can be easily modified once you know *what* to do.

> NOTE: For example, in our private lives we "pay bills" (*what* we do). Most remitters use some form of electronic funds transfer, but you could also send a check, use currency, use a credit card, and so on. *How* you pay bills becomes far less important than making sure the bills get paid (*what* gets done).

The larger the group, the more your meeting facilitation skills need to keep any one person from dominating online meetings. Remember, scope creep begins in meetings.

GIVEN THE CHOICE

Organizations justify online meetings to save travel time and money, along with reducing some risks associated with travel. While online meetings work particularly well for reviewing progress and sharing information, they are not optimal for all deliverables. The online platform becomes suboptimal when the meeting is a kickoff or attended phase-gate review, when consensus is critical, when the issues are contentious, or when the situation involves highly political decision-making and trade-offs. Figure 9.1 shows some of the different factors that affect the choice of online or in-person meetings.

Online meetings may be helpful when . . .

- Conversations are focused and brief

- Groups are geographically dispersed, typically intercontinental

- Ongoing work teams must continually update one another (for example, Daily Scrum, although colocation remains preferred)

- Diverse perspectives and rotational contributors are valued

- There is no alternative (for example, during a pandemic)

Online meetings are not optimal when . . .

- Challenging issues, arguments, or disagreements must be resolved

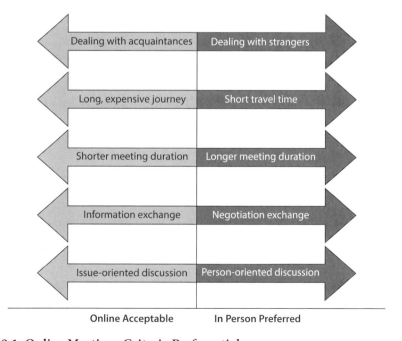

Figure 9.1. Online Meetings Criteria Preferential

- People are experiencing job assignments, organizational changes, or technology overload

- Relationship and trust building may be as important as sharing information

- Talking face-to-face simply makes more sense

- The technology keeps getting in the way

Research and results are quite clear. You can expect online meetings to take much longer to accomplish the same amount of work than in-person meetings, for these reasons:

- Participants stay more fully engaged when they are observed, can observe others, and "feel" nonverbal clues and intonations.

- Thirty to 60 percent of "meaning" (the intent behind the words or message) is communicated or expressed outside of the words that are selected.

- When English might be a participant's second, third, or fourth language, you cannot assume everyone is hearing or understanding the same message. In fact, it is wiser to assume participants are *not* sharing the same understanding and that at least one person has a different interpretation.

AVOID HYBRID MEETINGS

"All or none" (or colocation) is a better policy than holding hybrid meetings. When some participants gather in person and others remain remote, facilitation challenges increase. Remote participants frequently are treated and feel like "second-class" citizens. Yet the secret to creating equanimity is effortless. If some people must "dial in" or "Zoom in," then make everyone dial in. It is much easier and more effective to manage a full complement of remote participants than to try to blend in-person and off-site participants. And don't forget, strive to keep your group size between five and nine participants for optimal performance.

> NOTE: Don't forget the Agile principle of "all or none"—meaning to avoid hybrid meetings. Either everyone attends in person (colocated or in the same physical vicinity) or everyone attends online.

COMMUNICATING

Online meetings increase the likelihood of engaging multiple cultures. In the absence of some of the in-person intuitive and visual feedback, closely monitor:

- Clarity—From idioms to accents, people need to slow down their rate of speech, enunciate clearly, and project a bit louder.

- Grammar—Avoid interrupting. Rather, use feedback and reflection to correct for imprecise word or grammar choices. Be patient.

- Jargon and slang—Carefully monitor expressions like "silver bullet" and "on the same wavelength." Avoid idioms that are not universal, such as "don't make waves." In Islamic and Buddhist cultures, "thank God" may be considered blasphemous unless meant piously. There are thousands of other examples.

- "Officialese"—Your particular concern here ought to be acronyms—or what many people call acronyms (technically, an acronym needs to spell an actual word). Even basic English abbreviations may not be understood by everyone, such as "P & L" or "AC" (is air-conditioning or alternating current intended?).

- Vocabulary—After providing reflection, do not forget to confirm that everyone understands what has been stated. If you sense that someone is holding back, consider a roll call technique (round-robin) to have each person interpret how the most recent content affects him or her.

Special Preparatory Activities

Prepare thoroughly and allow twice as much time when possible. As meeting leader, you need to keep all your participants fully engaged. Thorough preparation requires planning your activities, scripting your questions, and creating backup plans. You will be responsible for keeping participants clear about what you need from each of them; therefore, do the following:

- Provide participants with a written meeting purpose, scope, objectives, and *Basic Agenda*. Stipulate broad expectations and detailed questions that your subject matter experts need to properly prepare for the call, even 50-minute calls.

- Highlight your dial-in number, passcodes, and attendance list.

- Encourage everyone to invest in quality cameras, microphones, and headsets to avoid feedback and noise that negatively affects both sound and video quality, causing distractions.

- For yourself, dual monitors are necessary: one for the gallery and one for screen-sharing. Optimally, the meeting facilitator uses three screens: one for the faces of the participants, one for static and temporary material such as legends or definitions of key terms, and one for the dynamically changing material such as focused on an easel, a whiteboard, or some shared screen platform.

- Invest in a second or third camera. Using a dedicated camera for standing, especially if at an easel or whiteboard, commands attention and prevents viewer fatigue. Affordable document readers are crisp and powerful.

- Place an analog clock in your background to indicate progress.

- Wear glasses that minimize gloss and flare-ups. When possible take off your glasses entirely.

- Instruct everyone to reboot their computer and their router before meetings. Encourage hard-wired internet connections in lieu of wi-fi.

- Inform participants about the files or sites that should be open and available. For more extensive workshops, send *Participants' Package* two weeks in advance with the items listed in chapter 5.

- Decide how to reach one another if a technical problem arises. Decide how participants will be informed about unplanned changes to meeting arrangements or technology failures.

Logistical considerations:

- Cultural differences (impacts timing)

- Language differences and competencies (impacts speed, efficiency)

- Time zone differences (impacts bio-breaks)

- Type or mix of technology and communications (impacts speed, clarity)

Facilitation considerations

- Nonmeeting titles and roles (everyone's an equal participant)

- Multitasking expectations (enforce "be here now")

- Organizational differences (truly collaborative or not?)

- Social factors (trust and team-building needs increase)

- Work histories (mitigate tenure and title "superiority")

Meeting design considerations

- Participant, product, and project interdependencies

- Team size (optimally, seven, plus or minus two)

- Technical skills (separating *what* from *how*)

Figure 9.2. Sample Artifacts for Online Sessions

SCHEDULING

Invest heavily in scheduling and preparation, because you cannot rely on your "charisma" when meeting with online participants:

- Allow extra time. An hour in an online meeting will *never* accomplish as much as an hour in a face-to-face meeting.

- Consider the impact of volume of comments when building the agenda. If everyone in a 10-person meeting provides input on a specific issue, and comments average two minutes each, you can only complete two issues per hour (in addition to your *Launch* [chapter 5] and *Wrap* [chapter 5]).

- Get your tech together. Something will always go wrong, so have a backup plan. Consider sending "hand notices" (figure 9.2) to provide visual indication of audio challenges. I've been frequently thanked for sending out the four cards in figure 9.2 in advance to each participant.

- Provide a map with thumbnail photographs of your participants showing their location and time zone on a map.

- Set up appropriate arrangements for accessibility-impaired participants (TTY, simultaneous transcriptions, and so on). Apple, Microsoft, and others should be commended for pushing the envelope on making modern technology available to most everyone.

During Online Meetings

ONLINE SEATING CHARTS

Greet each person as they come online and create an online seating chart. Seating charts (also known as roll calls) are indispensable and may be used frequently during online meetings. Assign a virtual seat in a circular sequence to everyone as they join the meeting. Tell them where they are sitting at your imaginary U-shaped table. Encourage them to create a mental picture of the room and their orientation to the other participants. Use their seating positions to determine the roll call sequence you may use at significant inflection points.

LAUNCHING

Getting and keeping people involved takes a concerted effort from start to finish. Get off to a good start by setting a good example:

- Log in first and early. Today, even experienced and expert facilitators continue to allow one hour, and sometimes more, to ensure all the technologics arc working properly (and sometimes more).

- Set camera at face height, or very slightly above (not below, looking up at rolled chins and nose hairs). Look at the green dot on the camera, not your monitor. Please smile.

- Introduce each participant to subsequent arrivals while assigning them their virtual seat.

- Lean forward into the camera to command attention. Your head should normally occupy about 25 percent of the screen. During points of emphasis, however, move closer and reach at least 33 percent of the screen when speaking, even cutting off your hairline.

- Confirm early that cvcryonc can hear each other clearly.

NOTE: *Icebreakers* remain particularly valuable with online settings. Even basic questions like "favorite ice cream" strengthen connections between participants remotely located from one another.

- Provide *Ground Rules* (chapter 5) and then enforce them. Add the *Ground Rule* "no hiding." This rule forces participants to remain live and not hide behind still photographs or icons of their favorite university mascots.

- Consider assigning people separate roles to help you, such as a time-keeper or a specialized note-taker for each of the following:
  - *Action Items*: to be assigned later
  - *Decisions*: agreements, inflection points, and issues that are closed
  - *Guardian of Change*: specific communications about *who* needs to be informed *what* updates
  - *Parking Lot*: open items

- Establish and enforce protocol demanding that speakers announce their names (or nicknames) when taking a turn speaking. The ideal protocol is "one name only," because verbs and prepositions do not add value.

NOTE: Most people do not use a protocol because they feel that saying "Hi, this is Terrence speaking," is a waste of time. They're right. We do not need the words "Hi, this is . . . speaking." They add no value. Simply identify and reinforce the name behind the voice with a single word or term, like "Metz" (then speak).

Heed this suggestion closely when you end up with hybrid meetings and a few remote people calling in. The participants attending in person don't bother to identify themselves because they can see who is speaking. Unfortunately, the remote people pay only partial attention when they cannot attribute the source of content. Their time is frequently wasted because we fail to treat them as active and fully engaged participants.

- Regularly remind participants where you are in the agenda, preferably with a visual indicator. Provide clear endings and smooth transitions for each *Agenda Step* as you progress.

- Texture is your friend. Rely on handheld artifacts that you can position in front of the camera. With artifacts, move your hands slowly and in full view on occasion.

- Load appropriate .jpg files to render green-screen versions as if you are a television weatherperson explaining a chart or graphic in the background.

- Based on who is attending and the brand of technology being used, set up your *Breakout* rooms in advance. Name them creatively with topics related to the issues at hand. Some topics need homogeneous groups who think alike, and others need to be stirred up with heterogeneous groups.

ETIQUETTE AND QUALITY

If you don't monitor participant etiquette, no one else will. While some of the following directives reflect common sense, your role as the process police officer mandates enforcing standards:

- Avoid paper rustling and other office noise. Have folks turn off notifications, both on desktops and on handheld devices.

- Be acutely aware of the impact of accents. Have everyone, including yourself, slow down the vocal pace and tempo, project louder, and fully explode the consonants, especially consonants in the middle of words, such as the middle *n* in the word "consonant."

CAUTION: When members of one team use a second language, or when members of one group are subcontractors, or when participants in one group clearly have higher pay or status, people build the perception that one group is "better" than the other. Such perceptions will quickly destroy the respect, trust, and commitment that are essential for true collaboration. Remind participants that facilitators treat everyone as equal, and see whether participants can support this equality. If not, you have serious problems, so consider delaying your meeting until after additional conversations.

- Carefully manage cadence and control pace. Slow down during transitions and speed up during the middle of your *Agenda Steps*.

- Demand punctuality, but consider more frequent bio-breaks, at least hourly. Consider body-stretching exercises during longer meetings. Before bio-breaks, consider a quick *Plus-Delta* assessment and ask for immediate feedback.

- Do not permit multitasking. Remind people to "be here now" and avoid keyboard sounds, side comments, and flushing toilets. Speak with violators after the meeting so that you do not embarrass them. Continuously strive to eliminate distractions.

- For video-presence meetings especially, beware of audio lag. Compression algorithms cause latency that extends up to three seconds. Be patient. Everyone does not hear everyone else at the same time.

- Silence is OK. Letting people catch up or catch their breath is natural.

- When possible, include one social learning event per hour. Strive for a balance, such as conducting a 10-minute instruction, a 10-minute *Breakout Team* (chapter 6) session, a 20-minute group interaction, a 10-minute social connection, and a 10-minute break.

PREPARING TO WRAP

Throughout, emphasize reflection and confirmation of content. Too frequently, online participants are distracted and do not capture as much as they do when meeting face-to-face. Summarize, summarize, summarize: a "clear group" may be an oxymoron.

- Use the four *Review and Wrap* (chapter 5) activities including review, *Parking Lot, Guardian of Change*, and *Meeting Assessment*.

- Be sure to review, affirm, and confirm assignments and deadlines. Summarize and conclude by confirming the schedule for the next meeting.

- Offer each participant an opportunity for final or closing comments. Offer participants the simple courtesy of saying "Pass." Alternatively, consider "Just Three Words," for example: "What three words describe your experience with today's meeting?"

- Use an evaluation form to improve subsequent calls. A *Plus-Delta* assessment (chapter 5) can also be completed at the conclusion of each call. Electronic polls may be used. For longer projects, send anecdotal forms out on occasion (see figure 5.4).

- Distribute notes within hours after the meeting and emphasize the follow-up actions and responsibilities in your email cover note. Include a set of comments and links copied from the chat room (if available).

Significant Online Differences

Use your intuition. Since you cannot rely as much on nonverbal feedback, remain firm but flexible.

- Avoid screen-sharing for more than 30 seconds at a time.

- Do not forget about the lag time. A latency that extends up to three seconds (or longer) affects everyone's comprehension because they fail to remember or understand the importance of nonverbal reactions when everyone does not hear everyone else at the same time.

- Dress for video presence. Stripes and patterns are not friendly during videoconferences. Plain-colored clothing is optimal. Also, avoid wearing white and red. With video presence, restrict or slow down movement when possible. Viewers may be disrupted by rapid movements, especially with poor video transmission.

- Embrace advanced collaboration technology to create shared electronic notes, flip charts, whiteboards, and so on. Do not hesitate to use a second camera by pointing it to an easel pad or whiteboard. You don't have to get fancy to be effective. Keep it simple.

- For decision-making or other inflection points, clearly restate or repeat key issues as they are precisely articulated. This is an appropriate time for visual reflection as well, whether handwritten or typed; provide visual feedback of inflection points.

- Since much of the nonverbal and intuitive feedback and observation has been minimized, use a roll call or "a round circle" (a round-robin using your online seating arrangement) to allow quieter people and people who may have been cut off by someone else to add input.

- Take extreme caution when imposing new platforms on participants who may not be familiar with the most current and "best" technology. When they are challenged, it is no longer the "best" for them and thus not the best choice for your group either.

- Use *Breakout Team* (chapter 6) sessions frequently. Don't hesitate to use *Breakout Teams* with only two people in each group.

- Use people's names to get their attention. In advance, provide everyone the opportunity to say "pass" when asked a question directly by name or during general roll calls.

ONLINE TECHNOLOGY

Many of the complaints registered against online technology are misdirected. Frequently, the complainer didn't know *what* to do in person either. Collaborative online meeting technology can speed idea generation and data collection. Technology can also change group dynamics by allowing people to contribute anonymously through polling and asynchronous arrangements that also give participants more time to think.[1] Consider the following about such arrangements:

- Anonymous contributions may remove political overtones.

- Everyone can see everyone else's contributions and build upon them.

- Participants may work on the same topic at once.

- Such arrangements can offer flexibility to adapt to schedules, time zones, and budgets.

REMINDER

If you know *what* to do in the role of meeting leader, you will find it remarkably easy to change *how* you do it. Once you integrate clear thinking about your meeting design, you could scratch participants' comments in sand or post them in the cloud: it doesn't matter *how* you do it when you want to build consensus. All methods, whether in-person or online, require leadership line of site, active listening, and appropriate meeting design and tools. In truth, most people who "fail" online are not particularly effective in person either.

The following pages outline some special-purpose *Tools* and meetings.

Breaks Tool

WHY?

Besides standard 10-minute breaks every 75 minutes or so, you may need to break up participants' saturation—for a change of scenery. "Special" breaks enable people to stand up, move around, and think of the situation in an unusual way (for example, by going outdoors).

"THEY NEED A BREAK" PROCEDURE

Whenever participants get stuck on a subject, in a circular argument, drowsy, brain-dead, and so on, take a break. Before you send them on their break, however, do the following:

- Give them 5 minutes in addition to the normal 10 minutes (15 minutes total).

---

[1] Polling and asynchronous arrangements enable participants to contribute at separate times from separate places.

- Post some question (visually) that participants need to address when the break is finished.

- Tell them to use 10 minutes for themselves as they normally would, but to take the additional 5 minutes and walk around, preferably getting some fresh air (outside), or doing some minor stretching.

- During the extra 5 minutes, tell participants to develop one or two compelling responses to the question you have posted.

- When participants return, begin by capturing the input they developed.

"YOU NEED A BREAK" PROCEDURE

If you are stuck, saturated, or brain dead—take a break. Before you send participants on their break, however, repeat the procedure above. Note the following benefits to this technique:

- Participants remain productive for five minutes of the break, while giving you a full quarter hour to "phone home," sort through your notes, or better ascertain what you should do next.

- You get to save face while at the same time creating a win-win scenario. Very few professionals in the history of the world have ever been disappointed in a meeting when told that it was time to take a break. They have plenty of other stuff to do.

"EVERYONE NEEDS A BREAK" PROCEDURE

Clinical proof tells us that you learn faster after exercise than after sitting still. Why? Exercise improves the blood's access to specific brain regions and stimulates learning cells to make brain-derived neurotrophic factor (BDNF), which acts like a fertilizer for neurons.

Especially during full-day or multiple-day workshops, you will note around 3 p.m. that energy is lagging. Biorhythms are lower mid-afternoon than at any point, even compared to our sleeping hours. So, be prepared to take a quick 30- to 60-second ergonomic break.

- Ask everyone to stand up.

- Lead yourself or have someone predetermined (such as someone who takes or teaches yoga, Pilates, and so on) to guide the group with a few undemanding exercises. For example, have participants roll their heads, twist their torsos, bend their hips, rotate their arms, and so on.

- Alternatively, substitute basic deep-breathing exercises.

- Experiment, based on how many participants, how much space is available, and how much time is remaining. Everyone will benefit, feel better, and stay awake longer.

Content Management Tool

WHY?

To develop consensual understanding about the impact of speakers' presentations, open issues, or otherwise newly obtained or developed information.

Using a slide presentation as an example, it's common to conduct a question-and-answer activity when the presenter has completed a presentation. Next, participants give the speaker a round of applause and take a break or dismiss. As participants, we assume that we all heard the same thing or that our interpretation will automatically lead to consensual changes and coherent behavior. Such is not always the case. In fact, meeting participants may take off in opposite directions based on their biases, filters, and interpretation of the presented content.

PROCEDURE

The following begins optimally before a speaker's presentation has begun, by suggesting that the listeners should be capturing takeaways (facts or evidence), why we should care (implications), and what we may want to do differently that will make us more efficient or effective (recommendations) because of the presentation we just sat through.

> NOTE: If nothing changes in our world, then the presentation was a waste of time. If we're not sure what changed, we need help or insight. If we disagree on what changed, let's find out now.

Since we're focused on what the participants will do differently, it's a clever idea to conduct a review activity with a technique that breaks down the "many-to-many" into uncomplicated logic and more manageable takeaways (see figure 9.3):

1. Solicit takeaways such as facts, evidence, or examples newly learned by meeting participants. This list provides the *what* factors.

2. For each *what* factor from step 1 (one at a time), develop consensual understanding about the implications and why we care. Strive to

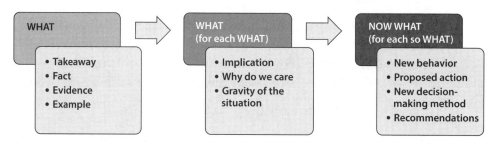

Figure 9.3. Content Management Tool

obtain objective measurements that properly scale the gravity of each implication. This list provides the *so what* factors.

3. For each *so what* factor or implication (one at a time), facilitate consensual understanding about what changes in our lives—what we should do differently. Develop recommendations based on the implications rather than the facts. This list of new behaviors is why we took the time and money to listen to the speaker—it comprises a list of *now whats*.

Flexibility Matrix Tool

WHY?

To help a group understand needed trade-offs. Executive sponsors want the best, the fastest, and the cheapest, but something's got to give. (For example, it's highly unlikely you can access a 5-star hotel at the base camp of a major mountain, which guarantees a successful ascent the next day, for USD$100.)

If you ask an executive sponsor, "Among time (for example, speed), cost (for example, price), and quality (for example, scope), which is most important?," the likely answer will be "all of them." Therefore, we concede that scope, timing, and cost are the crucial factors, but we seek to understand where we have the most amount of flexibility and, conversely, the least amount of flexibility.

PROCEDURE

Since the sponsor may not give us that information, we can ask the team to build it. This *Flexibility Matrix Tool* captures group assumptions to support consistent decision-making. Building consensus around flexibility early and up front helps drive consistent decision-making across the life cycle of projects or products.

Build the blank template in advance. Fully define or explain the terms "time," "cost," and "quality" for your situation.

- Be certain to use *Bookend Rhetoric* (chapter 6), and ask the team, "Where do we have the most amount of flexibility?" Then ask, "Where do we have the least amount of flexibility?"

- We know the moderate box by default: it is the remaining blank.

After participants have indicated their choices by placing check marks in the appropriate columns, have the group convert each check mark into a narrative sentence providing the rationale and support. For example, using the illustration in table 9.1, we might find that schedule is *least* flexible *because* we must be ready for use by October 1. Quality, defined as scope or feature set, is the *most* flexible *because* we can secure improvements, updates, or upgrades later.

Table 9.1. Flexibility Matrix

Flexibility	Least	Moderate	Most
Resources (Cost)		✓	
Schedule (Time)	✓		
Scope (Quality)			✓

Intervention Tools

ISSUE BAG (TIME FILLER)

When you need a productive time-filler for a few minutes, turn to your *Parking Lot* (chapter 5) and pick a quick-hit issue the group needs to talk over. By the time you are finished, lunch will have arrived. If not, continue with an additional open item.

PETER AND PAULINE (ANTAGONISTS)

This exercise enables people who do not necessarily like each other to get to know each other better. It forces antagonists to stand in each other's shoes, thus reducing the antagonism for a while. This exercise may take 30 minutes or more—so plan accordingly:

- Pair off into groups of two—especially pair off the antagonists.

- Tell one member of each pair to interview the other for five minutes. When the timer sounds, reverse the interviewer and interviewee for another five minutes. Interviewers could be asking for . . .

  - Background or special talents

  - Hobbies and talents

  - Scars and awards

  - Successes and fun factors

  - Other information that is appropriate and revealing

- Bring the groups back together.

- Tell people to introduce themselves as the person they interviewed.

As the first antagonist makes the other sound like a hero (because they want to prove that they are not the cause of any animosity), some people will giggle at the flowery remarks. The second antagonist, of course, must go a step further and make the first one sound like the best thing since "sliced bread." Now people are laughing. They know the two cannot be serious but having put a stake in the ground and publicly praising the other person forces them to maintain respect throughout the meeting in order to "save face."

THUMBS (CONTEXTUAL APPROVAL)

While it is critical to be sensitive to the meaning of nonverbal gestures for the people and cultures you facilitate, some groups in the United States rely on a quick thumb indicator to generate a quick sense of the level of consensus about consensual issues, such as, "Should we break for lunch now?":

 thumb up equals full agreement (but not in all countries)

thumb sideways equals partial agreement

thumb down equals full disagreement

FIST OF FIVE (CONTEXTUAL APPROVAL)

This *Tool* has the speed of using "thumbs-up" or "thumbs-down" and displays the degrees of agreement across participants. Using this *Tool*, people vote using their hands and display fingers to represent their degree or intensity of support:

Fist—A clear no vote, block to consensus: "I am opposed and need more information or changes with this proposal."

One finger—"I am opposed and need to discuss certain issues and changes that might be made."

Two fingers—"I have some reservations and want to discuss it further."

Three fingers—"It's not my favorite, but I can live with it and support it without further discussion."

Four fingers—"I think this is a reasonable idea. Wish I'd thought of it."

Five fingers—"It's a great idea and I am a major supporter."

Scoping or Framing Tool

WHY?

Groups need a *Tool* to help them stay focused on the same topic—to avoid scope creep. When participants agree about what something is, they might need to test their agreement by confirming what the thing is *not*.

Clarifying what something "is not" and "is" creates a *Scoping* statement— what may or may not be included in a field of work. Strong empirical evidence says you should always begin with what something "is not" (out of scope) and then continue with what something "is" (in scope).

PROCEDURE

Various means may be used to capture input, including *Breakout Teams* (chapter 6), Post-it notes, electronic templates, and off-line gathering. You can also gather input from multiple *Perspectives* (chapter 8).

Table 9.2. "Is Not—Is" Procedure

Is Not (Out)	Is (In)	Uncertain
✓ ~~~~~~~~~~~~~	✓ ~~~~~~~~~~~~~	✓ ~~~~~~~~~~~~
✓ ~~~~~~~~~~~~~	✓ ~~~~~~~~~~~~~	✓ ~~~~~~~~~~~~
✓ ~~~~~~~~~~~~~	✓ ~~~~~~~~~~~~~	
✓ ~~~~~~~~~~~~~	✓ ~~~~~~~~~~~~~	
✓ ~~~~~~~~~~~~~	✓ ~~~~~~~~~~~~~	

Consider using the "is not—is" procedure (table 9.2) concurrently with results or output from *Categorizing* (chapter 6). If not, there are typically similar or redundant components that can be eliminated or "chunked" together.

Once the group feels comfortable with how they have categorized what *is not* and what *is* in scope of the topic at hand, aggregate the inputs into a narrative statement. The statement, or brief paragraph, can then be appealed to during the project or product life to see whether something new should be included or not. Let the group know that the initial statement may be modified later if needed, and frequently is, usually to sharpen the edges and make the scope more detailed and clearer.

When needed, there is also an "uncertain" option. Most items should be "is not" or "is," but some remain undecided until they are resolved or escalated to a sponsor or review board to decide.

Staff Meetings

WHY?

There are good meetings, and there are long meetings, but there aren't many good, long meetings. Based on Agile's Daily Scrum, this procedure encourages self-advancing teams to meet daily, yet briefly. Time-boxed to 15 minutes in duration, the Daily Scrum may also be called a morning roll call, daily huddle, or a daily stand-up. You can use the following questions to improve your own regularly conducted staff meetings, whether you are the leader or a participant.

THE THREE QUESTIONS

Daily Scrum meetings provide team members insight about where each other focuses their activities. For instance, you may use the trichotomy formula of "yesterday, today, and tomorrow" to modify the questions listed here for your needs.

The classic three questions (with alternatives) are as follows:

1. What did you complete yesterday? (What did I accomplish yesterday?)

2. What are you focused on today? (What will I do today?)

3. What impediments are you facing that we might help you with? (What obstacles are impeding my progress?)

Here's a motivational version:

1. What did you do to change the world yesterday? (What did you accomplish since we last met?)

2. What are you going to crush today? (What are you working on until our next meeting?)

3. What obstacles are you going to blast through that may be unfortunate enough to be standing in your way? (What is getting in your way or keeping you from doing your job?)

COMMENTS

Use the same technique for your weekly, biweekly, or monthly staff meetings. Although not exhaustive, scope creep is prevented when progress reports are restricted to yesterday (past), today (present), and obstacles (future). Additionally, standing rather than sitting ensures that staff meetings remain brief, discourages wasted time, and keeps participants in scope.

> NOTE: The Daily Scrum does not provide the time and place to solve problems. Rather, the Daily Scrum makes the team aware of what people are working on. If detailed support is required, a separate meeting with appropriate participants is arranged *after* the meeting. Topics that require additional attention should always be deferred until every team member has reported.

Board and Committee Meetings

You may lead or participate in board meetings that rely on *Robert's Rules of Order*. However, you may still leverage your facilitative leadership skills to improve the clarity of meeting output and the quality of meeting outcomes.

In 1876, General Henry M. Robert wrote the rules of the U.S. Congress (parliamentary procedure) for common citizens and societal groups with his publication of the *Pocket Manual of Rules of Order*.[2] One hundred and fifty years later, his grandson, Henry M. Robert III, was living with an MG RUSH alumnus (also a monsignor) in the rectory at St. Mary's Parish, Annapolis. The two frequently argued at dinnertime over the value of "voting" compared with "building consensus." There is a time and place for both methods of decision-making. Never forget, however, that voting may not yield better decisions, only bigger numbers. For decision quality, strive for diversity of views and building consensus.

---

[2] Henry Robert, *1907 Pocket Manual of Robert's Rules of Order for Deliberative Assemblies* (1907).

CONSENT AGENDA ALTERNATIVE

For routine decisions such as approval of meeting minutes, committee reports, and other noncontroversial items, use a consent agenda to save a lot of time. Consent agendas enable the board to approve items that do not require discussion or independent action—in other words, items that do not need to be motioned, seconded, debated, and so on. After the *Launch Agenda Step* (chapter 6), make producing a consent agenda the next item, so that you spend precious meeting time on items that demand members' input.

> NOTE: The concept of using a consent agenda should be approved in advance. Consent agenda items should also be distributed at least one day before the meeting so that members can review the material before being asked to ratify it.

With traditional board meetings, parliamentary procedure expedites *Agenda Steps* and provides structure that ensures topics are considered, managed, and documented. As meeting leader, embrace the following facilitative tips.

GET YOUR MEETING OFF TO A SOLID START

Start every board or committee meeting with a solid, well-prepared *Launch*. Cover the seven required activities quickly, but thoroughly. In sequence, the introductory activities should do the following:

- Reinforce your role as meeting facilitator and their roles as equal voices

- Provide one statement that covers the purpose of the meeting (can be reused)

- Stipulate the scope for each specific meeting (typically time horizon)

- Provide one statement that distills the meeting deliverable (can be reused)

- Cover any administrative or noncontent issues

- Review the *Basic Agenda*

- Review *Ground Rules* (chapter 4) to ensure the group gets more done faster

SUSTAIN AN UPBEAT TEMPO

Your best meetings will conclude ahead of schedule. Do not overinvest in early topics and shortchange the value of later topics. "New business" often follows "department reports," and "new business" remains one of the most important topics of every meeting. Be sure that you get to that topic.

DO NOT ALLOW SCOPE CREEP

Do not allow your participants to wander, ramble, and extemporaneously talk too much. Keep them on point. Focus on *what* has transpired, *not how* they are accomplishing stuff. Most important, do not deviate from the agenda by jumping around to the topic of the moment. Cut people off when necessary with the caveat that their content will be covered in a later *Agenda Step*.

FOCUS ON OUTPUT, NOT OUTCOME

Satisfy the legalities of mandated meetings, but strive for clear and actionable results each time. Focus on change and what actions transpire because of shared learnings, experience, and suggestions. Carefully record and separately document decisions, actions, and other inflection points. Visualize your deliverable for every *Agenda Step*. What should we do now? What should we do differently? If nothing changes, we wasted our meeting time with material we could have reviewed on our own.

MANAGE OPEN ISSUES AND FOLLOW-UP

Make yourself comfortable with one of the three procedures for managing the *Parking Lot* (chapter 5) and making follow-up assignments. If board members' contributions need to be analyzed further, make the assignment clear so that they can prepare input when the issue is brought up again in a different forum. Conclude with any reminders that help participants show up better prepared for the next meeting. And remember, strive for consensus, rather than relying on voting as a painless way out. Consensus, as a more sophisticated way out than voting, will generate higher returns on the investment of your money and your board members' time.

Epilogue

Do not read this unless you are driven to help others.

First, there is you, the subject. As you wake up, you observe things external to yourself, outside objects. The observation itself establishes your connection. When visual, your connection may be called line of site. When invisible, I'll refer to your connections as "cords." Either way, think of a cord as a thin string that flexes, like a bungee cord, getting thicker or thinner with each flex and distance.

The objects connected with you are nouns, things. The cords that connect the object and you operate as verbs or predicates. The cords constantly contract, expand, and change direction, changing the relationship between you, the subject, and the outsider, the object.

Within you are an infinite amount of sparklines, emerging from an imaginary center point. Each sparkline possesses numerous attributes. Each attribute further divides into many characteristics. Like a single bar gauge that goes up and down (such as a speedometer), each characteristic, attribute, and sparkline is constantly moving up, down, and around—never static. For example, as your courage bar goes up, your fear bar goes down. As your confidence increases, your doubt diminishes. You, the subject, are seamlessly shifting in color and temperature—but more important, so is your sense of connectedness, as is consciousness. Your life, in constant motion, constantly affects everything else.

And like "relativity" or the "butterfly effect," as your consciousness increases, the distance between you and the objects outside you decreases, and that cord gets thicker. Likewise, as your consciousness drifts elsewhere, the cord lengthens and gets thinner—but never, ever does it disconnect entirely.

You see, we're all connected, inexplicably. On occasion, our cords get knotted. Think of your higher self as controlling your lower self as a puppeteer controls a marionette. The knots get in the way and cause some cords to work less effectively—sometimes, barely at all.

Our purpose in life is to serve and that means to remove the knots so that connections remain free and flowing. Positive or forward thinking helps by reducing or eliminating knots, allowing a freer exchange between the cords. Altruistic thoughts, words, and deeds are encouraged by the simple fact that we all strive to avoid pain.

Mother Teresa of Calcutta removed or eased a lot of knots in her lifetime. Beings like Adolf Hitler created knots, rather than removing them. Thank God that more of us would rather be like Mother Teresa than Hitler. Why? As consciousness increases, natural law becomes our driving nature—get rid of the knots (pain). Abraham Maslow referred to knots as a hierarchy of needs. Donald Miller emphasizes the needs to survive and thrive, to conserve energy. And on, and on, and on . . .

World-class facilitators are servant leaders. Potent servant leaders should be facilitating, because facilitating removes knots, making it easier for connections to flow. The first step to becoming a world-class meeting facilitator is to be a servant leader, and the first step to becoming a world-class servant leader is to become conscious of natural law and the importance of helping others remove their knots.

Appendix

Support and Reinforcement

Use the following supplements to understand yourself better. The two most important days of your life are the day you were born and the day you figured out why. The materials in this appendix are intended to shed light on why facilitation and being facilitative are virtuous, to help you understand the rules of nature and natural order, and to illuminate servant leadership. The golden rule variations, including the "silver rule" version, and the *Tao Message of Invisibility*, are here for you to appreciate.

The *Meeting Design Steps* and *Agenda Framework* are intentionally duplicated here (from chapter 5) for your convenience. An alphabetical list of *Tools* will help you quickly locate the chapter where you can find any *Tool* when you need it for a particular application.

Following these sections, the glossary will save you some time. Use the bibliography to conduct deeper dives into topics that interest you personally.

—Traits, skills, and strengths identified by Leonardo da Vinci

- Curiosita—*an insatiable thirst for knowledge*
- Dimostrazione—*the ability to learn from experience*
- Sensazione—*the discipline of continuing to hone one's senses*
- Sfumato—*the ability to cope with ambiguity*
- Arte / scienza—*holistic thinking*
- Corporalita—*what some people call sound mind and body*
- Connessione—*seeing deeply into the connection between things*

Being of service to others represents the most important effort in life. I hope you share that spirit with (as in "inspire") others.

The Golden (Silver) Rule

This list compiles 13 religions' versions of the golden rule.[1] The servant leader we envision understands natural laws, including cause and effect, and karma. While religion is a significant driver of past wars and violence, the religious founders would not necessarily be supportive of any actions taken without compassion for one another. Here is the proof:

Baha'ism

Lay not on any soul a load that you would not wish to be laid upon you, and desire not for anyone the things you would not desire for yourself.
—Bahá'u'lláh, *Gleanings*

Buddhism

Treat not others in ways that you yourself would find hurtful.
—The Buddha, *Udana-varga 5.18*

Christianity

In everything, do to others as you would have them do to you; for this is the law and the prophets.
—Jesus, *Matthew 7:12*

Confucianism (Silver Rule)

One word which sums up the basis of all good conduct: loving-kindness. Do not do to others what you do not want done to yourself.
—Confucius, *Analects 15:23*

Hinduism

This is the sum of duty: do not do to others what would cause pain if done to you.
—*Mahabharata 5:1517*

Islam

Not one of you truly believes until you wish for others what you wish for yourself.
—The Prophet Muhammad, *Hadith*

Jainism

One should treat all creatures in the world as one would like to be treated.
—Mahavira, *Sutrakritanga*

---

[1] Compiled by the Very Rev. Frederick A. Shade, *Communion* (Easter 2020), 16.

Judaism

What is hateful to you, do not do to your neighbour. This is the whole Torah; all the rest is commentary.
—Hillel, *Talmud, Shabbat 31a*

Sikhism

I am a stranger to no one; and no one is a stranger to me. Indeed, I am a friend to all.
—Guru Granth Sahib

Taoism

Regard your neighbour's gain as your own gain, and your neighbour's loss as your own loss.
—Lao Tzu, *T'ai Shang Kan Ying P'ien*

Unitarianism

We affirm and promote respect for the interdependent web of all existence of which we are a part.
—Unitarian principle

Zoroastrianism

Do not do unto others whatever is injurious to yourself.
—*Shayast-na-Shayast, 13.29*

The Tao of Facilitation

A servant leader can remain invisible. I would suggest that some of the fairest, kindest, and genuinely "good" people that you ever met, went unnoticed. You never knew what they were doing for the good of others, quietly in the background. The following verses are excerpted from Dr. Wayne Dyer's book *Change Your Thoughts—Change Your Life, Living the Wisdom of the Tao* (2007).

10th Verse

Can you love your people
and govern your domain
without self-importance? . . .
. . . working, yet not taking credit;
leading without controlling or dominating?

17th Verse

With the greatest leader above them,
people barely know one exists . . .
. . . The great leader speaks little,
He never speaks carelessly.

He works without self-interest
and leaves no trace.
When all is finished, the people say,
"We did it ourselves."

27th Verse

A knower of the truth
travels without leaving a trace,
speaks without causing harm,
gives without keeping an account . . .

. . . Be wise and help all being impartially,
abandoning none.
Waste no opportunities.
This is called following the light.
What is a good man but a bad man's teacher?
What is a bad man but a good man's job? . . .
. . . This is the great secret.

Quick Reference: Nine Activities for Your Meeting Design Solutions
Use the following guideline for every significant meeting you lead.

1. **Codify the purpose and scope** of the meeting: What project or product are you supporting? Stipulate what it is worth in currency and FTP: Why is it important? How much is at risk if we fail?

2. **Articulate the deliverables:** What is the specific content that represents the output of the meeting and satisfies what DONE looks like? What is my analogy for explaining it? Who will use it after the meeting?

3. **Identify known and unknown information:** What is already known about the organization, business unit, department, program, product, or project? What information is needed to fill the gaps?

4. **Draft *Basic Agenda* Steps:** Compose a series of steps from experience or other proven approaches that would be used by experts to build the plan, make the decision, solve the problem, or develop the information and consensus necessary to complete the deliverable and get DONE.

5. **Review *Basic Agenda*** for logical flow: walk through the *Agenda Steps* with others to confirm that they will produce the desired results. Link your analogy to each of the *Agenda Steps*. Rehearse your explanation of the white space.

6. **Identify meeting participants:** Determine the optimal subject matter expertise you require, the meeting participants who can provide the information required, or both.

7. **Detail the procedures** to capture information required: gather and assemble specific questions that need to be addressed, even questions for which subject matter experts are seeking answers. Sequence the questions optimally. Build your *Annotated Agenda* including the appropriate *Tools* and activities to produce the information.

8. **Perform a walk-through** with business experts, executive sponsor, project team members, and anyone else who will listen to you (grand-mothers are good for this and you might get a delicious, home-cooked meal).

9. **Refine:** Make changes identified in the walk-through, edit your final *Annotated Agenda*, firm up your artifacts, fill out your glossary, complete your slides, distribute your handouts, and rehearse.

Quick Reference: Meeting Design *Basic Agenda* Framework
Use this *Launch* and *Wrap* for every meeting—whether 50 minutes or multiple days.

Launch (Introduction) (chapter 5):

1. Introduce yourself: stress neutrality, meeting roles, and quantify impact.

2. State the meeting purpose and get agreement.

3. Confirm the meeting scope and get agreement.

4. Show the meeting deliverables and get agreement.

5. Cover the "administrivia" (for example, safety moment); have the attendees introduce themselves.

6. Walk through the meeting agenda (preferably using an analogy).

7. Explain the *Ground Rules* (chapter 4), emphasizing duty (fiduciary responsibility).

Middle Agenda Steps:
The meeting facilitator has an Annotated Agenda that details activities and procedures for each Agenda Step:

- *Agenda Step name*

- *Estimated time for each Agenda Step*

- *Agenda Step purpose (and analogy)*

- *Procedure for each Agenda Step*

- *Deliverable from each Agenda Step*

- *Graphical support required (such as legends, screens, definitions, and so on)*

- *Closure for each Agenda Step (and analogy)*

Wrap (Conclusion) (chapter 5):

1. *Review* the final output and deliverable: Restate or summarize what the group did.

2. Open items *(Parking Lot)*: Assign responsibility and detail how the group can expect to be updated.

3. *Guardian of Change*: Determine what group participants agree to tell their superiors and other stakeholders about what happened or what was accomplished.

4. Continuous improvement: Use *Plus/Delta* or a more comprehensive meeting and facilitator assessment form.

Meeting Design Tools (Alphabetically)

Actions Tool, chapter 6
After-Action Review Tool, chapter 8
Alignment Tool, chapter 6
Assessment Tool, chapter 5
Board and Committee Meetings, chapter 9
Bookend Rhetoric Tool, chapter 7
Brainstorming Tool, chapter 6
Breakout Teams Tool, chapter 6
Breaks Tool, chapter 9
Categorizing Tool, chapter 6
Clarifying Tool, chapter 7
Coat of Arms Tool, chapter 6
Communications Plan Tool, chapter 6
Content Management Tool, chapter 9
Creativity Tool, chapter 8
Decision Matrix Tool, chapter 7
Decision Quality Tool, chapter 7
Definition Tool, chapter 6

Glossary

2-by-4 — A mnemonic to remember a quick method for managing open issues. Represents **To** do what? **By** when and whom? **For** what benefit or purpose?

Agenda Indicator — A mobile arrow, tab, highlight, or some type of pointer indicating where we are in the agenda.

Agile — A mindset supporting various life-cycle frameworks used for product development, project management, change management, and others including popular frameworks like Kanban, Lean, and Scrum.

BHAG — Big hairy audacious goals.

Bookend Rhetoric — The opposite of analyzing in a linear fashion. Leading the analysis of any listing by working the two extremes (or bookends) and closing in on the gray area in the middle.

> **—Socrates**
> *The beginning of wisdom is a definition of terms.*

Breakout Teams — Assigning the large group into smaller teams and using teams to work on the same or different issues at the same time. Excellent for getting ideas and less optimal for conducting analysis.

Business Facilitation — A method that removes all distractions, thus enabling a group of experts to focus on the same question at the same time, being led by a meeting facilitator who knows how to sequence questions, ask questions with precision, and guide consensual understanding and agreement around optimal solutions for that specific group of experts — truly making it easier for your meeting participants to make more informed decisions.

Consensus — For a group, a level of understanding that appears reasonable and acceptable to everyone, meaning that everyone will support it professionally, even if it is not their personal favorite. They will *not* try to undo or unravel it when they get back to their office. No one will lose any sleep over it personally, even if it is not their personal favorite.

DONE — An expression that represents the objective or deliverable from some effort that could be a meeting, product, project, and so on.

DUMB — The opposite of SMART: Dull, Ubiquitous, Myopic, and Broad.

FTP — Stands for full-time person. Some use FTE for full-time employee or equivalent. Calculated as the value of one person for one year, typically around 2,000 hours of work contribution. For example, a project might require four FTP, but is completed within three months using 16 people.

Global Hunger — An analogy for a meaningful question that is difficult to answer because it is too broad or general, such as "What should we do about global hunger?" By understanding that hunger is a function of food manufacturing, food storage, food distribution, nutrition absorption, and so on, we can sharpen our questions and make it easier for participants to provide detailed answers.

Holarchy — A tabular view that unifies the purpose, scope, and objectives of an organization along with its business units, departments, programs, projects, products, meetings, and so on. The view enables and promotes consistent decision-making that intends to harmonize all of the operations within an organization.

Ishikawa Diagram — Also known as a fishbone diagram and the framework for root cause analysis.

Kumbaya — Activities designed to improve teamwork, increase trust, and so on, because those types of outcomes represent what most other resources publish about "facilitation."

Launch — The first *Agenda Step* in a session, in the English language, most frequently called the *Introduction*.

Life Cycle — A series of stages capturing the changes for various objects; notably arts, biology, business, software, and so on. For business purposes this term frequently refers to enterprise, product, project, and information technology.

Meeting — The two terms "meetings" and "workshops" are commonly used to denote, primarily, difference in duration, as meetings are frequently boxed in time. Sessions that last an hour or two are commonly called meetings while sessions that run three hours through three days or more are commonly called workshops. Regularly held meetings (staff meetings or board meetings) end when time runs out, usually with an understanding that unfinished items will be picked up in the next meeting. Roughly speaking, meetings deliver up outcomes or conditions, such as "increased awareness," while workshops document outputs such as strategic plans or detailed requirements.

OKR — Objectives and Key Results.

Pareto Principle (80-20 Rule) — A rule or expression suggesting that 80 percent of the incidences result from 20 percent of the causes.

Parking Lot — A place to temporarily put important items that should not be forgotten but cannot be discussed immediately. Optimally, these issues or items are important but not within the scope of the meeting.

Plus-Delta — A method of soliciting input from participants at the conclusion of a session, noting aspects they liked about the session (*Plus*) and aspects they would like to have changed (*Delta*).

PowerBalls — Icon symbols using circles ranging from empty to filled in to represent a lot, a little, or somewhere in between.

Purpose Tool — One of dozens of facilitation *Tools* supplied in this book, this *Tool* generates a consensual understanding of *why* something should be done before stepping into further analysis or design about *what* to do and *how* to do it.

RASI — Used to describe a *Roles and Responsibilities* matrix where R = Responsible, A = Accountable, S = Supports, and I = Needs to be Informed. Can also be called more than 20 other "acronyms" including RACI, RASCI, LACTI, and so on.

Refrigerator — An alternative term to *Parking Lot* that signifies more value or worth. Items in a refrigerator are preserved or protected until it's time to take them out of the refrigerator and "cook up a new meal" with them.

Rhetoric — Explained by Dr. David Zarefsky as the process of adjusting ideas to people and people to ideas. For our purposes, rhetorical precision implies clarity, not a universal standard—material that is clearly understood by the audience being served.

Scope — The boundaries of a topic that could range from an entire organization down to a highly specific question. Most frequently applied to projects to determine what is excluded or included within a project.

Scrum — An Agile framework used for change management, process improvement, product development, project management, and others.

Servant Leaders — Not engaged to change people's minds but to make it easier for people to make choices supported through more informed decisions. By speaking with people rather than at them, servant leaders create environments that foster breakthrough solutions. All skilled meeting facilitators are servant leaders, but not all servant leaders are meeting facilitators. Servant leaders may also be found serving as advisers, arbitrators, coaches, consultants, mediators, and ombudspeople and in other roles in which they share primary skills with meeting facilitators such as active listening, maintaining content neutrality, observing, questioning, and seeking to understand.

Silver Rule — "Do NOT do unto others what you do NOT want done to yourself."

SMART — Specific, Measurable, Adjustable, Relevant, and Time-based.[1]

Sparkline — A small intense, simple, word-sized graphic with typographic resolution.

Subject Matter Experts (SMEs) — Meeting participants, experts, or other stakeholders with needs, preferences, and requirements. These are people invited to a session because they bring valuable expertise or points of view.

SWOT Analysis — Frequently referred to current situation or situation analysis; identifies an organization's strengths and weaknesses to determine what to do with the environmental (or market) opportunities and strengths.

THRIVE LLC — A fictitious greenfield company built as an analogy for an organization; provides for-profit products and services to residential households, intended to make activities and resources easier to manage.

TO-WS (Quantitative) — Conducting situation analysis or traditional SWOT by reversing the sequence (threats, opportunities, weaknesses, strengths) when creating the four lists. Next, rather than concluding with four narrative lists, transpose them into a quantitative analytic. Use the quantitative framework to take the many strengths and weaknesses (controllable aspects) and focus on one opportunity or threat at a time (uncontrollable aspects).

Trichotomy — An expression that summarizes the nature of critical thinking, the transformation from the abstract to the concrete—from the *why* to the *what* to the *how*; from thoughts to words to deeds. Business life cycles refer to the trichotomy as planning, analysis, and design. A use case looks at the input, the process, and the output. Brainstorming relies on diverge, analyze, and converge, and so on.

Workshop — Commonly, given the way the two terms "meetings" and "workshops" are used, the primary difference between them is duration. Sessions that last an hour or two are commonly called meetings while sessions that run three hours through three days or more are commonly called workshops. Workshop facilitators risk total failure if they violate neutrality by offering up or evaluating content. When groups build toward a workshop deliverable, the sequence of the *Agenda Steps* is critical, and participants cannot leap ahead or advance until foundation work is completed. Roughly speaking, meetings deliver up outcomes or conditions, such as "increased awareness," while workshops document outputs such as strategic plans or detailed requirements.

---

[1] Deming's original definition used Achievable or Attainable for the "A." I prefer implying a gauge or a potentiometer that suggests an objective unit of measurement.

Wrap — The final *Agenda Step* in a session, in the English language, frequently called the conclusion.

Zoom — A company based in San Jose, California, that provides simplified videoconferencing and messaging across desktop and handheld devices.

Bibliography

Ackerman, Joshua M., Christopher C. Nocera, and John A. Bargh. "Incidental Haptic Sensations Influence Social Judgments and Decisions." *Science*, June 25, 2010.

Besant, Hanisha. "The Journey of Brainstorming." *Journal of Transformative Innovation* 2, no. 1 (Summer 2016): 1–7. https://www.regent.edu/acad/global/publications/jti/vol2iss1/Besant_JTISU16A.pdf.

Black, Harvey. "Stop Slouching! Good Posture Boosts Self-Esteem." *Scientific American Mind*, May 1, 2010.

Covey, Stephen. *The 7 Habits of Highly Effective People.* New York: Simon & Schuster, 2013.

Cuddy, Amy. *Presence: Bringing Your Boldest Self to Your Biggest Challenges*, illustrated ed. New York: Little, Brown, 2018.

Day, George. "Is It Real? Can We Win? Is It Worth Doing?: Managing Risk and Reward in an Innovation Portfolio." *Harvard Business Review*, December 2007.

De Bono, Edward. "Six Thinking Hats." https://www.debonogroup.com/services/core-programs/six-thinking-hats/.

Dyer, Wayne. *Change Your Thoughts—Change Your Life, Living the Wisdom of the Tao.* Carlsbad, CA: Hay House, 2007.

Erard, Michael. *Um: Slips, Stumbles, and Verbal Blunders, and What They Mean.* New York: Pantheon, 2007.

Getzels, J. W. "Problem Finding and the Inventiveness of Solutions." *Journal of Creative Behavior* 9, no. 1 (1975).

Gleick, James. *The Information: A History, a Theory, a Flood.* New York: Pantheon, 2011.

Gordon, Thomas. *Parent Effectiveness Training: The Proven Program for Raising Responsible Children.* New York: Harmony Books, 2000.

Hall, Brian, and Barbara Ledig. *Lifestyle Workbook: A Guide for Understanding the Hall-Tonna Inventory of Values.* N.p., 1986.

Icebreakers and so on. https://www.teampedia.net/wiki/Main_Page.

International Association of Facilitators (IAF). https://www.iaf-world.org/site/.

Jones, Morgan. *The Thinker's Toolkit: 14 Powerful Techniques for Problem Solving.* New York: Times Books, 1998.

Kahneman, Daniel. *Thinking, Fast and Slow*. New York: Farrar, Straus and Giroux, 2013.

Koestler, Arthur. *The Ghost in the Machine*. Last Century Media, 1982 (1967).

Maskin, Eric, and Amartya Sen. *The Arrow Impossibility Theorem*. New York: Columbia University Press, 2014.

Mezick, Daniel. "Connect and Communicate: How to Teach Online." http://newtechusa .net/danielmezick/.

Mintzberg, Henry, Bruce Ahlstrand, and Joseph Lampel. *Strategy Safari: The Complete Guide through the Wilds of Strategic Management*, 2nd ed. Toronto: Pearson Education Canada, 2008.

Moore, Geoffrey. *Crossing the Chasm*. New York: Harper Business, 1995.

NASA (National Aeronautics and Space Administration). "Survival! Exploration: Then and Now." https://www.nasa.gov/pdf/166504main_Survival.pdf.

National Speakers Association. https://www.nsaspeaker.org/about/.

Newseum. "Today's Front Pages." https://www.newseum.org/todaysfrontpages/.

North Carolina State University. "No Laughing Matter: Laughter Can Play Key Role in Group Dynamics." *Science Daily*, August 24, 2010. https://www.sciencedaily.com /releases/2010/08/100824103525.htm.

Osborn, Alex. *Applied Imagination: Principles and Procedures of Creative Problem-Solving*, 3rd ed. New York: Charles Scribner's Sons, 1963.

Osburn, Jack D., Linda Moran, Ed Musselwhite, and John H. Zenger. *Self-Directed Work Teams: The New American Challenge*. New York: McGraw-Hill, 1990.

Osburn, J. D., L. Moran, E. Musselwhite, and J. H. Zenger. "Self-Directed Work Teams. The New American Challenge." *Management Revue*, April 1991.

Pink, Daniel. *When: The Scientific Secrets of Perfect Timing*, illustrated ed. New York: Riverhead Books, 2018.

Pinker, Steven. *The Stuff of Thought: Language as a Window into Human Nature*. New York: Viking, 2007.

Robert, Henry. *1907 Pocket Manual of Robert's Rules of Order for Deliberative Assemblies*. Glenview, IL: Scott Foresman, 1907.

Saj-nicole, Joni, and Damon Beyer. "How to Pick a Good Fight." *Harvard Business Review*, December 2009.

Shade, Rev. Frederick A. (compiler). "The Golden Rules," ed. John Hawkins. *Communion*, Easter 2020.

Sommer, Tom. "Increasing Alignment." February 26, 2019. https://medium.com/redbubble /increasing-alignment-a33203fe8687.

Spangler, David. "A Vision of Holarchy," *Seven Pillars: House of Wisdom*, https://web.archive .org/web/20120218163022/http://www.sevenpillarshouse.org/index.php/article/a_vision ofholarchy1.

Surowiecki, James. *The Wisdom of Crowds*, reprint ed. New York: Anchor Books, 2005.

Taleb, Nassim. *Incerto: Fooled by Randomness, the Black Swan, the Bed of Procrustes, Antifragile*, boxed ed. New York: Random House, 2016.

The Nobel Prize. "Paul Krugman." Press release, October 13, 2008.

Toastmasters International. "Gestures: Your Body Speaks: How to Become Skilled in Nonverbal Communication." https://www.toastmasters.org/-/media/files/department-documents/education-documents/201-gestures.ashx.

Truss, Lynne. *Eats, Shoots & Leaves: The Zero Tolerance Approach to Punctuation.* New York: Avery Publishing, 2004.

Tuckman, B. W. "Development Sequence in Small Groups." *Psychological Bulletin* 63, no. 6 (1965): 384–399.

Tufte, Edward. *The Visual Display of Quantitative Information*, 2nd ed. Cheshire, CT: Graphics Press, 2001.

Tynan, Susan, and Ruth Feldman. *Communicoding.* New York: Dutton, 1989.

Wilber, Ken. *A Theory of Everything: An Integral Vision for Business, Politics, Science and Spirituality.* Boston, MA: Shambhala Publications, 2000.

Winchester, Simon. *The Meaning of Everything: The Story of the Oxford English Dictionary.* Oxford: Oxford University Press, 2003.

World Future Society. https://www.worldfuture.org.

Acknowledgments

A special thanks is owed to my editor, Charlotte Ashlock, whose keen spirit sensed the value of serving others by building consensus through more effective meetings, especially around evidence-based planning, deciding, and problem-solving challenges.

Thanks are also owed to the following people:

To Maxine Attong, who encouraged me with her stellar personality and vigor to write; it's hard to imagine that people came up with the word "effervescent" before meeting Maxine.

To Kevin M. Booth, the clearest thinker, speaker, business process illustrator, and business writer I've ever met. Highly practical, he represents the opposite of my predisposition toward psychobabble. Kevin introduced me to his version of the trichotomy: (1) a foundation of evidence (2) that gives rise to conclusions (3) that justify optimal recommendations. Kevin inspired me by setting high standards with his ability to integrate complex relationships in a clear and thoughtful manner.

To Catherine Cambron for her brilliant copyediting support. She has no idea how much I value the tweaks she made so that some of the complexity we face has been made much simpler to understand.

To Gary Rush for his background and legacy of integrating IBM's JAD and structured analysis into a technique he called FAST.

And to Scott Wild, a genuine servant leader, whose wisdom oriented me to make things clearer and simpler than they would have been; my message reaches far beyond what is included in this book, but as a meeting primer for most people, Scott created the traction of making this easier for you.

Thanks is also owed to the MG RUSH alumni, and specific individuals who continue to provide invaluable support with their social messaging of our hundreds of best practices articles. While listing names is risky, because no doubt I am missing some important people, it feels better to mention the many and then apologize to the few: Kristen Avery, Steven Bailey, Christopher Bittinger, Nachmi Braver, Julie Bruski-Kuennen, Justine Burdette, Jeff Cagle, Alvin Calicaran, Tiffany Chanell, Roxanne Felton Christopher, Rockwell Clancy, Lindsey Clawson, Raquel Clement, Michelle DeLauer, Josephine Delgado, Grace

Denman, Nathan Diercks, Douglas Ferguson, Ildemar Ferreira, Roger Fla-haven, Charlotte Germain-Aubrey, Sevak Ghazaryan, Thomas Gibbs, Lisa Gonzalez, Diego Guerrero, Sasha Gumprecht, Robert Hammond, Molly Her-rington, Earl Humphrey, Ron Itnyre, Jan Kaderly, William Kaplan, Bruce Kish, Monica Kleve, Dorothy Littleton, Lewis "Chip" Locke Jr., Tanaka Macharaga, William Malek, Sana Manjeshwar, Michael Manning, Deepika Marisetty, Greg Michael, Linda Moineau, Louis Mollon, Mark Morgan, Jennifer Munson, Ven-kat Narayanan, Gordon Ng, George M. Okantey, Ray Ontko, James Pennella, G. Perez, Dwayne Phillips, Michael Ramos, Mitzi Rapkin, Tracee Rice, Larry Richard, Joren Scharn, Stacy Shireman, Ling Sondersted, Scott Sowell, Maria Steinhoff, Brent Stewart, Ben Stutzman, James Vera, Tricia Vincent, Brittany Williams, Jessica Williams, Letty Zazueta, and Erin Zocco.

Index

About the Author

As a Certified Structured Professional Facilitator (CSPF), lead instructor, and managing director of MG RUSH Facilitation Training and Coaching, Terrence Metz is passionate about training students to lead meetings that produce clear and actionable results *every time!*

In addition to earning his MBA from Northwestern University's Kellogg School of Management, his professional certifications include a Six Sigma Green Belt from Motorola University, Scrum Master (CSM) from the Scrum Alliance, Certified Scrum Product Owner (CSPO), and How To Teach Online (HTTO) Certification from the Open Leadership Network, among other certifications.

Terrence's professional experience has focused on mergers, organizational design, problem solving, process improvement, product development, and strategic planning. He also has P&L experience in highly engineered products and services (Honeywell, for example).

He has taught classes on facilitation and leadership with the Broad Institute (a research venture of Massachusetts Institute of Technology and Harvard University), Purdue University, the University of Arkansas (Sam Walton School of Business), and instructors from the Stanford University Advanced Project Management Program (who wedged in his five-day professional class between Christmas and New Year's), along with numerous private organizations and departments of local and federal governments.

His decision-making tools for galvanizing consensus, including *Perceptual Mapping* and *Quantitative TO-WS Analysis*, are used worldwide. In 2004, he introduced the concept of holism to the field of structured facilitation as a method for keeping discussions on target, aligning deliverables within and throughout an organization, and creating traction for facilitators to lead meetings that get results.

Having taught over 300 classes and more than 3,000 students, Terrence is a talented instructor, focused listener, and equally adept at both teaching the *MG Rush Facilitation Training* curriculum and at facilitating consensual agreement around important and challenging issues for groups, organizations, and teams.

Berrett–Koehler
Publishers

Berrett-Koehler is an independent publisher dedicated to an ambitious mission: *Connecting people and ideas to create a world that works for all.*

Our publications span many formats, including print, digital, audio, and video. We also offer online resources, training, and gatherings. And we will continue expanding our products and services to advance our mission.

We believe that the solutions to the world's problems will come from all of us, working at all levels: in our society, in our organizations, and in our own lives. Our publications and resources offer pathways to creating a more just, equitable, and sustainable society. They help people make their organizations more humane, democratic, diverse, and effective (and we don't think there's any contradiction there). And they guide people in creating positive change in their own lives and aligning their personal practices with their aspirations for a better world.

And we strive to practice what we preach through what we call "The BK Way." At the core of this approach is *stewardship,* a deep sense of responsibility to administer the company for the benefit of all of our stakeholder groups, including authors, customers, employees, investors, service providers, sales partners, and the communities and environment around us. Everything we do is built around stewardship and our other core values of *quality, partnership, inclusion,* and *sustainability.*

This is why Berrett-Koehler is the first book publishing company to be both a B Corporation (a rigorous certification) and a benefit corporation (a for-profit legal status), which together require us to adhere to the highest standards for corporate, social, and environmental performance. And it is why we have instituted many pioneering practices (which you can learn about at www.bkconnection.com), including the Berrett-Koehler Constitution, the Bill of Rights and Responsibilities for BK Authors, and our unique Author Days.

We are grateful to our readers, authors, and other friends who are supporting our mission. We ask you to share with us examples of how BK publications and resources are making a difference in your lives, organizations, and communities at www.bkconnection.com/impact.

Dear reader,

Thank you for picking up this book and welcome to the worldwide BK community! You're joining a special group of people who have come together to create positive change in their lives, organizations, and communities.

What's BK all about?

Our mission is to connect people and ideas to create a world that works for all.

Why? Our communities, organizations, and lives get bogged down by old paradigms of self-interest, exclusion, hierarchy, and privilege. But we believe that can change. That's why we seek the leading experts on these challenges—and share their actionable ideas with you.

A welcome gift

To help you get started, we'd like to offer you a **free copy** of one of our bestselling ebooks:

www.bkconnection.com/welcome

When you claim your **free ebook**, you'll also be subscribed to our blog.

Our freshest insights

Access the best new tools and ideas for leaders at all levels on our blog at ideas.bkconnection.com.

Sincerely,
Your friends at Berrett-Koehler